The Misadventures of
Russell Quigley
Photographer's Mate, United States Navy

by

David Griffiths

Copyright © 2000 by David Griffiths

All rights reserved. No part of this book may be reproduced or transmitted in any form by any means, electronic, mechanical, photocopying, recording, or otherwise, without the written permission from the author.

ISBN: 143826545X
EAN-13: 9781438265452

Cover: Official U.S. Navy Photo by
Photographer's Mate Craig McClure

The Misadventures of Russell Quigley

Russell Quigley was the kind of man that irritated everyone. But, Russell was a man of principle. It didn't mater how small an incident was if it violated one of his principles, he just had to let someone know. Russell also had a problem with bullies. He could not let a bully go unchallenged.

Russell had a fear of authority and; therefore, of making mistakes. If he couldn't make any mistakes, then you shouldn't be able to either.

When Russell reenlisted, he vowed to do better. And, he did—for a while. You see, it was not something Russell could easily control. The Navy violated a lot of principles. And the Navy had a lot of bullies

**Dedicated to
Chief Petty Officers,
past, present, and future**

Acknowledgments

Special thanks to Jane Hyer, who first suggested that I write a book; to Mike Nichols, who insisted that I write a book; to Carol Owens, for her editorial assistance; and to my wife Perla, who, without a single complaint, endured many nights alone while I hacked away at the computer.

TABLE OF CONTENTS

RUSSELL QUIGLEY 1

BOOT CAMP 5

AIRMAN PREP SCHOOL 23

PHOTO SCHOOL 25

TREASURE ISLAND 35

THE FLEET AIR PHOTO LAB 39

THE NAVAL PHOTO CENTER 79

A CIVILIAN AGAIN 101

USS *WASP* 107

USS *ENTERPRISE* 129

NAVAL PHOTOGRAPHIC INTERPRETATION CENTER 173

THE DEFENSE INTELLIGENCE AGENCY 181

USS *OBSERVATION ISLAND* 173

PHOTO SCHOOL, AGAIN 211

USS *MIDWAY* 229

KADENA AIR FORCE BASE 255

RUSSELL QUIGLEY

I grew up in South Dakota during the depression. I remember eating a lot of biscuits and gravy and getting a whipping for putting both butter and jelly on the same piece of toast. I also remember my mom complaining, when things got a little better, that my older brother wouldn't stop hiding cookies under his clothes in his chest of drawers. They would get old, crumble, and get all over everything.

I think I was born afraid. Maybe it was my father's explosive temper. Anyway, I spent a lot of time hiding out behind the garage. And I was angry all the time. I don't know why I was angry; I just know that I don't ever remember seeing a picture of me where I wasn't standing a foot away from the rest of the family, arms folded, pouting, and looking down. I started selling papers on the street when I was in the third grade as much to get out of the house as for the money.

And it wasn't just the family. I was the kind of person everybody loved to dump on. I attracted the attention of the school bully, Abel Leaman, who was a year ahead of me. He wasn't satisfied just to beat me up; he had to beat me up everyday after school, and everyday I went home crying.

My mother complained to my dad; my dad complained to me. He said the bully would never stop bothering me until I showed him that I wasn't afraid of him.

"Dad, I fight back as hard as I can, but—"

"No buts," he interrupted, "if you come home crying and upsetting your mother again, I'll give you something to cry about."

Well, I was more afraid of my father than I was of Abel, so I knew what I had to do.

Abel always managed to get out of class first and be waiting for me. He beat me up again, but this time when he got up to leave, I tackled him from behind. As a result of his surprise, I managed to hit him once in the face. He rewarded me with the most severe beating ever. He bloodied my nose and puffed both of my eyes.

But when he turned to leave, I tackled him again. He beat me up again; I tackled him again. He never got more than 10 feet before I tackled him again. He started crying when it got dark. He wasn't hurt; he just wanted to go home. He kept asking me to let him go home, but I wouldn't stop.

Our parents and the police caught up with us at the same time. My mom was furious. Abel's mom called me a monster. The police were annoyed. But there was a twinkle in my dad's eyes.

Whenever I saw Abel after that, I turned towards him just to watch him turn and go the other way. I vowed never to be afraid again and to stand up against all bullies including my father.

Not long after, I walked in on my dad while he was building a breakfast nook in our kitchen. It was not going well and my mother made the mistake of laying a plate on the tabletop before it was finished. He picked up the plate and hurled it at her as if it were a Frisbee.® She jumped back, and it smashed against the refrigerator.

I stepped forward and said, "If you do that again, I will smack you." I was eleven.

He picked up a hammer and came after me. I fled down into the basement. He followed me with the hammer raised over his head and I knew he meant to hit me. I spotted a hatchet, grabbed it, and spun around. He stopped dead in his tracks and glared at me. He dropped the hammer, turned around, and went upstairs. I stood there for the longest time, hatchet raised, body trembling. Finally, I put the hatchet down and crept upstairs. I had to sneak by his bedroom to get out of the house. He was crying. We never got along after that; but then, to the best of my recollection, we never got along before that either.

I was petrified by an emotional account of Pearl Harbor being bombed emanating from a radio hidden in a cathedral that was taller than I was. I also read about the war in my newspapers, and listened to the war every night. And, I watched the war every Saturday afternoon when my uncle took me to a 12-cent western with my cousins. It seemed like the war would never end, and I was sure that I would have to fight. I ran to and from school to keep in shape. I lifted weights. I fought every chance I got. I had my own paper route by the time the war was over.

My older brother, Roger, seemed to fare better than I did. He didn't get along any better than me at home, but he got along great at school, and he had lots of friends. He was a stranger to me by the time he left for the Naval Academy.

We prospered along with the country, and by 1953 my dad was a radio engineer with the Voice of America in Tangier, North Africa. My father mellowed some. My mother was delighted to have a maid.

My little brother, Rolland, was more like me. He was 12 when we went to Tangier, an international free port. Tangier was the smuggling capital of the world and a center of international intrigue. It was often described as the world's wickedest city. Rolland was deported when he was 15 for socially and politically incorrect behavior.

I weighed 135 pounds when I decided to join the Navy. I was five feet, nine inches tall, had unruly red hair and hazel eyes. A little thin, otherwise, I was pretty average all around. I thought joining the Navy was a great idea. I wanted to be a photographer, and I also wanted to go to school eventually, so the G. I. Bill was just what I needed.

I didn't realize how unprepared I was for the Navy. You see, I was a man of principle. It did not matter how small an incident was, if it violated one of my principles, I was compelled to let someone know. I was loyal to the Navy, to my country, and to my God, but not so much to my supervisors. In fact, I was frequently referred to as a sea lawyer, that is, someone who thought they knew more about Navy regulations than anyone else. If a petty officer missed a rule, or regulation, he would hear from me.

Warrant Officer Butz wrapped me up in one sentence: "Quigley," he said, "you are the most arrogant, condescending, self-righteous bastard I ever met."

I was destined to have problems and I did: a dozen captain's masts and a hearing for a summary court martial in my first four years. It wasn't all my fault. The Navy violated a lot of principles, and the Navy had a lot of bullies.

With all of my problems, you'd think that I wouldn't have any friends; however, I was always the instant leader of the downtrodden and the malcontents. I was the leader of the opposition. If you stepped on someone, I instantly became his or her champion. For all the trouble I had, I don't know of any other organization that would have put up with me. And back then, they wiped the slate clean when you reenlisted.

BOOT CAMP

When the last line is removed and a US Naval ship breaks away from the pier, the officer-of-the-deck announces, "Underway, shift colors" over the speaker system. And so it is that I begin my story by breaking family ties and moving out on my own.

I left Tangier, Morocco, by train with $35.00 in my pocket. Not knowing it was illegal to transport American dollars from Spanish Morocco to French Morocco, I didn't try to hide my money when the Spanish Militia at the border asked to see what was in my wallet. They took all my money. They were nice about it, but they took it. When I asked how they expected me to travel without money, they told me there was a Red Cross office in the next train station. I never expected to see my money again, but they sent it to my folks in Tangier just like they said they would.

The Red Cross people said it happened all the time and they were very sympathetic. They loaned me $15.00 even after I told them I wouldn't get paid for three months. They said it was no problem. So I arrived at the Port Lyautey Naval Base happy and well fed.

I was given a physical and a bunch of shots that were duly registered on an international shot card so they wouldn't give them to me again in boot camp, but of course, they did. The dentist said they didn't usually take people in with braces; however, I needn't worry, because according to Navy Regs, once I was sworn in, the Navy would have to take care of them even if they had to send me to a civilian dentist. The personnel office handled my enlistment and I was soon on my way to Bainbridge, Maryland for recruit training. I landed in Baltimore, Maryland, where a bus was waiting to take me the rest of the way.

Boot camp was the Naval Recruit Training Center, Bainbridge, Maryland. In the winter of 1953-1954, it was a barren little base with buildings as gray as the weather. Boot camp, as it was called because we all wore those high-top shoes the Navy called boots, was drills, marching, classes, swimming, more classes, remedial swimming, too many watches, too little sleep, and an endless stream of all-you-can-eat buffets. I gained 11 pounds in three months.

SIR

"Chief's ass, SIR to you," bellowed the bellicose, potbellied chief glaring down at me through the window of his white, wooden outhouse in the center of the road. Well, I didn't know much, but I knew those anchors on his collar meant he was a chief, so I said, "Sir?"

"Yes, SIR," he said. "While you are here, you will address all senior petty officers as SIR."

"Yes sir, SIR," I said.

Naked City

He took my orders and pointed me towards another bus that would take me to a gym where a new company was forming up. I glanced at the clock behind Chief SIR; it was 11:15 p.m.

A bunch of people was standing buck-naked on the gym floor like rows of corn, but with more space between them. I was handed a cardboard box and told to undress and put all my belongings in the box. I was told I would get it all back when I graduated, but of course, I never did.

"Hurry up Quigley; we ain't got all day," barked First Class Petty Officer SIR. So I hurried up, and then I stood there buck-naked like a fool along with the rest of the men for forty-five minutes while they "formed" a company. Nobody looked happy, but a tall redhead, shoulders slumped, knees bent, and rocking back and forth was saying to no one in particular because all of the SIRs had left the area, "It ain't right; they can't do this to us; it ain't right." Finally, we were asked to march our nakedness down a narrow hallway lined with small rooms with half doors with junior petty officers behind them, which I SIR'd anyway.

"Pants," screamed Junior Petty Officer SIR.

"Size 28," I screamed back, but it didn't make any difference because he gave me the ones he already had in his hands, which were two sizes too big. I was still wearing baggy pants when I got to my first duty station.

"Shirts." "Skivvies." "Shoes." "Sea bags." And so it went until I had more new clothes than I had ever had in my life.

We marched our naked bodies back to the gym with our arms full. All our boxes were gone. We dressed in boots, dungarees, white hats, and P-coats. It only took a minute to see that I was not being picked on. Only a handful had clothes that fit. There seemed to be a correlation between big, good looking guys and well fitting clothes. That would explain my baggy pants. We stuffed our remaining new clothes in our new sea bags, threw them over our shoulders, and marched through wet snow and mud to our new barracks.

Moving In

The barracks were pre-World War I buildings. They were built about four feet off the ground with brick supports on the corners and about every 20 feet in between. The first deck consisted of an open bay with rows of bunks and lockers and an office for Company Commander SIR.

We marched inside, not realizing that we would have to clean all the mud off the floor—soon to become a deck—before we could get some sleep. Mud is revered in South Dakota, but here it was used for punishment. We stowed all of our gear in our lockers, and figured we would be hitting the sack. It was none too soon, either, because it was nearly 3 a.m. However, it was not to be. We weren't even ready to scrub the deck yet. It was time to go over to the mess hall and take our General Classification Tests. My "GCT" was 69. I wasn't used to scoring that low, and I was sure I could've done better with a full night's sleep. Years later, after several years of college and a full night's sleep, I scored 70.

We never made it to bed that first night. We began the day with a huge breakfast, and then we went to medical. I had a 28-inch waist, a 32-inch chest, and weighed 137 pounds. We had a huge dinner and went to dental. The dentist told me that I wasn't supposed to be in the Navy with braces, and that they wouldn't be able to adjust them while I was in boot camp. I asked if I could see a civilian dentist. He smiled, and then we had a huge supper and learned how to "fall in" and "stand at attention" and "stand at parade rest" and finally to be "at ease."

The next day, after another huge breakfast and a skinhead haircut—I was the only one whose appearance improved—we began our classification interviews. I told Petty Officer SIR that I was going to be a photographer. Petty Officer SIR said my scores were too high, and that I shouldn't be so cocky. I really didn't understand. I wasn't being cocky; if anything I was a little embarrassed; I was used to scoring in the 70s and 80s. Anyway, Petty Officer SIR said I would be a sonarman. Being a sonarman was the last thing I wanted to be.

We were forming up to march to the mess hall for lunch when Company Commander SIR ordered me to "fall out" and report to Regimental Headquarters. "You must have really stepped in it, Quigley," he hollered after me as I began trotting across the parade grounds.

A Commission

"Russell Quigley, you are being considered for the Naval Reserve Officer Training Corps. How would you like four years of college and a commission?"

"That would be great sir, SIR," I replied. My heart began to pound. I would be an officer just like Roger.

"We are impressed with your scores and the fact that you have a brother at the Academy. All you have to do is answer a few simple questions and you'll be on your way. Who is your regiment commander?"

"I, ah, I don't, I, um, oh, that's you sir, Lieutenant Commander Love, sir," I read from the plaque on his desk. He obviously wasn't impressed, and his tone became less friendly.

"Who is your battalion commander?" he asked sternly. I felt sick. I didn't know. He was introduced somewhere between field day and breakfast.

"I don't know, sir," I said flatly.

"Who is your company commander?" he asked. My spirits lifted. I had heard his name a hundred times already. But it wouldn't come to me.

"Well, Quigley," said Lieutenant Commander Love, "It's obvious why your brother Roger is at the Academy, and you are here. Dismissed"

The Red Cross

When I got back to the barracks, I was told to report to Battalion Headquarters, which of course, was in the same building I just came from on the other side of the parade ground. The name on the desk was Ensign Bonham. I sure could have used that information a few minutes ago. He said, "Quigley, it says here that you owe the Red Cross $15.00."

"Yes sir, SIR," I said, "But I told them I wouldn't get paid for—"

"Goddamn it, Quigley, I didn't ask for any excuses. You owe 'em; you gotta pay 'em. We don't need any deadbeats in the Navy. And what the hell is this, I hear you don't know my name?"

"Well, sir, I remember you came over, but I just didn't remem—"

"Damn it Quigley, I just told you I'm not looking for any excuses. My name is Ensign Bonham and don't you forget it. You ever forget my name again you'll be one sorry son-of-a-bitch; you understand me, Quigley"?

"Yes sir, SIR," I said.

"Get outta here, now," he hollered, "If I see you again, you will automatically be in trouble."

A Tale of Two Cities

A number of New York City street punks were allowed to enlist as a group and they immediately started bullying and intimidating people. The leader was a big homely man named McMurdy, who later became the Sixth Fleet boxing champion. One of the gang made the mistake of picking on a big good-looking guy from Boston whose clothes fit perfectly. Boston picked up New York City and threw him out a window, which wasn't open yet.

New York City made Boston an instant member of the New York City Street Punks Association, but Boston never really fit in because Boston kept warning people about what the punks were up to. Friction grew between the cities until one night Boston asked, "How many of you punks want a free trip to the hospital?"

McMurdy stepped forward and said, "Just one, Boston, just one."

Boston looked surprised. McMurdy was usually an instigator, not a participant. "Okay," Boston said with a stone face. McMurdy was much bigger, had huge muscles, and ill-fitting clothes, but if Boston was intimidated, he didn't show it.

The two Titans stepped to the center of the quarterdeck and a crowd formed around them. McMurdy landed the first blow and it caught Boston square in the mouth and sat him down. McMurdy's training took over; rather than going in for the kill, he stepped back and waited for Boston to stand up. That was a mistake. Boston was a street fighter and promptly kicked McMurdy's feet out from under him. McMurdy bounced right back up and landed two rapid punches, and this time he didn't step back. Boston grabbed McMurdy's left fist with both hands, turned it to the outside, and pushed back and down so hard that McMurdy's feet went into the air, and he crashed through the deck shoulders first. McMurdy landed flat on his back on the ground about four feet below the deck.

It was too cold to get much sleep that night with winter coming up through the hole in the deck. I had learned to respect those skinny green wool blankets, but this was too much even for them. Reveille was louder than usual the next morning, and we had to fall in outside before we had a chance to clean up. Standing at attention, we could see Lieutenant Commander Love SIR and Ensign Bonham SIR coming towards us across the parade ground. Company Commander SIR called us to attention and saluted smartly.

They kept us at attention for an hour and a half waiting for someone to tell them who made the hole in the deck. Finally, Lieutenant Commander Love SIR said, "You've got until 1600 to tell your company commander who did this, or I'm going to come back and run you around the parade ground until you drop."

We returned from classes at 1600 and, of course, no one had told. There was a ten-foot square of new wood where the hole had been. Company Commander SIR had us fall in where we could all see it.

"Men," he said, "have you ever heard of holystoning a deck? Well, you're in for a treat. We used to holystone the old wooden carrier decks to get the gunk off them. You take an old brick and some sand, and you use them to grind off a layer of wood. I want everyone to go outside and get a brick off the pile out there, and I'll show you how to use it. Now we ain't got no sand, but I'm sure you can do the job without it.

"Now then, you get down on all fours, put your weight on the brick, and slide it back and forth on the deck until you see it making a difference. Remember, you got to keep it up until that old deck looks just like this new one. One more thing before I go men, don't bother going to supper, and don't bother hitting the sack until I say you can."

Well, we all stood around looking at each other in disbelief, then we started going outside and getting our bricks. We formed two rows across the barracks about ten feet apart. As luck would have it, I wound up in the center of the new deck. I sat there for a minute wondering what to do when I remembered seeing an old bucket out by the bricks. I got up, went outside, got the bucket, filled it full of mud, came back, and dumped it in the middle of the new deck.

Some of the guys went into an instant panic, certain that I would get them into even more trouble. Others, frustrated by the impossibility of the task, cheered, and came over to help spread it around and rub it in. The new deck was soon a more reasonable gray and the task did not seem quite so impossible.

Most of the guys were busy "holystoning" the deck, but to no avail. The deck was gray all the way through and no amount of rubbing with bricks was going to make any difference. We had actually lost ground with all the mud we tracked in getting the bricks.

The Punks called a meeting. They emerged in a few minutes, and one of them said, "We're gonna go buy some bleach. Anybody wanna chip in?" They had $30.00 in no time. "Why don't some of you guys clean the shit can, so we can have something to put it in when we get back?" Again, some of the guys were moaning that we were going to get into more trouble, but nobody was going to stand up against the Punks.

The trashcan was ready for them, and they literally filled it full of bleach. We had plenty of swabs, so we drenched the deck in bleach in a matter of minutes, but to our amazement, it didn't make any difference either. In desperation, they started pouring bleach on the deck by the buckets full, and all of a sudden the deck was so slippery guys had trouble standing up. We all started coughing and opening windows. The temperature quickly dropped to below freezing, and we started huddling together and asking, "What the hell do we do now?"

One man, that same redhead from Naked City, kept right on holystoning even though he was engulfed in a river of bleach. We hardly noticed until he screamed in a wild and raspy voice, "I can't see! I can't see!" The watch called an ambulance, which carted the redhead with his tie-dyed bell-bottoms off to sickbay. Now, I was scared. I figured they would court martial the whole company.

"ATTENTION ON DECK." It was the watch announcing the return of Company Commander SIR. "Out, out, everybody out. Open the windows; Open all the windows. Watch, call the fire department." Company Commander SIR toured the barracks to make sure everyone was out. Then he told us to fall in, and put us at ease.

The fire department arrived. They hosed and squeegeed as much of the bleach off the deck as they could. They left after about an hour, but we couldn't go in until we got an "okay" from the medical department representative. The corpsman kept making phone calls; he finally said we could go in, but we would have to keep the windows open.

We all expected to catch hell, but we were so cold by that time we didn't much care; however, none of the SIRs said a word. They didn't even seem to notice that our bell-bottoms were turning white, or that the guys who had fallen down were beginning to look like Casper.

The Redhead

It didn't take long to figure out boot camp: the goal was to weed out the weenies by making life as miserable as possible. That way, the Navy wouldn't have to go to war with anyone who couldn't take it. One day I said to Company Commander SIR, "SIR, why don't you feed us some germs? That would really weed out some weenies."

"Quigley let me show you how I weed out weenies and smart asses. Drop down and give me 20 pushups while I figure out what it is about you that I don't like."

Well, our first casualty was Raymond Squigley. We all saw it coming; if you stepped on his heels while marching, he would cuss a blue streak and take a swing at you.

One morning, after noticing Ray's bunk was empty, we were asked to empty his locker, pack his gear in his sea bag, and turn it in to Petty Officer SIR over at Battalion Headquarters. We never saw Raymond again, but the rumor was that he had taken a swing at Company Commander SIR.

I didn't think much about it, but that night I was called in to Duty Petty Officer SIR's office and placed on report for leaving my clothes on the clothesline outside the barracks. Well, I hadn't left any clothes anywhere let alone outside, so I instantly created a ruckus. Duty Petty Officer SIR calmly said he had them right there in the box. "See for yourself," he said.

Well, I looked at the clothes in the box, and of course, they belonged to Raymond Squigley, so I showed Duty Petty Officer SIR the difference between the name on the clothes and the name on my shirt. Duty Petty Officer SIR apologized nicely, and told me not to worry about it and that was the end of it.

That is, until Saturday morning when the phone rang and some ill-tempered SIR informed me that since I failed to muster for extra duty, I had an additional 20 demerits. When I tried to explain, I was told to shut up and get my butt over there, or I would have an additional 40 demerits to work off. Well, I figured there would be at least one SIR over there that would listen to me so I hustled on over. It was snowing and there was a half-foot of snow on the ground. I remember being thankful for the boots.

"You Quigley?" asked Chief Petty Officer SIR.

"Yes sir, SIR" I replied.

"You being a smart ass?" Before I could answer, he said, "Fall in over there."

"Excuse me chief, I mean SIR, but I ain't supposed to be here—"

"You are being a smart ass," he growled. "Get your ass over there before I kick your butt."

"Yes sir, SIR," I said.

"Ski, give that asshole 20 pushups."

"Right away Chief. You heard the man; give me twenty, now," said First Class Petty Officer Ski SIR.

Everybody stopped—they were doing calisthenics—and watched me do my best to do 20 pushups. Petty Officer Ski SIR soon got tired of waiting and ordered me to get a rifle and join them. We turned that rifle every way but loose for the next two hours, and then marched to chow. To my amazement, Petty Officer Ski SIR worked and marched right along with us. The other SIRs just stood around barking orders.

Most of the guys got to go back to the barracks, but those of us who were late reporting for extra duty had to return to shovel wet snow off the parade ground. They issued about 30 of us the flimsiest snow shovels I'd ever seen. The curved blades were about two feet wide and held a heap of snow, but the handles were only a half-inch in diameter.

Well, the shovels started bustin' left and right and the SIRs were getting madder and madder and accusing us of breaking them on purpose so that we wouldn't have to shovel snow. It wasn't long before my shovel broke, and it was the proverbial shovel that broke Petty Officer Ski SIR's back. Petty Office Ski SIR dragged me into see Chief Petty Officer SIR who dragged me into the Duty Officer-of-the-Day SIR who commenced to chew my ass after Chief Petty Officer SIR explained how I was being disrespectful and destroying government property.

"It ain't my fault your puny shovels are busting like match sticks. I mean, I'm from South Dakota, and I know what a real snow shovel looks like."

Duty Officer-of-the-Day SIR kept trying to interrupt me and tell me to shut up until finally he screamed, "Goddamn it Quigley, don't you know how to talk to an ensign? As far as you're concerned an ensign is God, and when an ensign speaks, you shut up."

"But sir, I wasn't even supposed to be—"

"Shut up" he interrupted again, getting up out of his chair and coming towards me. "Quigley, you're on report for disrespect and for destroying government property. Report to building 12 at 0800 Monday morning, and tell your company commander because he has to be there with you."

Well, you know, I was scared, and I worried all weekend, and I told my company commander everything when I saw him. I expected him to be sympathetic because it wasn't my fault to begin with, but he was irritated and told me it would be good riddance, and that he was tired of my mouth anyway.

There were 42 recruits lined up outside the captain's office waiting for captain's mast. The thought of justice didn't even enter my mind; I just wondered what kind of punishment I would receive. When my turn finally came, I was surprised at how calm and how cordial the captain was. "Quigley, why don't you tell me what happened," he asked.

I started to pour out my story, getting more and more emotional as I went along. I did not leave out a single detail. I even told him what the ensign said about being God, and in a burst of self-pity, said that if he was God, I didn't belong in this Navy anyway because I sure wasn't going to pray to any ensign.

Well, I was sure I overdid it because I could tell the captain was mad; he was glaring at everyone. Finally he asked, "Bishop, who had the watch Friday night?"

"Mildred had the watch, sir," replied Company Commander Bishop SIR, and when he saw the captain's eyes widen added, "That's his last name, sir."

"Did you ask Mildred if Quigley is telling the truth?" the captain asked.

"No sir," answered Company Commander Bishop SIR.

"Bishop, you're supposed to be here representing this man, and you can't even tell me if he is telling the truth?" asked the captain, his voice getting an edge on it. "Don't ever bring anyone to me without doing your homework. Get Mildred here on the double, and don't bother coming back."

We didn't have to wait long for Duty Petty Officer Mildred SIR to appear. The captain told him what I said, and asked him if it was true.

"Yes sir, Captain, it was my mistake. I tore up the chit, but I forgot about the hard card," replied Duty Petty Officer Mildred SIR.

"Do you have any idea how much trouble you've caused this man by not paying attention to detail? All of you, you remind me of Keystone Cops. Mildred, I want you to stand a couple of training watches until you get the hang of it. You can go now," Captain Postel said while turning his attention to Chief Petty Officer SIR.

"Mahaffy, it says here that Quigley broke the eighteenth shovel. Where are the other 17 sailors?" asked Captain Postel.

"Sir?" replied Chief Petty Officer Mahaffy SIR.

"If 18 shovels were broken, I should have 18 sailors on report. Don't tell me the first 17 were accidents? Why did you single this man out?"

"Because he has a rotten mouth," blurted Chief Petty Officer Mahaffy SIR. "He is extremely disrespectful."

"I would be too," said the captain, "if I had been treated as he has. Mr. Becker, did you really tell this man you were God?"

"Yes, sir," Ensign Becker SIR replied. I was surprised at his truthfulness.

"Mr. Becker, do you remember where I live?" asked Captain Postel.

"Yes, sir," Ensign Becker SIR replied.

"Good. I want you to accompany me and Emily to church for a while until you learn the difference between an ensign and God. It won't take long because one's on top and one's on the bottom, and I'm going to explain which is which."

"Yes, sir, Captain Postel."

"Quigley, I apologize for these clowns. I can assure you the real Navy is not like this. If you have any more trouble, you just come over here and tell me about it."

"Yes, sir. Thank you, sir, SIR," I stammered.

"Dismissed," he said.

Loose Buttons

The SIRs were on a scavenger hunt for loose P-coat buttons. They inspected all of us at quarters, and then came around anytime, day or night, and inspected the watch standers. When they found a loose button, they slipped their fingers under it and snapped it off. It would cost a dollar over at Battalion Headquarters to get it back.

The P-coat material was thick, and the buttons were forever coming loose. We were always at risk. I watched my bunkmate solve the problem. He removed his buttons and sewed them back on while holding the buttons about a quarter inch away from the P-coat. Then he would wind thread around the loose threads behind the buttons until the buttons were fastened with a thick cord.

I imitated him. I sewed my buttons on loosely and then wrapped thread around and around the loose threads, and then sewed some more until I was sure I had the most secure buttons in the Navy because I didn't have a dollar. There was a small problem. The thread held the top button out a little too far and the button drooped. I wasn't worried because there wasn't any way it could be pulled off.

A week later I had the mid watch in the barracks. Ensign Bonham SIR, himself, came by to inspect me at 0200. He should have been sound asleep. Anyway, he spotted my droopy button. I saw him smirk as he slipped his fingers under the button and jerk. I nearly came out of my boots, but the button held. He jerked again, harder this time. I fell forward to the deck, almost taking him down with me. He backed up, turned around, and left with my button. It had a three-inch triangle of my P-coat attached.

I was furious and I refused to pay for a new button. I wore my P-coat defiantly, daring anyone to say anything about the large hole where my button used to be. After about a week, Company Commander SIR took me back over to Naked City and swapped my P-coat for a new one. I got a bonus; it fit.

I'll be Home For Christmas

Tall poles with lights and loud speakers surrounded the parade ground. They started playing Christmas music about two weeks before Christmas; it was my first experience with surround sound. It was pleasant. The ground was covered with snow reminding me of South

Dakota, and listening to *White Christmas* made me feel good, if not a little homesick.

The music had a positive effect on the SIRs; there was less bullshit. About a week before Christmas, the music was interrupted by a young sailor bawling like a baby and an impatient SIR trying to calm him down.

"Why do you have to keep playing *I'll be Home for Christmas* over and over and over when you know we won't be home for Christmas," blurted the young sailor between sobs, unaware that his lament was being broadcast over the loud speakers.

"Look, kid, it's only a song and it's in the middle of a record; I ain't gonna stop playing it," said the impatient SIR.

"But I can't go home and I can't keep hearing that song," the young sailor cried. "If you don't stop playing that song I'm going to call my mom and—"

"You're gonna do what?" screamed the impatient SIR. He immediately switched to a sarcastic tone and said, "Well son, I wouldn't want you to tell your mother. Why don't we just reach over here and turn it off."

Silence.

I figured the music would start again after a while, but it never did. We had a quiet Christmas. The bullshit returned. I was depressed.

The Red Cross, Again

I had to see Ensign Bonham SIR again. They had received another letter from the Red Cross saying that I owed them $15.00 and that I was delinquent and that they needed their money, so they could do great things. I thought Ensign Bonham SIR was more reasonable this time, but it did seem like he was speaking through clenched teeth. Anyway he asked nicely if I would write a letter explaining everything, and I said I would and I did. I expected that would be the end of the Red Cross thing.

Non-Qualified Swimmer

I spent more and more time in the swimming pool as the swimming staff was determined that I was not going to leave boot camp a non-qualified swimmer. They tried hard, but I just kept sinking to the bottom of the pool. They seemed to think if they kept teaching me new swimming strokes; surely, one of them would work. The dog paddle was the worst. I wound up walking on my hands on the bottom of the pool. The backstroke came the closest to working. I still sank to the bottom, but I sank more slowly.

The Navy took swimming seriously, and I had to sign a waiver to stay in. They said if I didn't learn to swim by the time I got to my permanent duty station, I wouldn't be able to stay in the Navy.

Classification

I missed the final classification interview because of remedial swimming classes. I had to go over to the classification center for a make-up session. I dreaded being a sonarman. I saw a different Petty Officer SIR this time around and he was more cordial. I think everyone was more polite because we were getting close to graduation.

Anyway, Petty Officer SIR said, "Quigley, I have bad news for you. The sonarman rating is all full up; there are no more quotas. Is there anything else you want to try for?"

"Well, SIR," I said, "I guess I could tolerate being a photographer."

"Great," he said, "I'll send you to Airman Prep School."

I thought I had been sucker punched again, but I was told I had to go to Airman Prep School before I could go to photography school. I made it. I was going to be a photographer.

AIRMAN PREP SCHOOL

"Knock off that boot camp shit," said the chief at the duty outhouse. "I am a chief petty officer and damn proud of it, and furthermore I ain't no SIR, and I'm damn proud of that too."

"Yes, sir," I said.

When I got to the personnel office, I found out I was already on report. Ensign Bonham had felt compelled to forward all letters from the Red Cross along with a summary of the counseling I had received for refusing to pay back a loan.

"I have no use for a man that would short change the Red Cross," said my new commanding officer.

"But sir, I had an agreement with them to—"

"I don't want to hear any excuses. What I want is for you to give my secretary a $15.00 money order and a stamped envelope addressed to the Red Cross within an hour. Failure to do so will seriously jeopardize your career. Do you understand what I'm saying?"

"Yes sir."

"I don't understand you kids now-a-days; you have no sense of responsibility. Dismissed."

I liked Airman Prep School. I learned about all the aviation ratings including Photographer's Mate. I also learned some practical things like welding and soldering. And I learned a lot of exciting stuff about aircraft carriers and airplanes and I figured I was in the right place.

I had remedial swimming lessons three times a week. I didn't mind because I really wanted to learn to swim; however, the two instructors weren't very helpful because they concentrated on helping the women. They didn't say five words to me all the time I was there. I tried swimming on my back, but it was hopeless; I just kept sinking to the bottom. After a while I gave up and just watched the instructors play with the women.

We had Cinderella liberty every Friday and Saturday night. Friday was out because I didn't finish swimming until 2000, but I was ready to go, come Saturday night. I had a great time. Norman, Oklahoma, was a great place. The people were friendly, and I was overdue for a good time. Mostly, I just talked to people and drank a few beers. I headed back to the base about 2330 because I sure didn't want to be late. But, of course, I was. Can you believe it? Cinderella liberty ended at 2300. I was put on report at the gate.

Because it was my first Cinderella liberty, and because of my superior knowledge of literature, the captain actually let me off with a warning.

I was not so lucky the next time around. I guess the captain had to do something because it was the third time he'd seen me. Without any warning, the swimming instructors had put me on report for dereliction of duty. They told the captain I never made any effort to learn to swim. I couldn't believe it. These guys had hardly said a word to me. Anyway, I told the captain about the women, and he relieved them of instructor duty without even asking them if it was true. Captain's mast is a real crapshoot. I received another official reprimand.

I saw the captain again before I left. I was honor man for Class 254. I was off to photo school, and I was excited.

PHOTO SCHOOL

The U.S. Naval Schools of Photography were located at the Naval Air Station, Pensacola, Florida. The large, elegant, white sandstone building looked more like a hotel in the Alps than a military school. Its four-inch-thick doors, 14-inch-thick sandstone walls, brass expansion bracelets, brass periscope, and intricate beams that held the roof up without any nails made a unique home for the Photo Schools.

The building, formerly the Bachelor Officer's Quarters at Fort Barrancas, housed the basic photo school, a motion picture school, and a camera repair school. The building faced the ocean, and the white sand beaches of Escambia Bay were only a few blocks away. We fell in for quarters every morning on the parade ground immediately in front of the building. Beyond the parade ground was a large park that was separated from the beaches by a road that ran along the bay.

It was a great place for a photo school for Southerners. For people from South Dakota, there was a little problem with the heat, the humidity, and the roaches. The heat was unbearable. The humidity was oppressive, and I was terrified of the roaches. I don't ever recall seeing a roach in Rapid City, South Dakota. They mustered in front of my bunk every evening for the sole purpose of intimidating me. It worked. I had nightmares of being carried off on a bed of roaches.

I was given one sheet and one pillowcase when I checked into the barracks. "Is this all I get?" I asked.

"It's all you need," came the flat reply.

I lay awake all night listening to the roaches call cadence and wondering when it would cool off. By morning, I understood why I didn't need a top sheet. There was a wet imprint of my body on the bottom sheet when I got up.

The school was 15 weeks. I wondered if I could go that long without sleep.

We marched from the barracks to the school, sat through an hour of indoctrination and three hours of class. We bused to the galley and back; sat through four more hours of class, held a 30-minute field day, and marched back to the barracks. The instructors seemed cold and indifferent, but they were good. We did everything by the numbers; there was no room for creativity. Most would become artisans; few would become artists.

I was placed on report my second night in the barracks for sleeping in the windowsill.

The school was about 75 percent theory and about 25 percent practical. The first time I saw a photographic image appear in a tray of developer, it was pure magic. I have been hooked ever since. I was enthralled, and I studied simply because I enjoyed it, something I had never done before.

A Hole in the Wall

I was called downstairs to the Barracks Master-At-Arms office the evening of my third night in the barracks.

"Quigley, I've been told that you punched the holes in the wall outside my office, and I am officially notifying you that you are on report."

Something inside me exploded. I spun around and hit the wall with my fist so hard that it went all the way through.

"What the hell do you think you're doing?"

"If you're going to put me on report for punching holes in the wall, then by God at least one of them is going to have my name on it."

"Well, you didn't have to do that. You could have just told me."

"Yeah, like you would have believed me."

"You shouldn't have done that; you really shouldn't have done that. Go to your room and stay there until I get back to you."

He never got back to me, and he didn't put me on report, which was a relief because I hadn't seen the captain yet for sleeping in the windowsill.

When I finally went to mast, all I got was a warning, but I was really starting to worry. Do they keep count? Are they going to kick me out when I hit a certain number?

Step to the Back of the Bus

I made my first friendship with a colored man—well, that's what we called them back then. His name was Henry Mason. Henry was much more outgoing than I was and a lot of fun to be with. He could mimic all of the instructors and all the rest of us with uncanny accuracy. He seemed to be aware of everyone's relationship to everyone else, and was a constant source of insight and amazement.

Henry was always happy and could see humor in almost everything. I don't know how anyone could not like him, but the instructors were all down on him except for one we all called Big Jim. The instructors were always asking Henry questions that were beyond what was being taught and then ridiculing him for not knowing the answer. I was given two hours extra duty one day for telling an instructor that the question he asked Henry had not been covered, and that none of us could answer it. Henry came and marched right along with me. We had so much fun we almost got another two hours.

When we were back in the barracks, I said, "Big Jim is okay, ain't he, Henry? I mean he is powerfully good looking, and his clothes fit so well I think he has them tailored. He is the only one that doesn't give you a bad time."

"Well, he really is something. You know he is banging every broad in the joint. The girls are crazy about him."

"How do you know all that stuff, Henry?"

"Open your eyes, Russell. They follow him up and down the hall everywhere he goes. Yesterday, one of them even followed him into the head, but he run her out. Rumor is, he has three of them pregnant."

"I still don't know how you pick up on all this."

"Russell, the next time you see him, count the number of girls with him, look at their faces, and watch the way they touch him, and then tell me they ain't all crazy about him. Women don't touch men like that unless they've been intimate."

"How do you know they're pregnant? You can't tell that by looking at them. Ain't nobody showing."

"That's what the girls are saying. Don't you talk to the girls, Russell?

"Not much."

"Well, that's your problem, Russell. If you don't talk to girls, you'll never know what's going on. You know they're into everything."

I was amazed that all this was going on around me, and I didn't have a clue. I made a vow to be more observant and to learn how to talk to girls. I really didn't like to talk to girls unless I was drunk and horny. Henry enjoyed talking to everyone. I wanted to be like Henry. I still do.

Henry and I took the shuttle bus downtown one Saturday just to look around. We got off at Garden and Palafox and walked over to the Saenger to check out the movie. It didn't interest us, so we went across the street to the Sears and Roebuck Company. Henry says, "If they don't have it at Sears and Roebucks, you probably don't need it."

We ate at a corner café, walked back to Garden Street, and decided to catch a city bus back to the base. We got on, paid our fares, walked back to the middle of the bus, and sat down. Well, the bus wasn't going all that fast, but it stopped so suddenly that we all were thrown forward. I heard someone curse behind me.

The bus driver came back and looked at Henry and said, "Would you please step to the back of the bus?"

Henry didn't say a word; he just stood up, squeezed by me, and went to the back of the bus. I was stunned. I had heard about segregation, but it really caught me off guard. The bus was moving again by the time I decided to move to the back of the bus and sit by Henry. Henry didn't give me his usual smile.

This time the bus came to a gentle stop. The bus driver opened the doors before coming back and pointing to me. "You, off the bus."

I was about to challenge the bus driver when he shoved me towards the door. The stairwell was behind me, so when I stepped back, I fell completely out of the bus on to the road. I was surprised, hurt, and angry. I was about to tear back into the bus and into the driver when he said, "Officer, a little assistance, please."

A police officer helped me up, and then held on to my arm.

"What's wrong, driver?"

"That man is trying to make trouble with the coloreds. Make sure he doesn't get on another city bus."

The police officer was still holding on to me when the bus pulled away. I wondered why Henry didn't get off the bus.

"What did you do?" the officer asked.

"I sat with a friend."

"You mean you sat with a colored friend, and that's not legal."

"I can't believe that it's illegal for one sailor to sit with another sailor."

"If you like, I can arrest you, and you can see for yourself how legal it is."

"No thanks. I believe you. Do you know how much it costs to take a taxi to the base?"

"You don't need to take a taxi; you can take a bus. That driver runs a bus, not the whole city."

To this day, I do not understand why Henry did not get off the bus, but even more puzzling is why he never spoke to me again. They dropped Henry from the school about half way through.

Mustang

Big Jim was selected for the Limited Duty Officer (LDO) program. It caused quite a stir because the three girls really were pregnant. LDOs, or Mustangs, as they are called, have to go to "Knife and Fork" school to learn how to be gentlemen. Big Jim was transferred. The three girls were dropped from Photo School and put out of the Navy.

Another Redhead

His hair was blond and his eyes were blue, but I could see that he was another redhead. I clipped his heel while we were marching. He spun around and hit me so hard three of us went down. I knew better than to fight back. I could see the adrenaline pumping through his veins and popping out his eyes. I'd seen that look before. I just listened to him swear a blue streak and let it go at that. I wondered how long he would last.

A few weeks later, I had the 0800 to 1200 barracks watch on the second deck. There were stairs on each side of the lobby with an open-air railing between them. It was Saturday morning. Normally, it would be a quiet watch because everyone would be on liberty. However, the Officer-of-the-Day was Lieutenant Asshole, who said we didn't get the barracks clean enough yesterday, so he ordered another field day, and said he would be here at 0900 to inspect.

Well, all I could do was walk around and watch, but everybody else pitched in and the place was ready for inspection by 0900. I stood by the railing so I could see down into the lobby to watch for Lieutenant Asshole. Everybody was anxious to go on liberty, so of course they were annoyed when he didn't show up. Everybody quit cleaning and stood by their room ready to sound off whenever Lieutenant Asshole showed up. Everybody that is, except Red. He kept cleaning his room over and over and imploring his roommates not to touch anything.

An hour went by. Red must have cleaned the top of his locker with a damp cloth 20 times. Another hour went by, and finally I saw 220 pounds of asshole climbing the stairs. I gave him a snappy salute and he gave me a clipboard. I guess I was supposed to record the discrepancies.

Red's room was next to the stairs and that's where we were, so that's where we started. Lieutenant Asshole stepped into Red's room wearing white gloves. He reached up and swiped his finger across the top of Red's locker, turned the finger towards his face and without looking at it said, "Dust on top of the lockers."

What happened next happened so fast it was a blur. Red knocked me down on his way to the railing above the lobby. Lieutenant Asshole was actually circling over Red's head. Before I could get up, Red threw the lieutenant over the railing and down to the lobby 18 feet below. I stood up and watched Red fly down the stairs. He picked up the lieutenant again and ran outside holding the man over his head again. I got outside in time to see Red hurl the lieutenant into the middle of the street.

About a dozen of us surrounded Red, thinking we ought to hold him there. We all tackled him at once, and he threw us all off at once. We tried again and he threw us off again. He just walked away as if nothing happened.

When I first heard I was on report, I knew it was a mistake. They just needed me as a witness. I was wrong. I was on report.

"How could you let this happen on your watch? You should have warned the lieutenant. Why didn't you help him? Couldn't you see he needed help?"

They could tell I didn't know how to stand a proper watch, so they gave me more of them.

Aerial Photo

I volunteered for the extra two weeks of aerial photography training because I heard you make more money if you fly. We took our flight physicals right alongside of the cadets in flight training. I enjoyed learning about aerial cameras and all the related equipment. I even enjoyed the equations we used to determine image size at different altitudes.

Veggies

A holding company is made up of sailors waiting for something to happen; in this case, we were waiting for orders to our first duty stations. Sailors in a holding company are available for odd jobs and working parties. It is better to work than to just sit around, but for some reason, transients in holding companies were always treated poorly, so we were always on guard.

Our first assignment was to weed the lawns and gardens on admiral's row. There was a lot of noise in Congress about officers using enlisted men for personal chores, and we all thought this was just such a case, but it was my idea to buy the vegetable seeds.

The country store was only a block away, so everybody chipped in and we bought corn, watermelons, tomatoes, onions, squash, the works. Every time we weeded a flower garden, we planted vegetables. We mixed the seeds together and divided them up, so that we didn't even know what we were planting. After a while we started planting them anywhere we could find a bare piece of ground.

We were long gone, of course, when the veggies started sprouting, but we heard from new graduates that they made quite a stir, especially since most of the residents let them grow to maturity. I don't know if they let them grow because they had a sense of humor, or if they were just being cheap.

I received orders for the Fleet Air Photo Lab, at Barbers Point, Hawaii. Six of us from the aerial class were going to the same place. We would go by train to Treasure Island and then fly to Hawaii.

TREASURE ISLAND

We came by train to this manmade island under the Golden Gate Bridge. It was a place where sailors were imprisoned while the naval bureaucracy arranged for transportation to their final destination. It was Treasure Island, more commonly known as TI.

Upside Down
If boot camp made a farce of discipline, Treasure Island turned it upside down. Fortunately, the average stay was only a few days, and most people could stay out of trouble for that length of time. Working parties were standard fare at such places, and let's face it, they usually helped to pass the time; however, TI added a new wrinkle. The executive officer had invested "master-at-arms" authority in seamen and junior petty officers. This meant that as long as they were wearing "MAA" armbands, their orders carried the same weight as an order from the executive officer, a privilege normally reserved for senior petty officers.

These masters-at-arms were in charge of the working parties, and each and every one of them was a little Hitler. It didn't matter whether you were an airman apprentice or a chief petty officer, they were in charge, and they loved it. All day long, they barked orders at juniors and seniors alike, and studied how they could make menial tasks even more humiliating. It was obvious by their nasty attitudes that they had all the backing they needed, so everyone did as they were told.

WHAAAAAP
My barracks consisted of four large door-less rooms big enough to hold 12 bunk beds each. The rooms were bordered by a long hallway that went from one end of the building to the other with a door on each end. The offices,

heads, and main entrance were on the other side of the hallway. The bunk beds were made of lead pipe just like you would have put in your house at the time. I was the only one assigned to my room, so I chose a bunk in the middle and was making it up when I heard the damndest "WHOOOOSH!" I ever heard. Then, there were a lot of "ohs" and "ahs" and "wows" and then a lot of excited conversation.

I continued making my bed, but then I heard it again, WHOOOSH!" And again, I heard a bunch of guys whooping it up, so I just had to wander next door to find out what was going on. Well, it was the damndest thing I ever saw; they had screwed the end cap off one of the corner poles of a bunk bed and were pouring lighter fluid into it. Then they held a lighter over the pole and flicked it. "WHOOOOSH! A large blue flame shot out of the pole and nearly reached the ceiling. It only lasted for a few seconds, but oh, what a sight.

Well, I couldn't wait to try it. I rushed back to my room and was delighted to see that an end cap was already missing from one of the corner poles on my bunk. I poured even more lighter fluid than the other guys because I wanted it to be a good one. I turned out the lights to increase the effect, and then took my Zippo® and set it on fire, but instead of a "WHOOOOSH!" I got a, "WHAAAAAP! WHAAAAAP! WHAAAAAP!"

My predecessors had used the open pole for an ashtray and stuffed it full of cigarette butts. It went off like a Roman candle, but with all the fireballs coming out at once. Instantly, the whole room was on fire. Burning butts were everywhere, on the beds, on the chairs, on the deck. I scurried around in a panic brushing the burning butts off the beds and furniture. Then, I scurried around stomping on the burning butts; I was so busy stomping I didn't even notice I had an audience that was getting bigger and bigger, and that right there in front was one of those little Hitlers with an armband.

I asked the captain, "How can you bust me? Ain't I already as low as I can get?"

I didn't realize I had been promoted when I left boot camp. I did realize that my pay was a few dollars more a month. I didn't know I had been a seaman recruit because we didn't wear any stripes and nobody called us that. Most of the time, we were called skinheads.

Fact is, I was a seaman recruit in boot camp, and I was promoted to seaman apprentice when I graduated. The captain explained all that, and then busted me back to seaman recruit.

THE FLEET AIR PHOTO LAB

The Naval Air Station, Barbers Point, Hawaii, sprawled over 3500 acres. You could get lost on the back roads. The Naval Air Station was host to Utility Squadron One (VU-1), which included the Fleet Air Photographic Laboratory (FAPL). The Fleet Air Photo Lab was primarily concerned with aerial reconnaissance and mapping photography.

Although the Korean peace treaty had been signed several months before, the Fleet Air Photo Lab at Barber's Point was operating as if we were still at war. There was enough work to keep 75 photo mates busy processing and printing intelligence photography and doing some mapping. In fact, one of my first aerial assignments was a high altitude map of the Formosa Strait.

I arrived in June of 1954. I had opted to become an aerial photographer while at Photo School so I could receive "flight skins," which is the Navy's way of saying flight pay. I got an unexpected bonus when the leading chief told me that I wouldn't be going mess cooking because they had plenty of junior people, and I would be needed to help with their aerial assignments.

There was some serious friction among the upper echelons. The Leading Chief Petty Officer (LCPO), Chief Buckley, was always fighting with Warrant Officer Connally, and both of them fought with Commander Anderson. The aerial chief, Chief Matheeny, hibernated in the mapping room, and Chief Maynard, the duty alcoholic, stayed in the Chief's Club except for field days and other shit details. He was the only one that was decent to the junior troops. The four first class section leaders seemed to be in competition with each other, and in general, nobody got along with anyone else.

There was also friction between the squadron we flew with (VU-1) and the photo lab. I don't know how it started, but it seemed to be headed for a showdown.

There was another chief, Chief Pointer, whom we never saw. He kept to himself. It was rumored that he was an ex-marine, and that he shot over 30,000 feet of Victory at Sea. Anyway, he worked in a Quonset hut on the other side of the hangar where all the motion picture work was done.

Whenever it rained, Chief Pointer would flatten cardboard boxes and throw them into the stream that quickly formed in the alley between the Quonset hut and the hangar. The alley drained into the large parking area in front of the hangar. The boxes would flow down the alley, out into the parking area, and then plug up the drains. The parking area quickly filled with water. The people in the main lab were afraid of being trapped, so they turned the photo lab over to the duty section and secured everyone else. The water would eventually dissolve the boxes, so no one ever caught on.

Chief Buckley, after being introduced, warned me that he couldn't stand whistling, and then he cocked his leg and farted loudly.

"Quigley, I rotate new people every 90 days until they learn their way around. You'll start in the print room with Petty Officer First Class Reggie Sinclair. You should be ready to fly whenever we need you."

It was great training, and eventually I got to know everyone. I started out processing prints, and then I flew photo missions two or three times a week. We worked closely with VU-1, a utility squadron with small planes and helicopters. Most of the petty officers were a pain, but I loved the work.

Stripes

I was still wearing my photographer's mate aerial airman apprentice (PHAAA) badge with two green stripes when I checked into the base at Barbers Point. That night, after I settled into the open bay barracks, I used the seam ripper in my sewing kit to remove the stripes from all of my uniforms.

The next day, when I returned to the personnel office to finish checking in, a first class personnelman, Sharon Denton, spotted my missing stripes and said, "You need to get your stripes sewed on. You can't check in without them."

Embarrassed, I told her about the fire and my mast and the reduction in rate.

She said, "I checked your page 13s. You've been in and out of a lot of trouble, but I don't remember anything about a bust. Let me double-check that for you. It's right here; your last mast was at the Photo School. Take a look; you got an official reprimand. There is no page 13 entry from Treasure Island.

I didn't know what to make of it. I clearly remembered asking the captain how he could bust me. I remember asking, ain't I already at the bottom? I also remember he explained that I was being busted from airman apprentice back to airman recruit.

That night, I sewed the stripes back on all my uniforms, and never said another word about it.

My First Day

I was assigned to the photographic print room, which had four enlargers, and huge marble sinks filled with chemistry. The first sink was filled with D-72, a print developer. The second sink was filled with shortstop, an acid bath that stopped the action of the developer. The third sink contained hypo, a chemical that makes photographic prints permanent.

The four people making enlargements gave me 15 to 20 prints at a time. I would fan them out, slip them into the developer one at a time, shuffle them for two minutes, and then transfer them to the short stop in the same order that they went into the developer. After agitating them in the short stop for a few seconds, I transferred them to the hypo where they stayed for 20 minutes. Then I rinsed my hands for another run of prints through the chemistry.

Whenever I had a bunch of prints that had been in the hypo for 20 minutes, I was instructed to scream, "PRINTS OUT," into the fresh air vent loud enough for the finishing room crew to hear me. Someone would then come in with a large print tray on a cart and take the prints out to be washed and dried.

The four printers kept me busy all day; although, we did have a work stoppage about 1400 when an angry chief petty officer barged in and bellowed at me for more than a few minutes. I did not understand a word he said, but I kept saying, "yes sir, yes sir, yes sir," until he was satisfied and left. I did get the impression that I was screaming, "PRINTS OUT," into his office rather than the finishing room.

The guys were snickering. "Russell," said Petty Officer Sinclair, "Perhaps it would be better if you went out to the finishing room before you holler prints out." When we finished for the day, they advised me to rinse my hands in the tray of clear liquid set up in the finishing room. A printed sign over the tray read, "HAND RINSE: Prevents photochemistry from staining your hands." I rinsed my hands and secured for the day.

I didn't notice my purple hands until I picked up a tray to eat in the galley. Oh oh, they played another trick on me. Since I'm already here, I might as well eat. I'll go back to the photo lab when I finish and see if someone in the duty section will tell me how to get it off.

About halfway through my supper I noticed a mess-deck-master-at-arms talking to two civilians in suits and pointing to my table. They came over.

"Would you mind standing up?"

"Why, what's going on?"

"Just stand up. You're under arrest."

I stood up. "What the hell is going on?"

They put handcuffs on me right there in front of everyone. "Well son, Ma Bell doesn't like thieves and neither do we."

"What are you talking about?"

"You can stop pretending. The evidence is all over your hands. We put dye on every nickel in every telephone on the base to catch your ass. You've been robbing phones for a long time, but we've caught you red handed, and now you're going away for a long time."

"Can I make a phone call before we leave?"

"You can make all the phone calls you want. It won't do you a damn bit of good."

They unlocked my handcuffs, and I called the photo lab hoping someone there could help. To my surprise, Chief Buckley was still there. I explained the problem, and he told me to put one of them on the phone. I handed the phone to the nearest man. He stood up straight and his chest swelled.

"Robert Snell, FBI. To whom am I talking?"

In a minute, he cupped the phone and said to his partner, "This kid's chief wants us to come by the photo lab where he works."

"Sure, we can do that. Let the chief get a good look at his purple hands before we take him downtown."

The men exchanged pleasantries with Chief Buckley and talked amicably until the chief said my hands were purple when I left work.

"Don't try to protect this kid, chief. He's been robbing phones for six months. We finally caught him red handed. Believe me, he isn't worth it. Besides, if you aren't careful, you could get your ass in a whole lot of trouble."

"If you'll just step back into the dark room, I'll show you exactly what happened to Quigley."

"We don't have time for this shit," said Mr. Snell.

The chief's voice took on an edge. "If you leave without allowing me to demonstrate his innocence, I'll be on the phone with the commanding officer before you're out the door, and I guarantee you will not be allowed off the base with this man after I tell the CO that I have proof of his innocence, and that you refused to listen to it."

"Okay. Okay. But make it quick. We haven't got all day."

Chief Buckley turned to go into the print room, but stopped to dip his hands in the tray with the hand rinse and dried them on the towel. "You will have to rinse your hands first."

"Don't play games with—"

"Rinse your hands." Chief Buckley could be very insistent. Reluctantly, they both rinsed and dried their hands. They went inside and Chief Buckley explained every step of my job.

When we were all back outside, Mr. Snell said, "I thought you were going to explain his innocence."

The chief held up his hands and said, "I did. Take a look at my hands. Now take a look at your hands"

Their hands were as purple as mine were. I was beginning to enjoy this.

"Son-of-a-bitch! What the hell are you trying to pull, chief?" The men had skipped angry and slipped right into livid.

"My men played a joke on Quigley. The same joke they play on all new guys coming into the lab. I don't know what you guys used, but we use potassium permanganate."

"How do we know you didn't just set this up?"

"Would handling nickels give you such a nice even tone? Especially, on the back of the hands? Would it leave that nice even ring around your wrist?" Besides, you said someone has been robbing the phones for weeks, Quigley just arrived this week.

"Okay, you've made your point; now get this stuff off of us."

"Take the handcuffs off Quigley."

They removed my handcuffs and demanded again that the chief get the stuff off their hands.

"I told you, it's a joke. You guys should have at least as much fun as Quigley's had."

"Chief," said Mr. Snell, "I don't appreciate this. I'm the one that's going to be talking to the CO this time. This isn't over. Not by a long shot." They stormed out of the lab.

"Bastards," said the chief. "They don't think an enlisted man is capable of telling the truth. They should have come straight over here when you told them what happened. You're lucky I was here, Quigley. They would've locked you up and thrown away the key. All we have to do to get this stuff off our hands, Quigley, is to rinse them in the same hypo you've been using all day."

The Airman Test

Since I wasn't busted, I was eligible to take the Airman test. It was given at the squadron once a month. I studied my notes from Airman Prep School, and I was ready. The trouble was, they didn't test on anything I learned in Airman Prep School. Utility Squadron 1 made up their own Airman test based on their mission and their aircraft. Well, besides hauling photographers to and from aerial jobs, which wasn't mentioned, I didn't have a clue what their mission was.

I flunked the test. Can you believe it? I was the honor man at Airman Prep School and I got a 62 on the Airman test. I was humiliated, and I was furious because I wasn't told in advance what to expect. I didn't get any sympathy.

Even after I knew what the test was about, I couldn't find any study materials. All I could do was ask everyone who had taken the test what was on it and what did I need to know. I passed the test the second time around, but I ain't telling by how much.

Once again I removed all my airman apprentice stripes, but this time I replaced them with Airman stripes. A week later I got called back to the personnel office and told that the paper work for my mast at Treasure Island had arrived and that once again, I was an airman recruit. I removed all my airman badges.

Chief Buckley got a call from the captain the next day. "Chief Buckley, PN1 Denton just called my attention to one of your new people. It seems he had already made airman by the time we got word of his reduction to airman recruit. I read the report and it sounds like it was an accident. If you have no objections, I would just as soon let him keep his airman stripes."

"I don't have any objections, Captain. He seems like a nice enough kid to me."

Telephone Mast

As soon as I could, I made an appointment with the senior dentist, Captain Sacks. He was not an amiable man. As a matter of fact, I might as well tell you right now that in 30 years, I never met a dentist with four stripes that wasn't mean.

I told him about not being able to get my braces adjusted, and that when I enlisted the dentist assured me that the Navy would take care of them.

Captain Sacks said there was no way the Navy was going to take care of my braces and that they damn sure weren't going to pay a civilian to do so.

I argued with him. I had paid for my braces myself and they cost me a bundle. I told him the Navy should not have accepted me if they were not going to take care of my braces.

Captain Sacks lost his patience and told me to get out. I got angry and said I was going to request mast. Captain

Sacks picked up the phone and called the commanding officer.

"Bob, this is George Sacks. I have a smart-ass kid here who won't listen. I have tried to explain to him that the Navy doesn't have orthodontists and that we can't take care of his braces. They should of never let him in with those braces on, but there is nothing we can do about it now. He says he is going to request mast and put me on report. I thought you might like to save us all some time." He handed me the phone.

They must have a correspondence course on how to chew ass because I never met a senior officer that wasn't good at it. It cost me $75.00 to have my braces removed. My page 13 said I got a warning, but I can tell you, I got a reprimand.

Open Bay Barracks

We lived in open bay barracks with screened in walls instead of windows. I was on the second deck, but both floors were the same. A gym-sized room was divided into four man cubicles by double rows of lockers, back to back. There were ten cubicles on each side and a row of picnic tables down the center of the room. A large head and a community shower were located at each end of the room.

I rather liked it. The lockers were large enough to hold everything I owned. There was usually a card game going on at one of the tables. I was never lonely. If I felt like going on liberty, there was always someone around that felt like going with me.

I was annoyed at how often I had to stand night watches in the barracks. Walking around a darkened room with no one to talk to for four hours is not very exciting. It was the only watch I had to stand besides duty photographer, so it wasn't so bad.

I knew the building was really old, but I was shocked when it was condemned. We didn't move out right away because there was no place to go. Then one day one of the photographers, Victor Lacarrio, fell through the floor, just like in boot camp except Victor wasn't fooling around and he fell all the way down to the first floor. Victor was banged up, but he didn't suffer any permanent injuries. That did it though; we started moving out the next day.

They had wanted to keep us together, but they had to split us up. Victor Lacarrio, a few others, and I moved in with squadron pukes that weren't at all happy to have us. It was another open bay barracks just like the one we left, and it was right across the street from the Navy Exchange, which was convenient, but with all the tension, it just wasn't the same.

Victor and I wound up in the same cubicle. I tried to make friends, but Victor was a real loner. He was a little man with olive skin and heavy black-rimmed glasses. Victor was the only guy I ever met who purchased his glasses on the outside, and wound up with glasses that were uglier than standard Navy issue.

Victor was always quiet and very polite, the kind of person everyone seems to love to pick on. And pick on him they did. He never complained, but he never seemed happy.

Victor made the mistake of coming through the first deck drunk one night and waking up some of the squadron pukes. They beat him up so badly, he spent a week in the hospital. I don't know why I felt guilty, but I did. I noticed that he had standard Navy issue glasses when he returned. He didn't talk at all after that, but no one picked on him anymore. It was like he wasn't even there.

Late one night, our old barracks burned to the ground. They said it only took eight minutes. I never complained about standing barracks fire watches after that.

Duty Photographer

Accident photography is much like combat photography. You are apt to see things that you cannot erase from your memory. These memories do not seem to fade over time, and they come to visit whenever they feel like it.

I had been at the Fleet Air Photo Lab about a month when such an accident occurred. An 18-wheeled tractor-trailer was speeding on one of the back roads when a man in a pickup estimated to be doing 80 miles per hour hit it from the left. The cab was jackknifed to the right by the pickup and then hit a second time by a passenger car, also traveling at a high rate of speed, with two couples and a baby onboard. Everyone was dead.

The call came into the photo lab at 2300. I was the duty photographer. There was no moonlight. Photographers define black as the absence of light. It was black. I shot 150 pictures over a two-and-a-half-hour period. Most were focused by flashlight, but eventually we had more powerful lights run by portable generators. Exposure was based on the size of the flashbulb and the distance to the subject and had to be calculated for each shot.

We were just about finished; a tow truck was straightening out the cab so that it could be separated from the trailer. That's when I saw her. The force of the impact had thrown her out of the car against the trailer, and then she had been pinched in-between when the cab jackknifed. I was doing okay until I saw her. She seemed to be standing in mid-air looking down at me.

There was a crowd in the photo lab when I returned: a dozen officers and chiefs that I didn't know, Commander Anderson, Chief Buckley, all the section leaders, and a bunch of photographers. Several darkrooms were set up for film processing and I was directed to turn over my film to Petty Officer Second Class Morehead who seemed to have everything organized and ready to go.

Chief Buckley cornered me and asked me if I had remembered to open up three f-stops since there were no walls to bounce the light back into the subject.

"I don't know. I can't remember." I started to shake. The more I tried to remember, the more I shook. I told the chief I thought I was going to be sick, but I really just wanted to get away from his questions. I poured myself a cup of coffee and sat in a corner out of the way. I could remember each and every picture, each and every face, but I couldn't remember if I focused, let alone opened up three f-stops.

The lab was nearly empty when I got up. The Chief was manning the finishing room, and prints were starting to come out of the enlarging rooms.

"Good work, Russell. You had me worried for a while, but all of your negatives are good. Sharp and well exposed. Your coverage was excellent. The XO and all of the investigators praised your work and your demeanor on the job. You'll be getting a letter for sure."

"Thanks, Chief." I was relieved. It was a scenario that would repeat itself many times. Whenever life got scary, I would go on autopilot. I would be fine until it was over.

Survival Training

The first part of survival training was fun all except for when I panicked and pulled the cord on my life vest before I hit the water. They told us not to do that. The vest inflated, so when I went into the water, it snapped my head back so hard I thought I broke my neck. I was okay, but I vowed not to make that mistake ever again.

We had to inflate our life rafts and find our own way back to land. It took us all day, but we made it. Some of the guys got sick, and all of us were exhausted by the time we reached shore.

I dreaded the second part of survival training: swimming. We had to swim four laps in the pool or tread water for 30 minutes. I couldn't do either. I wondered if they would really put me out of the Navy or just tell me I couldn't fly anymore.

"Russell, what do you mean, you can't swim," asked Petty Officer Mackenzie.

"Petty Officer Mackenzie, I mean exactly what I said. I can't swim. I've had hundreds of hours of lessons and I still can't swim."

"Just call me Mack, Russell. Well, I never met anyone in the Navy who couldn't swim, but don't worry about it. I will teach you the dead man's float. Anyone can do that, and all you have to do is stay afloat for 30 minutes."

He took me to the deep end of the pool, and demonstrated the dead man's float and showed me how to breathe. I was inspired by how effortlessly he floated. He got out of the pool.

"Now then, you try it, Russell."

I assumed the position full of confidence. I was still confident when my first effort to breathe didn't work because I was too far under the water. I did start to worry when I realized Mack was just a blob against the light and my feet were touching the bottom of the pool.

Mack was in the pool and pulled me up in a flash. "My God," he said, "no wonder you can't swim, you have negative buoyancy. Didn't any of those clowns that were teaching you to swim ever notice that you sank to the bottom of the pool?"

"What's going to happen to me? Am I going to be put out of the Navy? Can I still fly?"

"Relax, Russell. All you have to do is sign a permanent waiver so the Navy won't be held responsible if you drown. It's your choice."

"Good. I want to stay at least long enough to qualify for the GI Bill."

The Formosa Strait

I didn't know what all the fuss was about. The Korean truce had already been signed, but there was a lot of talk about a lot of Sampans forming an intelligence network. Anyway, somebody wanted to map the Formosa Strait from a high altitude, flying all of the flight lines at once. It would take 11 P2Vs all rigged with mapping cameras and all flying parallel flight lines. Chief Matheeny was in charge, and laid out the flight lines on charts for everyone. We were all issued high altitude flight gear.

We touched down at Midway for refueling and then took off again. We landed in Formosa and spent the rest of the day playing tourists. I took a liking to Chinese cooking. We couldn't communicate, so we all had to go outside and point to the sample dishes in the window. We were asked to return to the base early because we had a long hard day in front of us.

We got up early, had a big breakfast, and were checking out our camera systems when the pilots and crewmembers arrived. We started taking off at 0830, one after the other. We were all on station and began flying our flight lines by 0900.

It went well for about half an hour, and then all hell broke loose. Three Chinese MIG 15s attacked us from the rear. I thought we would run for cover, but we held our course, and stayed on our flight lines. Two American jets arrived promptly and chased the MIGs away, but not before one of our photo planes was forced into the water. Only one of the crew was lost: the photographer, Victor Lacarrio.

Years later, I would learn that a cousin was flying one of the jets that chased the MIGs away. I would also learn that brother Roger received a large cash bonus from the State of South Dakota for sitting at a desk at the Naval Academy during the Korean War while I was getting shot at, and that I wasn't eligible for the bonus, because the truce had already been signed when I joined the Navy.

Doctor Quigley

My big toe started swelling one day for no apparent reason. It kept getting worse and worse until I could hardly walk. I developed a large lump in my groin that seemed to be related to my toe, so I decided it was time I went to sick bay. I hobbled to the photo lab, which was only a few of blocks away, expecting to get a ride to sick bay, which was several miles away. When I asked for a ride, Chief Buckley said, "They took the pickup to the flight line. It won't be back until they're through flying."

Well, I sure didn't want to walk, but I figured somebody ought to look at it, so off I went. My toe was twice as big when I got there. One of the two corpsmen on the desk took me into a little room, set a pan of cold water on the floor, and handed me a pack of Epsom salts.

"Don't I get to see a doctor?"

"For a sore toe?"

So I soaked my toe, and walked back to the photo lab. I could tell by now that it was an infected toenail. I didn't know what to do. I couldn't get my shoe on. I could hardly walk. I knew I was not going to walk to sick bay again. I had an idea. That evening, I went to the exchange, which was just across the street from the barracks, and bought an Exacto® knife, two rolls of cotton, two bottles of iodine, some gauze, and a bunch of bandages.

The next day I went to work and locked myself in the film developing room. I noticed right away that I could move my toenail around. I thought maybe I could just pull it out, but it wasn't going to be that easy. I used my lighter to sterilize the blade. I soaked my toe in iodine, and then I began to cut. I had to stop and let the infection ooze out.

A voice came over the loud speaker, "Quigley, come out to the office; I need to see you." It was the leading chief.

"I can't," I said, "I'm operating on my toe, and I'm right in the middle."

"You're what? You come out of there right now."

I ignored him. I wasn't leaving until I got all of the infection out of my toe.

Chief Buckley had seen my toe when I got back from sick bay and was feeling guilty for not getting me a ride. He was also upset when I told him I didn't get to see a doctor. Anyway, he called for an ambulance. Then he called sick bay and asked to talk to the officer-in-charge.

A doctor arrived at the same time as the ambulance, but I wouldn't open the door. They were banging on it, swearing, and threatening me with everything from a beating to a court martial. It took about an hour to cut around the jagged edges of my toenail and remove it. It didn't hurt; in fact, I didn't feel a thing.

I packed my toe with cotton and gauze soaked in iodine. I didn't come out of the dark room until I had it bandaged and all taped up. I not only wouldn't go with the doctor to sick bay, I wouldn't even remove the bandage so that he could look at it.

Chief Buckley, the ambulance driver, and the doctor all put me on report.

My toe healed beautifully.

Tampering with a Sacred Tradition

My best friend was Curtis Manning. He was a third class petty officer who hated the Navy and the morons that ran it as much as I did, so we got along famously. It was nice to have a friend with some horsepower on his sleeve even if he was on the outs with all the other petty officers.

Curtis said he had been a second class, but was busted for drinking on duty and busting up six marines. I took all of that with a grain of salt until one day I plopped a carton of cigarettes on top of my locker while I did my combination, and then I couldn't reach it. Curtis was no taller than I was, but from a foot away, he reached on top of my locker and handed me my cigarettes. I stopped and looked at his arms; his hands hung down to his knees. He was built like a gorilla; from that day on, I had no doubt that he could whip six marines.

One day, Curtis up and reenlisted in the Navy. I was devastated. He had been bitching about the Navy with ever-increasing intensity for the last few months, and then, he up and reenlists. I couldn't believe it. Before I even had a chance to talk to him, an alarm went off signaling that a plane coming in for a landing was in some kind of trouble. The person nearest to the duty motion picture camera had to grab it and run to the roof—the lab was located in the air tower—and photograph the landing. That was me, so I grabbed the camera and ran.

The plane landed without a hitch. While I was breaking down the camera and tripod, I noticed the flag, and I remembered that dropping the flag to half-mast was an appropriate thing to do for sad occasions. Since I viewed Curtis's reenlistment as an especially sad occasion, I lowered the flag to half-mast. I returned to the lab, put away the duty camera, and returned to the film processing room where I now worked when not flying.

About 30 minutes later, I was called out into the office where two marines were talking to Chief Buckley.

"Quigley, you were up on the roof a minute ago, weren't you?"

"Yes sir, I went up to cover that emergency landing."

One of the marines—he was ugly, but his clothes fit well—said, "You're under arrest for tampering with tradition sacred to our country."

Oh Lord, that sounded serious.

They put me in their jeep and hauled me over to the brig. Five minutes later I was a skinhead again. They gave me a pretty bad time, and threatened me with a blanket party if I didn't do everything they said, so I did everything they said. That night they gave me a blanket party. They made a lot of noise, but they didn't really hurt me that much. I wondered if I could whip six of them.

The next morning I received a visit from the motion picture chief, Mark Pointer. The marines seemed to respect him. He offered to be my defense counsel.

"Don't I need a lawyer?" I asked.

"All you need to be a defense counsel is a six-month correspondence course. I am better than any lawyer you can find in Hawaii, and besides, I'm free."

I accepted him as my defense counsel.

He asked if I had any trouble with the marines during the night. Apparently, he was familiar with their routine. Then he asked me if I had breakfast and I said I hadn't had supper or breakfast. He got me released into his custody and we had breakfast at the chief's club.

"The blanket party and not letting you eat will give me some leverage at your hearing."

"What hearing?" I asked.

"You are slated for a hearing for a Summary Court Martial."

Chief Pointer was as good as he said he was. He got the charge dropped based on my youth, inexperience, stressful working conditions, and the abuses. I wouldn't even have to go to mast. There was a catch, however. I had to see a psychiatrist. I guess they thought I was a little crazy.

I thought I would see a shrink one time and that would be the end of it, but it didn't work that way. I had to see a shrink once a week until the shrink told the Commandant that I didn't need to see a shrink anymore. Apparently, they never talked, because I had to see a shrink every Wednesday for the rest of my tour.

Buddha Belly Bob

I was taking judo lessons. Two hours every Saturday afternoon cost me $15.00 for three months. I loved it. We did a lot of calisthenics, but we also learned a lot of neat things. I was particularly fond of the hand flip and some of the defense maneuvers. I was impressed with myself, and I guess I did a little bragging.

A chubby kid named Bob Fletcher, said good naturedly, "Hey, tough guy, how about a little one-on-one, just you and me?"

He kind of put me on the spot. I liked him and I didn't want to fight. I said, "I don't want to hurt anyone; I'm just learning how to defend myself."

"Come on, no one is going to get hurt. We'll put some mattresses on the deck and have some fun. Come on, Russell, you can show me what you've learned."

"Well, okay," I said.

We made a 15-foot-square ring out of mattresses and everyone crowded around to watch the judo demonstration.

We squared off across from each other; I took my balance position; Bob took off his Hawaiian shirt, and just stood there, bare bellied, with his hands behind his back. I have never seen so many muscles in a belly, a kind of Buddha belly at that. Well, he scrunched his Buddha belly up into a basketball and bounced it up and down, and just stood there grinning. I didn't know if he was making fun of me, or what, but I decided it was time I showed him a thing or two.

It was clear he wasn't going to move, so I stepped in close and tried for a straight forward take down, but the next thing I knew I was flat on my back, and his hands never moved, and everyone was laughing. That little Buddha belly had bounced up and out with such force that it knocked me down.

Well, that does it, I thought, I am not going to be beat up by a belly. I'll grab his right hand with my right hand, wrap my fingers around his thumb, and twist his hand to the outside and then pull down. I'll show him how a little guy puts a big guy down.

But once again, his Buddha belly became a battering ram and knocked me on my butt. Humiliation is fertile ground for anger, and mine started to grow. "Forget judo, how about some old fashioned street fighting," I mumbled.

The grin left his face; arms came out from behind his back and were raised to show his biceps. Well, I wasn't about to be intimidated. I lowered my head and ran straight into him. This time, Bob stepped forward, swung his arms back for leverage, and belted me in the solar plexus with that damned belly of his. I staggered, stumbled back, slipped off the mattresses, and banged into a row of lockers. I slid to the deck, stunned and sucking for air.

The crowd hushed as they realized the fight had just gotten serious.

I tried to hold it back; I was angry, humiliated. I could not. My mind had glimpsed an image of what it must have looked like, this jolly Buddha beating me up with his belly. It started with a giggle, and then I laughed out loud. "Bob, you just beat me up with your belly."

"Yeah, I did, didn't I?" The grin was back.

The Pacific Fleet Photographic Supply Depot

The Pacific Fleet Photographic Supply Depot was a warehouse for photographic supplies for the whole Pacific fleet including Japan, Korea, and the Philippines. It consisted of a large Quonset hut across the parking lot from the motion picture hut, which put the main photo lab across the parking lot on the left. I guess I was an embarrassment, what with me operating on my toe and the incident with the flag. Anyway, they transferred me over there to the photo supply depot.

I processed and shipped orders from the fleet, of which there were surprisingly few. My main customer was the lab itself. So I was kind of a receptionist, and I processed chits from my fellow photographers, which was kind of nice because it was the only time I got to see them. Most of the time, I just sat on my behind except when I got to fly. Since I was the only one there, I figured I was in charge.

After I read and reread Photography Volume 1 and Volume 2, I was so bored, I started reading supply instructions. I learned I was supposed to hold inventory every six months, but I didn't learn how I was supposed to do it. I found some records in a dusty old file cabinet. It looked to me as if there hadn't been any entries in a couple of years, so I locked up and went over to see Chief Buckley.

"Chief, ain't I supposed to hold inventory or something?" I asked.

"Quigley, we'll hold inventory when we're goddam good and ready. Get back over there where you belong."

Well, I was always one to worry. What if there was a bunch of stuff missing and I was held responsible because I never held inventory? I looked around for books and things, but I couldn't find anything that helped. Finally, I remembered that the base supply depot was only a few blocks away. All I had to do was go over there and ask somebody.

Everybody was tucked away in a bunch of tiny offices, and I didn't know where to go. I spotted an old warrant officer walking down the hall towards me.

"Excuse me sir, do you know anything about supply?" I asked.

His eyes opened wide. "Yes, I might know a thing or two. How can I help?"

"Well," I said feeling important, "I'm in charge of the Pacific Fleet Photographic Supply Depot, and I'm trying to determine if I should be holding inventory."

His mouth formed a perfect O as he looked down at my three green stripes and back to my face. "Well, how long has it been since you took inventory?" he asked.

"Well, sir, that's just it, I haven't, and I know it's overdue, but the chief told me not to worry about it, but I'm afraid I'm going to get in trouble if I don't," I replied.

"Well, son," he said, "why don't I just go over to your Pacific Fleet Photographic Supply Depot, and have a look for myself."

He took a look at the same files I did, and apparently he couldn't make any sense of them either because pretty soon he called for help. When two first class and two second class petty officers came in, he told them he wanted a complete inventory and he wanted all of the records updated. "And, I want a complete report on my desk when you're done."

"Quigley," he said to me, grinning from ear to ear, "you done good. I'd like you to come over to my office; I have a few questions I want to ask you. You know, your photo lab hasn't been too responsive to my requests for photos of goods damaged in shipment. They keep saying, 'Don't you know there's a war on?' so I'm setting up a little lab of my own, and I could use your help."

I wanted to tell him that I thought it was illegal to set up your own photo lab, but I bit my tongue because he was being so nice to me and all.

Well, it took several days to complete the inventory. Boy, could that warrant officer chew ass. He didn't mind about rank either. He dressed Commander Anderson down to parade rest. Seemed he checked out a new experimental press camera and couldn't find it. Warrant Officer Connally had all kinds of equipment checked out that he kept saying was around here somewhere. And one of the first class petty officers had requisitioned thousands of feet of movie film, but hadn't shot any official movies. The supply warrant officer assured them that everything that couldn't be found would be paid for because he was certain that they didn't want this matter to go any higher. They all agreed.

Chief Buckley did not have any equipment checked out and did not have to pay for anything. He did not say so in words, but it did seem to me that he was tickled with this turn of events. In any case, it seems my aerial photography abilities weren't as essential as I had been led to believe because they sent me mess cooking.

Mess Cooking

The only things missing were the bullwhips. We worked 14 hours a day seven days a week, 20 minutes for meals and no breaks unless you smoked. That's right, unless you smoked. Smokers were an exalted group in 1954. They were authorized two five minute breaks in the morning and two in the afternoon, but it was impossible for the mess deck masters-at-arms (slave masters recruited from mafia enforcers on the lam) to keep track, so you could have as many breaks as you could con them out of. Everybody smoked by the time they finished their three-month tour of mess cooking. The Navy was probably getting kickbacks.

We were all exhausted and short-tempered within a few weeks. There was more petty bullshit here than there was in boot camp. We ate great in boot camp and with no hassles. Here, a slave master guarded the shit can by the scullery, and if a mess cook took more than he could eat, the slave master made him sit down and finish it. One time when I wasn't paying attention, the people around me put their leftover crackers on my tray. I started to dump my tray and this Neanderthal came unglued and screamed all over me. I had to eat 30 crackers without anything to drink.

I didn't really get into trouble, though, until a cook threw a large pan (30" X 15" X 12") of mashed potatoes my way and expected me to catch it. Well, I couldn't even lift it let alone catch it, so I stepped aside and let it hit the deck.

You know, an angry cook can be just as mean and unreasonable as a slave master.

"You stupid son-of-a-bitch, I'm gonna kill you," he screamed as he charged towards me with his fists doubled up.

I almost didn't move fast enough, but I managed to grab his shirt, turn around, bend my legs, and pull down as his momentum carried him over on top of me, and then I stood up, flipping him all the way over my head onto his back. It wouldn't have been so bad landing in the middle of the steaming hot mashed potatoes the way he did, but that damn pan caught him right in the middle of his back. Naturally, he put me on report.

The captain decided it was the cook's fault as much as it was mine, so he let me go with a warning; although, he did tell them to assign me to the scullery.

"And make sure he has full-time supervision."

The scullery was reputed to be the worst job in the galley, but I liked it better than being on the serving line, or being out on the floor. All I had to do was scrub the pots and pans three times a day and then clean up after myself. My full time supervisor was Chief Cook Don Lapone, the senior cook in charge of the galley. He looked after the pots and pans himself, and he wanted everything done just so.

"No soap. You don't need any soap when you steam clean. And coat every pan with lard when you're finished with it while it's still hot." He demonstrated while he talked. "If I find a dirty pan, or catch you working without gloves, you will go back out on the floor. One thing more, I get some weirdoes back here; if I ever catch you spitting on the pans or anything else, I'll put you in the hospital. Are we clear on that?"

"Yes, sir," I said.

I worked hard and did everything just like the Chief said. He was actually very nice. No screaming and hollering like the rest of them, and once he realized that I was doing everything just like he asked me to, he even seemed to take a liking to me.

"So you flipped Rodney over your head? How did you do that? He must weigh 220 pounds."

I showed him how to do a basic body flip, and he really got into it. He practiced flipping me over his head, breaking my fall so I didn't get hurt.

"What else can you show me? I can probably use it where I'm going."

I immediately thought of the war, but then I remembered it was over.

"Where are you going?"

"Eventually, I'm going to prison. The investigation will take a few more months, but then it's all over for me. Nineteen years down the tubes."

"What did you do?"

"It started about five years ago in San Diego when I was still a first class and recently divorced. My child support was too high and I couldn't make ends meet. A man I knew from the commissary offered me cash for meat from the galley. It wasn't much at first, but then they wanted more and more stuff. They were selling galley food in the commissaries and somehow putting the money in their pockets. I thought it would be over when I got transferred, but it wasn't.

I finally couldn't take it any more, so I turned them in. It was hard because some of them used to be friends. It was a smart move, though. I'm looking at five years, but the rest of them are looking at more like twenty. We would have been caught anyway. Most of them were living large."

I taught him everything I learned at the USO. We got along fine after that. Once in a while, one of the slave masters would try to borrow me when I was caught up, but the chief would run them off.

One evening, a seven-man flight crew headed by Commander Albertson came in just after we tore down the serving line. Commander Albertson demanded that Chief Lapone set up the entire line. The Chief refused and they got into an argument. The Chief tried to explain that it would take too long and be too difficult to set up the line, but the commander wasn't hearing any of it. Finally, Chief Lapone offered to cook each of them a porterhouse steak and they became friends instantly. Commander Albertson strode back to his crew and announced victory. A cheer went up when they heard about the steaks.

Chief Lapone was grinning when he emerged from the freezer with the steaks. Puzzled, I kept an eye on him while he prepared to cook. I didn't see where it came from, but I saw the Chief pouring motor oil on the grill.

"Gees, Chief, what is that gonna do to them?"

"Believe it or not, the steaks are going to taste great, but they're going to have the shits for a week."

The rest of my three months was pretty uneventful. There was that one day when we all ran to the barracks, got our mattresses, and hauled them out on the runway, so that a helicopter with only one landing strut could land safely. It worked, and we all felt pretty good about it. Next thing I knew, I was back in the photo lab.

Permanent Burn Petty Officer

Chief Buckley was still down on me. He said I couldn't go up for third class because I missed all their training while I was mess cooking. Well, I knew that was wrong. They specifically told us during our indoctrination as mess cooks that mess cooking was not a punishment and that we would not be held up from advancement. I requested mast.

CDR Stevens, VU1 Executive Officer, suggested that I talk to him first, so I explained my problem to him.

"You're absolutely right," he said. "Mess cooking is not supposed to be a punishment. Tell you what I'm going to do. I'll recommend you from here. That way we won't have to get into a pissing contest with Chief Buckley, and he'll probably forget all about it by the time the exams arrive."Well, sure enough, I did take the third class test, and Chief Buckley didn't miss me while I was gone. However, he did notice my name on the list of people to be promoted.

"Quigley, I told you that you could not go up for third class, and I meant it. You are on report, and you are not going to make third class."

"Chief, the XO said—"

"I don't give a damn what the XO told you, I told you you couldn't go up, and you ain't making third class, not after what you did, you ain't. You can't go behind my back to the XO or anyone else and go up for third when I said you couldn't."

"Chief, I didn't go behind your back. I put in for request—"

"Get out of here and go to work, Quigley, you ain't making third class."

The Chief and I were waiting on the XO for screening mast, when the XO stepped out of his office and said, "Chief Buckley, I need to see you alone."

Well, I don't know what they said, but the Chief was breathing fire when he came out. He walked right by me and out of the building. He got into the photo lab pickup and took off without me. It took me twenty minutes to walk back to the photo lab.

"Quigley," he said, as I walked into the lab, "You are the lab's permanent burn petty officer. From now on, you will make all of the burn runs to the incinerator. All of them, you understand?"

"Yes, Chief, I understand. Who's gonna help me?"

"Nobody."

"But Chief, we have to have two people on classified runs."

"Quigley, I said nobody, and I meant nobody, and I don't want to hear another word out of you, not one word. If you say another word, I'm gonna hit you."

Twice a day I packed all the waste from the lab into a pickup and hauled it to the base incinerator. Once there, I had to carry it all up a flight of stairs and dump it into a large outdoor fireplace with 30-foot chimney. A third class boatswain's mate named Timothy Barnsworth ran it.

"It ain't my job to help you. You're supposed to have someone with you."

"I'm being punished," I said. "They ain't going to send anyone with me."

"Well, that's your tough luck because I ain't here to take your punishment either."

The trashcans used for movie film were almost as tall as I was. I was supposed to ensure that all of the film was unraveled, so that it would burn thoroughly. I couldn't reach the bottom, so when I couldn't reach anymore I just dumped it. One day I dumped a load of tightly wound nitrate-based film. What they taught us in school about nitrate-based film was that it was too dangerous, so the Navy didn't use it anymore. Well, it exploded and knocked Timothy and me off the platform, about a six-foot fall. He was off to the side, so he didn't get burned like I did, but he was hurt. From then on he gave me a hand, and I dumped the movie film on the platform before I dumped it in the fire.

After a while, I kind a got to liking it. I could still fly and I got a reputation for being a good still photographer. Whenever anyone blew a job, they would come get me to reshoot it. I was still the permanent burn petty officer when I got transferred a year later.

A Routine Assignment

I enjoyed shooting ship's identification photos. Pilots from Utility Squadron One would fly their helicopters in circles around the ships at an altitude of about 500 ft, while we took pictures with F-56 cameras. It would seldom take more than a couple of hours to fly out to the ship, take the pictures, and fly back. The weather was always great, and it was a nice break from working in the lab.

The helicopter door was always removed for photo assignments, and we would sit in the doorway to shoot our pictures. We wore a safety harness that was attached to a deck plate in the helicopter. The camera had a separate harness that was attached to the radio cabinet. We checked the harnesses religiously, because the gravitational pull caused by the sudden rising, falling, or turning of a helicopter is enough to snap the camera out of your hands, or dump you out into mid-air.

I was just about finished with such an assignment when it happened. The helicopter lurched up and the camera was pulled from my hands, and the weight of my body plus the gravitational pull put a strain on the strap from my safety harness to the deck plate. The deck plate came loose, and suddenly, I was in mid-air.

My life did not flash before my eyes. I just said, "This is it." And then, whap! I was hanging in mid air with my back to the wheel. Several times, I have had to look death in the eye, and I was not afraid. But, when it catches you by surprise, it is terrifying. I turned around and wrapped all four limbs around one of the helicopter wheels. It rocked, and I was even more terrified.

I looked down, and saw people on the ship waving frantically, trying to get the pilot's attention, but he just kept circling the ship. I looked up, and saw a square deck plate caught diagonally in the doorway. If the deck plate had turned, or lined up with the sides of the door, I wouldn't have been stopped.

I was shaking violently as I inched my way back inside. I could not uncurl my body from the fetal position it had assumed. I grabbed my microphone and double clicked it, a signal to the pilot that I was about to talk, but I couldn't say a word. The pilot thought that I had signaled him to indicate that the mission was complete.

I lay there shaking all the way back. I completely forgot about the camera dangling down below. After we landed, the pilot walked by and saw me still curled up in a ball.

"Damn photographers, always getting sick. Clean it up before you leave."

My Pride and Joy

It was love at first sight. It wasn't much more than a motorbike, but it looked like a real motorcycle. It was a 50cc Royal Enfield. The note attached to the picture said the owner, a Lieutenant Stevens, lived in officer housing on base. He was asking $200.00 and I only had $111.00, but I had to see it anyway.

I could tell I was too late. A moving van was already in front of the house and men were busy taking stuff out to the van. A crew cut and a big smile came out of the house and down the street to meet me.

"I hope you're coming about the motorcycle," he said, "because we're leaving in a few minutes."

"Well, kind of," I replied. "I only have a hundred and eleven dollars."

"It's yours," he said, "Come on. I'll take you over to Motor Vehicles and we'll transfer ownership and everything. Over here. We can take John's car; mine has already been shipped."

I hadn't even seen it yet, but I said, "Okay."

It was beautiful. It had a red gas tank, red fenders, a black seat, and lots of chrome. It had a top speed of 35 miles per hour. That was too slow to take me to Pearl or Honolulu, but it would take me all over the base. It took me to and from work, to and from the club, and to and from the beach. My friends loved to borrow it. It was my pride and joy.

One day the ancient mariner, a small, white haired, prune-faced chief with eleven hash marks came out of the exchange parking lot without looking in either direction. I plowed straight into him. My cycle suffered a bent frame and died on the spot. His car had some minor cuts and bruises.

The ancient mariner put me on report for doing 60 mph in a 25 mph zone; however, the captain referred it to the base traffic court, which was run by the marine commandant.

"Are you calling a chief petty officer a liar?" demanded the commandant.

"No, sir." I knew better than to say anything else. I was fined $25.00 and ordered to pay the $35.00 it cost the ancient mariner to bandage his car.

A Used Car Salesman

I never meant to become a used car salesman; it just happened. A friend had to go back to the States suddenly and needed to sell his car. He offered it to me for half of what it was worth, but I still couldn't afford it. He dropped the price with every passing day until I just had to try to scrape up the money. I wound up buying a 700-dollar car for 200 dollars.

No more buses. I really enjoyed having a car, but I couldn't resist when someone offered me $600.00 for it. I bought an old Packard for $200.00 and put $400.00 in the bank. Not long after, a fellow came to me and said, "I hear you buy old cars."

"Oh, no," I said, "I was just helping a friend. I don't need two cars."

"Aw c'mon," he says, "you can double your money in a couple of days, but I gotta have it right now. At least take a look at it."

It was a really nice looking Hudson coupe. I kept it and sold my Packard. My reputation was born. I was the last chance car dealer for the little guy in trouble. People didn't come to me expecting much for their cars, and I didn't give them much. I was buying and selling three to six cars a month, and I really enjoyed the prosperity.

This went on for most of a year, and then one day all of my cars disappeared, every last one of them, even my Hudson. I got the word at quarters. "Quigley," the chief said, "you gotta report to the Motor Vehicles Office—something about having too many cars on base."

"According to our records," the marine sergeant said, "You have five cars and a motorcycle on base. What are you trying to do, run a used car lot?"

"Oh, no," I lied, "the motorcycle is busted and I was just trying to help out some friends who had to leave suddenly."

"It really doesn't matter what you're doing because you can't keep that many cars on base. They're in the compound outside the gate. It's going to cost you $10.00 each to get them out and $10.00 a month to keep them there."

I paid the ransom for my Hudson, but I couldn't afford to pay the ransom or the monthly fees for the rest of them. It was my turn to sell cars at panic prices; however, the lot owner agreed to take my dead bike; all I had to do was sign the papers. A month later, I saw his kid riding my pride and joy.

Mattress Brigade

The marines never failed to hassle us at the gate. They searched our car for booze and cigarettes every time we came through and would confiscate them when they found them. My old Hudson had hidden compartments in the armrests in the back seat. I brought a bottle of booze back and forth every time I went on liberty just so I could sneak it by them.

After a good night on the town, we would gather at an all night cafeteria on base. I think it used to be a mess hall. We would sit at these big, old, picnic-style tables, drink coffee, sober up, and talk into the wee hours of the morning.

One night, the conversation turned to the marines on the gate and how they never seemed to tire of giving us a bad time. We kicked it around for a while until suddenly I remembered something from my mess cooking experience. A helicopter had come in for a landing with one strut missing. If it hit the runway that way, it would tip over, smashing the rotor blades into a million pieces, putting the crew at risk. The mess cook barracks was next to the runway and we were called upon to haul our mattresses to the runway to form a soft landing pad. It was a tremendous effort hauling our mattresses downstairs and out on the runway and then back again when it was all over, but it was worth it because it worked, and no one was hurt.

The marine barracks, however, was two miles from the runway. We began to plot. What if we started a fight out front and made enough noise to get the night watch to come outside? What if the rest of us slipped inside, turned on the lights, woke everybody up, and told them a helicopter was coming in on one strut and that their mattresses were needed on the runway to form a landing pad?

Well, you wouldn't believe how well it worked. Once a couple of sergeants woke up, they took over for us and started barking orders better than we ever could, and the next thing you know a bunch of half-dressed marines were in formation outside the barracks with their mattresses over their heads. I felt a slight twinge of guilt when a sergeant bellowed, "Double time, march," and off they went into the darkness.

We were so tickled with ourselves that we didn't notice how serious every one was at quarters the next morning. We fell in and did dress right and open ranks march as if we were going to be inspected or something. And then we just stood there at attention. And we stood there and stood there. Nobody said a word. Finally, after several hours, we were approached by a platoon of marines led by the marine commandant. I have never seen so much anger in a man's face before. My knees started shaking.

The commandant stopped in front of the first man in ranks and asked, "Is this one of them?"

"No sir," they all replied.

The commandant went from man to man. I knew I would be spotted, if for no other reason, because I was shaking so hard. The commandant looked me straight in the eye and asked, "Is this one of them?"

"No, sir," they all replied. I couldn't believe it. They didn't recognize a single one of us. When they were gone, Chief Buckley ordered, "Close ranks, march." But he didn't dismiss us. He didn't even put us at parade rest. After about twenty minutes or so, Petty Officer Silas Morehead was brave enough to ask, "Aren't you going to let us go, so we can go to work?"

"We'll secure when the commanding officer says we can secure," came the angry reply. We were still there at noon.

Silas Morehead

I'd like to tell you about my friend Silas for if ever a man had the soul of a sailor, his name was Silas Morehead. He literally loved the sea and all the ships that go to sea. He loved the ladies in port and the absence of ladies at sea. He loved living in a man's world. He wanted to be where the action is. For him, that meant being aboard a carrier, although he would take any ship over shore duty. You would think the Navy would love such a man, but it was not so.

Silas was what was called a professional second class petty officer, meaning he didn't want to go any higher. He would say, "I'm too junior for any real responsibility, and too senior for any shit details." Silas had memorized the *Bluejackets Manual*. It carried a lot more weight back in 1954 than it does today. And he knew the history of ships. He would keep us mesmerized with all the battles they had endured. He knew all the names and all the details.

I stood next to Silas at inspection one day. The captain's jaw dropped when he looked Silas up and down. "Why, son, you haven't even pressed your uniform."

"Yes, sir, I have," came the firm reply. "I pressed them under my mattress as prescribed by the *Bluejackets Manual*, sir."

The captain looked perplexed as if he wanted to challenge this assertion, but couldn't bring himself to do so. The captain looked down at his shoes, and said sharply, "Well, you could at least have shined your shoes."

"My shoes are well buffed, as they should be, sir. The manual says nothing about a spit shine."

The captain stared at Silas thoughtfully as if to determine if he was being put on, or if the man was in earnest. He must have decided on the latter because he moved on without another word.

I didn't just like Silas; I was drawn to him, for Silas carried the weight of the entire naval bureaucracy on his shoulders. Silas had reenlisted for sea duty and had been caught by a technicality: the Navy considered overseas shore duty to be the same as sea duty. Silas did not. He did not want to be stationed at Barbers Point, Hawaii; he wanted to be stationed aboard a ship, preferably an aircraft carrier.

Silas had written a letter to the Chief of Naval Operations (CNO) every day except Sundays for the last two years. He told the CNO that the Navy had not honored the spirit of their agreement. In the process, he had learned the name of every man in the chain of command between himself and the CNO. He had also incurred the wrath of each and every one of them. They told him to stop writing letters. They ordered him to stop writing letters.

Every day at quarters, the leading chief would say, "Silas, if you write one more letter, you're on report." And every day Silas would respond by telling the chief where in the "Bluejacket's Manual" it said he could write letters if he used the chain of command. This went on for another six months until Silas wrote his congressman. After two and a half years of writing letters, Silas was transferred to the USS *Midway*.

Turning Pro

The new photographic strobe lights were really something, 1/50,000th of a second. They were so fast that you had to increase the development time to compensate for the fact that film could not react fully to such a short burst of light. They were also fast enough that they did not disturb your eyes, even when the strobe light was popped right in your face. Later strobe lights would have a much longer flash duration, and were as apt to blind you as a flashbulb, but the first models were unique.

I was delighted at the prospect of not having to carry a large leather pouch of flash bulbs everywhere I went. I was excited. I took my camera everywhere and took pictures of everything. I even took it on liberty. In fact, I took it to my favorite watering hole, a bar in Pearl Harbor with half a dozen floorshows every night.

Normally, no one was allowed to take pictures during the shows, but I convinced the manager, Jerry Coates, that I could photograph the floorshows without disturbing the entertainers or the audience. I convinced him by flashing the strobe light in his face. He hardly noticed it. Even the monkeys ignored it. He said I could try it, but if anyone complained, I would have to stop. No one complained.

I did a great job. I captured every entertainer, every action, and every expression. I was really pleased, so I bought an album to show off my pictures. I was sure it would be good for a couple of drinks.

Mr. Coates was so impressed that he called the owner, Big John, who came in to look at them. Big John liked them so much, he said he wanted to buy them. He took a month's salary out of the register and slid it across the bar. I had to refuse because I had shot the pictures as a self-imposed training assignment. I used a Navy camera, strobe unit, film, paper, everything. It was barely legal as long as I didn't charge for them.

The owner would not take no for an answer even when I said he could have the pictures for free. He told the manager to get all the entertainers that were not on stage to look at their pictures. Then he picked his money up off the bar, stuck it in my shirt pocket, and asked me to step into his office. "You're good," he said. "I see a couple hundred publicity pictures a year, acts coming to the club and acts wanting to come to the club. None of the stuff I see is as good as yours, and most of it is shot by Hollywood photographers."

"Thank you."

"How much would you charge me for that album if you were a commercial photographer?"

"Oh," I said, "I would charge at least $1.50 for each 8X10. The album cost me $2.00, so I guess I could stretch that to $5.00. That would be $59.00."

"Not even close," said Big John. "If you give these Hollywood types a price list like that, they won't even talk to you. They will consider you an amateur. If you want to shoot for these people, and you should, you will have to multiply all your prices by ten. How much money will you need to get your own outfit?"

I had to think about that. A Speed Graphic, strobe light, film, paper, chemistry. "I would need at least $400.00."

"Well," he said, pulling another two hundred out of his wallet, "this will get you started. By the way, what's your name?"

"Russell, Russell Quigley. Are you going to trust me with all that money?"

"Not for long, Russell. I wouldn't be surprised if Jerry hasn't already sold that many pictures. One more thing, Russell, don't let them know you're in the military. They'll drop you like a hot potato."

We returned to the bar and sure enough people were writing their orders on the backs of the pictures. I told Big John I would make him new ones. When they were finished, I had orders totaling $540.00 and had been invited to seven other clubs. I was in business. I was a pro.

I bought the equipment and supplies, and laminated a base sticker, so that I could tape it on my windshield and take it off when I was working. Big John continued to coach me.

"If you sit with these people, they will be very generous with the booze, but when it comes your turn, they will expect you to buy a round for everyone, not just the people you're sitting with. These people hang around together, so you may be buying drinks 30 or 40 at a time. Don't ever get caught short. Carry at least $200.00 with you at all times. Keep track of what you spend. It's a business expense."

It was a lot of fun and very profitable. I drank too much at first, but I quickly got it under control when I realized that I couldn't shoot sharp pictures through fuzzy eyes. I met a lot of interesting people.

One night I was bumped into and knocked on my keester by a drunk while I was shooting. I got up, picked up my camera, and stepped toward the man who knocked me down. A second man pushed me down again. This time I got up, set my camera down on my table, and took after them in earnest. I was mentally rehearsing my judo moves when a big man stepped in front of me.

"You don't want to tangle with those men," he said. "That's Mel Torme," he said pointing, "and those other two men are his torpedoes, two of the nastiest people you could ever meet. Here, sit down a minute and cool off. Let me buy you a drink. By the way, I'm Count Basie. Who might you be?"

I was convinced. This is the life for me. No more worrying about college. Why should I go to school when I can make this much money doing something I love? Instead of going home when I finish my tour of duty at Barbers Point, I'm going to stay right here and run a full-time photography business.

Chief Buckley made the following announcement at quarters the next day: "Listen up: Quigley, Taylor, and Patterson. You have been caught in an emergency draft to the Naval Photographic Center in Washington, D. C.. Start packing and making the necessary arrangements. You will be leaving within a week. Don't forget to check in your high altitude flight gear."

THE PHOTO CENTER

The Naval Photographic Center, Washington, D.C., referred to as NPC, or simply as the Photo Center, the largest photo lab in the Navy, was built in 1942 to help in the war effort. The three-story brick and tile building contained over 5,000,000 cubic feet of space, including a motion picture sound stage complete with Hollywood connections. It housed the Naval Photographic Interpretation School, The Naval Photographic Interpretation Center, a huge still photography lab, an art and animation section, a movie theater, and libraries for movie film, still photography, and aerial intelligence.

The Photo Center worked closely with the motion picture and television industries on a large number of films during and after the war. Productions such as 20th Century Fox's *Fighting Lady* and the TV program *Navy Log* displayed the work of Navy photographers. The award winning historical documentary *Victory at Sea*, a 26-program series produced by the NBC television network, was based on footage shot by Navy and Marine Corps photographers.

But, to me it was just a factory where I would probably get stuck doing the same job over and over. The two major divisions were motion picture production and the still photo lab. I was assigned to a print darkroom in the still photo lab. There were eight of us assigned to the room: six printers, a developer, and a hypo puncher. We averaged 2,000 prints a day; it was as I expected it to be; I did the same thing over and over, but I did get good at it. I averaged nearly 400 enlargements a day with few remakes. Of course, the man in the developer was a genius at saving under- and over-exposed prints.

A Tradition

I was told upon checking in that I was on report. All my high altitude flight gear was missing from the Fleet Air Photo Lab back in Barbers Point. Everyone assumed I was guilty, and treated me accordingly, so once again I was at war with the Navy. I never missed a chance to put the Navy down, which I know endeared me to my chain of command. They hung this thing over my head for six months, telling me that at the very least I was going to have to pay the $400.00 to replace the high altitude flight suit.

About three months after I checked in, Petty Officer Sinclair, my section leader from the Barbers Point photo lab, was transferred to the Photo Center. He testified that I had checked the gear into him when I left; still they wouldn't let me off the hook.

After another three months, the command received a letter telling them they had caught the thief and that it wasn't me. It was that prissy little Chief Matheeny, the one in charge of the aerial section. I never would have figured him to be a thief. The command did not apologize.

Rope Yarn Wednesdays

I had forgotten all about my weekly visits to see the shrink. I received a phone call from Bethesda Naval Hospital setting me up with weekly appointments with a psychiatrist every Wednesday afternoon at 1300.

"Russell, how about bringing me up to date. What kind of problems are you having?"

I never knew what to say. If I told him how I really felt about things, he would probably kick me out of the Navy. I usually just talked about petty aggravations. "Well, you know there are no chairs in the barracks and the barracks masters-at-arms always bitch if you sit on the beds. I don't know how we're supposed—"

"Are you putting me on, Russell? Would you mind telling me exactly why you're here?"

"Well sir, I had this hearing for a summary court-martial for lowering the flag to half mast, and—"

"For what?"

"I lowered the flag to half mast, and it pissed off the marines, and they were gonna court-martial me, and my defense counsel told them it wasn't my fault because I was under a lot of stress, so they made me see a shrink—"

"Russell, do not refer to psychiatrists as shrinks. I am a psychiatrist. I don't like your attitude, but other than that, there is nothing wrong with you. I do not want to see you again. I have serious work to do, and I don't have time for this nonsense. I don't care what you tell your command. I will instruct my staff to tell anyone who calls me that I am seeing you once a week on Wednesdays."

I took that as an invitation to rope yarn every Wednesday afternoon. I went to places like the National Museum of Art, the Smithsonian, and the Library of Congress, places where I knew I would not run into anyone I knew.

No Jokers Allowed

We were all serious poker players. We played five-card draw, jacks or better, five-card stud, and seven-card stud, no jokers allowed. We played almost every noon hour and sometimes on weekends. I fancied myself a better than average player. I rarely lost money and I sometimes made a bundle.

I learned not to join the games that lasted all weekend until Sunday afternoon or evening. I would go against the big winner, who was usually exhausted and playing recklessly, with $20.00. If I lost it, he remained the big winner, but frequently I won it all in the last few hours of the game.

Our noon hour games were nickel ante with a quarter limit on raises; therefore, they were relatively harmless. It was rare that anyone lost more than $15.00 or $20.00. However, there was this one hand that was one in a million. Six of us were playing seven-card stud and everyone had a winning hand. I had two aces down and one up from the beginning, so I bumped every chance I got and to my surprise and consternation everyone stayed.

It was not until just before the last card that I realized I could lose. The player across from me had three kings showing and was betting like he had the fourth one buried, and the fellow to his right, with four straight clubs showing, was betting like he could beat four kings. I was expecting to have a full house by now, but it wasn't happening, and everyone was raising. The man with four clubs showing was dealing.

"Does anyone want to take off the limit before I deal the next card?"

"Great idea!"

"I'm for that."

They were all anxious to remove the limit, and they were looking at me to make it unanimous. "Well, okay."

The betting became real serious real fast. Paychecks were being pledged. We all knew each other well enough to trust each other. The bet was three hundred by the time it got to me. The man on my left had folded without a word. I called. The fellow on my right folded, cursing a blue streak. The last man bumped it a hundred. We all called and received our last cards down.

I was afraid to look at my last card. Recently, a girlfriend had taken a series of pictures of me while I was playing cards. Much to my chagrin, every winning hand was reflected in my face. However, I had to see it before the betting started. The man with four clubs showing could have a straight flush, so I prayed for a pair to give me a full house, but what I got was the fourth ace.

The betting went crazy. All I did was call. After all, I was looking at a possible straight flush. The man across from me had kings full, and was an extremely poor looser. He refused to play with us anymore. The dealer had his flush on the first five cards but the straight flush eluded him. He, too, was irritated. Bob Ericson had stayed in with a flush and was kicking himself.

I requested the afternoon off, went downtown, and bought a car.

Silas, Again

I was on my way to the galley for lunch when I saw him. I couldn't believe my eyes. It was Silas Morehead.

"Hey Silas! What are you doing here? You're supposed to be aboard the *Midway*."

"Hey, Russell! I got caught in the same damn emergency draft you did. I told them sonsabitches I reenlisted for sea duty and by God I wasn't leaving until I finished my tour, but they said it was either the Photo Center or a court martial."

"You gonna write letters again?"

"Damn right I am. I've already started. I wrote my congressman yesterday and I'm writing the CNO tonight. I'm going to write a letter a day until I get a full tour of sea duty just like they promised me."

"Where are you working, Silas?"

"I'm over in the MOPIC department. I think I'm going to be printing movies. They wanted me to be an editor, but I told them no way. I'd go nuts. How 'bout you?"

"I'm in the still department. I'm in the big enlarging room. There're eight of us. We're putting out over 2,000 prints a day. Can you believe it?"

"Hey, you want to hit the beach tonight? I found a country western bar over on 14th Street with a great singer. Name's Jimmy Dean. Ever hear of him?"

"Sounds good. I'll see you back at the barracks."

Silas stood me up. I didn't see him again for a couple of days. He seemed depressed. He was writing letters again, and soon incurred the wrath of the entire chain of command again. We went on liberty together, and Silas would still tell me stories of the great carrier battles of World War II, but we saw less and less of each other as he became more and more depressed. He seemed to prefer to be alone, and when we did go out, we just drank. He had no more stories to tell.

I remember feeling guilty when Silas was mugged at the gate. He didn't even know where he was. Silas was still writing letters when I left the Photo Center.

Liberty

Washington, D. C. in 1956 and 1957 was the greatest liberty port in the world. Every summer, fifteen thousand young women came to D.C. to be clerks, clerk typists, and secretaries. We used to go to the Mall near the Washington Memorial at lunchtime just to look at the thousands of women who came there to eat their lunches. We weren't very successful in making out, possibly because we were in uniform, but we did manage to learn that most of them lived in Alexandria, Virginia.

Silas and I decided that we had to have an apartment in Alexandria. It wasn't as easy as you would have thought. Most of them were too expensive and most of those that we could afford wouldn't take men, but we finally found one.

We were the only men in the building, and as far as we knew, we were the only men in the complex, if not the whole neighborhood. Our apartment was on the second floor right over the front door of a large three-story brick building. We watched and listened to all the women as they kissed their dates good night. Sometimes it was an x-rated event.

We learned about women. Clothes and cosmetics come before food and beer. They were always broke and their refrigerators were always empty. We learned that as long as we kept our refrigerator well stocked, we would have women knocking on our door day and night. True, some of them came and ate and drank and left without so much as a thank you, but enough of them stayed to make it worthwhile.

In order to get some sleep, we finally put a sign on the door:

THE DOOR IS ALWAYS OPEN
BEER AND FOOD IN THE FRIDGE
DONATION BOX ON THE TABLE

The strangest thing we learned is that women would say no to their dates and yes to us. I listened to Carol Beardsly, who had a fantastic everything, smooching and saying "No" to her boyfriend for an hour before she came panting into my bedroom, pulling her clothes off, and climbing into my bed. She was so hot she exploded before I was fully awake.

"How can you do that?" I asked.

"Do what?"

"Say no to your boyfriend and then come running up here."

"You could hear me? What did I say? How long were you listening?"

"I wasn't listening on purpose. I sleep with the window open. Every time I woke up I heard, 'I'm not that kind of a woman, I haven't known you long enough, what would you think of me?' and on and on."

Carol started crying. "You just don't understand, Russell. Women either have to be nuns, or they have to have double standards. Men don't marry easy women. I can't just have fun like you do. I'm in love with Ronnie, and I want to marry him. Besides, I thought we were friends."

I assured her that we were, and that I understood, but I didn't.

I was happy to have Silas as a friend again. He still drank too much, but he seemed happier. We talked about the girls that visited our apartment. Silas was annoyed that some of them took beer and never paid. He really wasn't his old self.

There were disadvantages. We never went out any more, and we missed the thrill of the chase. In fact, Silas got tired of it, and moved back into the barracks after watching a girl take money out of the donation box. Getting a new roommate would not be a problem, but I was getting serious with a girl at work, and she couldn't understand why she couldn't come over to my apartment. I finally had to make a choice, and I wound up moving back into the barracks myself.

There are memories that come sneaking in the night to terrorize me, and there are memories that are welcome anytime day or night.

The Paper Caper

Our job status board, a listing of all the printing jobs in house, usually contained between 15 and 50 jobs. In addition to our military customers, the Photo Center serviced the entire country, so there was no such thing as being caught up, or so we thought. One day, after about six months of working at a frantic pace, the job status board was empty. We had no work. We did what sailors always do under such conditions. We held a field day. While we were cleaning, we noticed we were almost out of paper.

There was a large paper bin under each of the six enlargers. Each bin held nearly a hundred boxes of paper. We filled all six bins to the top. The next morning we got two surprises. One, we were not caught up; the woman who processed the job orders had been out sick. There were now 75 jobs on the status board. And two, we were almost out of paper again.

There were nine men on the night crew, but they would have to have printed over 250,000 prints to account for the missing paper. Something was definitely wrong, and I needed to report it to my division officer, Chief Warrant Officer Larry Butz.

"Mr. Butz, we have a serious problem in the print room."

"Not now, Quigley, I'm busy."

"But sir, this is real serious."

"I said not now, Quigley. Can't you see I'm busy? Whatever it is, take care of it."

Mr. Butz was typing a letter, which obviously was not his strong suit.

"Mr. Butz, this really is urgent; I think—"

"Not now, damn it! What does it take to get through to you?"

I backed off, but I was all the more upset. They're not going to pin this on me. Could Mr. Butz be in on it? I'd better go see Lieutenant Ball.

"Mr. Ball, can I see you for a minute?"

"What's on your mind, Quigley? Russell isn't it?"

I wonder why he knows my name. "Well sir, I think somebody stole $15,000.00 worth of paper out of my darkroom."

"What makes you think it was stolen?"

I could tell Mr. Ball was a little anxious. This was a secure building full of secret and top secret material. Supposedly, nothing could go in or out of this building without being noticed, certainly not $15,000.00 worth of photo paper, which would be about 500 boxes. I explained what happened.

"Can the supply people back you up? Have you talked to Mr. Butz?"

"I tried to talk to Mr. Butz, but he said he was too busy. I just got the paper yesterday morning, so I'm sure supply will remember.

"Okay, Quigley, I'll take care of it. Tell Mr. Butz I'd like to see him."

Mr. Butz's desk was in the Job Order Control office, which he shared with three clerks and the Still Department secretary. I was called into his office as soon as he returned. He looked angry; I wondered if Mr. Ball was upset with him.

"Quigley, you slimy little piss ant. You just had to go to Lieutenant Ball behind my back, didn't you? He asked me if I was trying to cover it up. You just couldn't wait two minutes for me to finish what I was doing."

"Mr. Butz, you told me to take care of it, and I didn't know what—

"I didn't tell you to rat on me like I was one of the thieves; you little son-of-a-bitch."

But Mr. Butz, I didn't know what else—"

"Goddamn it, Quigley, you are the most arrogant, condescending, self-righteous little bastard I ever met. From now on, you work in the office where I can keep an eye on you."

"But, sir, I don't know how to type, and—"

"Bastards like you always know how to type. That's your desk in the back," he said, pointing at it. "Mary, give this man something to do. And keep him busy."

I looked at him in disbelief. Typical goddamn Navy. You do what's right and they screw you every time.

"Russell, the film comes in from the library in these canvas pouches," Mary said, pausing to look at me. "There is usually a letter inside describing what the customer wants. You take the letter and transfer the critical information to the job order."

"Can I fill it out by hand? I really can't type."

"No, they have to be typed. You just came from the dark room, so you know how hard it is to read these job orders under a safe light. It would be even harder if they were handwritten."

If you have ever seen a nontypist fill out a form with a typewriter, you know what an exquisite form of torture it is. And every day Mr. Butz accused me of faking it and of just plain goofing off. I was rather depressed by the time I remembered my friend, Silas. He was, once again, putting in a chit a day asking for sea duty. I will do the same thing. I will put in a chit a day asking to be transferred to the Motion Picture Department.

Of course Mr. Butz disapproved it. And Mr. Ball disapproved it. And it came back to me without the XO's or the CO's signature. I knew Silas would insist that the chit go through the chain of command like it's supposed to, but I also knew it wouldn't do any good. I decided to put in one a day and save them, so that when I saw the XO I would have a bunch of chits that hadn't gone through him. Perhaps he would be annoyed enough to transfer me to another department.

After seven chits, Lieutenant Ball called me into his office and asked me what was going on.

"I am being punished for reporting the loss of paper from my darkroom."

"Nonsense. Mr. Butz says he needs help, and that you know how to type."

"I don't know how to type, and I am being punished. Why haven't any of my requests gone to the XO?"

"Because, Russell, we take care of our own problems in this department without bothering the XO. I will not go against Mr. Butz, and the XO will not go against me, so you will be wasting everyone's time if you insist that I forward your requests. Are you going to force me to waste the XO's time?"

"No, sir," I said, wondering how Silas did it.

The next day I was summoned to the captain's conference room and introduced to two FBI agents and a recorder. The captain expressed his concern that if that much paper could be taken out of the building without being seen by one of the guards or watches, then so could classified material. The captain went back to his office and the investigation began.

"Mr. Quigley, would you tell us why you set a barracks on fire when you were at Treasure Island?"

"Wait a damn minute. Am I a suspect here?"

"Well, Mr. Quigley, you have been in a lot of trouble, and you are the number one suspect in the theft of some high altitude flight gear."

"Sir, I was cleared of all charges. A chief petty officer stole that flight gear, and it's because of bullshit like this that I am always in trouble. It wouldn't make any sense for me to tell Lieutenant Ball the paper was missing if I was the one that stole it."

"Mr. Quigley, we are sorry if we have offended you, but we—"

"You can take your apology and shove it. I don't have anything else to say to you."

"Now wait a minute, young man, you don't have any call to speak to us that way."

"Well, then, it's my turn to apologize," I said as I stood up. "I won't make that mistake again, because I am not going to talk to you again." I left and went back to work. I expected to catch hell, but I didn't.

The FBI solved the mystery. Seven members of the night crew were court-martialed. The other two were probably guilty of other thefts, but one was on leave and one was in the hospital when this batch of paper was stolen. Several people from commercial photo labs were also arrested and tried in civilian courts.

It was really quite easy to get the paper out of the building. Photography generates a lot of waste. They filled large waste cans full of good photo paper and put a little trash on top. They rolled the cans right by the guard and on to the elevator, which took them down to the back platform and the trash dumpsters. They removed the trash, put the paper in their car trunks, and went back inside.

After another month of fill-in-the-blanks torture, Mr. Butz went on leave. I immediately put in another request chit for a transfer, and to my surprise, Mr. Ball approved it. The XO, Commander Bartel, called me in to discuss the matter. He had my record open and made me explain every problem I had ever had.

Finally, he said, "I need someone to run the mail room. I have too many security violations, and nothing I have done so far has had any effect. The worst offenders are my own department heads.

"Looking at your scores, I know that you can learn the rules, but I also need someone who can stand up to my department heads and division officers. And I mean without being offensive. I won't tolerate any insubordination or disrespect. If you don't think you can take a little heat and still be polite, just say no, and I'll transfer you to the Motion Picture Department. Do you think you can handle the job?"

"Yes, sir," I said.

"Good, you can start this afternoon, but understand, one incident of disrespect and you're history."

"Yes, sir," I said again. "Oh, by the way sir, I have to go to the hospital every Wednesday afternoon."

"Yes, I know."

The Mail Room

CDR Bartel took mailroom security seriously. He personally went over all the details about how classified material should be wrapped and marked. Then he gave me a copy of the *Security Manual* and told me to study it. Two weeks later, the commander gave me a thorough oral test, and then told me he was pleased with my progress.

Three of us worked in the mailroom. Petty Officer Third Class Bill Mason was my guard mail petty officer. Airman Robert Bell helped me sort mail and covered the mailroom whenever I had to leave. By the time I was promoted to Photographer's Mate Second Class a month later, I knew the name of nearly everyone in the building.

I discovered Commander Bartel could be devious. He followed me upstairs one day when I had to return an improperly packaged box of classified material to the librarian, Commander Bellinger. There was something wrong with Commander Bellinger. For one thing, he was always angry. For another, he was senior to Commander Bartel, and yet he wasn't the XO. And finally, he was the most flagrant violator of security regulations in the building. He and his staff treated everything in the library as ordinary mail.

Anyway, Commander Bartel stayed out of sight, and I pretended that I hadn't seen him, but you know I am going to be extremely polite.

"Commander Bellinger, I have been ordered to check every package going to this address, and this one doesn't appear to be double-wrapped."

"Look' Quigley, I know you mean well, but I only have three people up here and there isn't any way that I can take the time to double-wrap everything that leaves here. It takes everything I've got just to get the right stuff to the right people."

"Well sir, you may need more people, but I can't do anything about that. All I know is that this package has to be double-wrapped, and if I open it, and it's not double-wrapped, I'd have to write you up, and I don't want to do that. It would be much better if—"

"Goddamn it, Quigley, don't tell me how to do my job. You do whatever you have to do, but don't come up here and tell me what to do."

"I'm sorry, Commander, I didn't mean to sound like I was telling you what to do."

CDR Bellinger turned and walked away. I took the package back to the mailroom and opened it. Sure enough it was secret material and it was not double-wrapped. I wrote it up.

CDR Bartel came in to tell me that Commander Bellinger had complained that I had been rude and disrespectful.

"I told him that you were just following my orders, and that I was very pleased with your work, and that I was counting on you to put a stop to all these security violations. By the way, I'm going to transfer Petty Officer First Class Williams to the library, but I'm going to let him work in the mailroom for a week before I send him upstairs. I want you to check him out on how things should be done."

It felt good to have my boss' confidence. I was beginning to feel good about myself and the Navy, and just when I thought it couldn't get any better, a big man with a big smile leaned in over our half door and said, "Hello, men, what do you do in here?" It was President Eisenhower.

"We sort the mail and keep track of classified material coming in and going out of the building," Airman Bell said proudly.

"Well, keep up the good work, men."

Guard Mail

Sailors, like water, usually seek their own level. I guess this is true for most people. Of course, some people try to get ahead of themselves. One way they do this is to identify with their bosses. Some secretaries become all-powerful in this manner, but if there is one place you would not expect this ploy to work, it is in the military.

First Class Petty Officer Mike Mullens was an exception. Mike was a guard mail petty officer and personal courier for Admiral Ballentine over at the David Taylor Model Basin. Mike was an arrogant son-of-a-bitch. I don't know of any other way to put it.

Part of my job as the mailroom supervisor was to ensure that classified material coming in and going out of the building was wrapped, marked, and handled properly. This included meeting people in the lobby who were bringing classified material into the building and accompanying them to their destinations.

I had to write Mike up every time he came in the building. He didn't do anything by the book. His packages were not properly wrapped or marked. He never carried a gun, never locked his truck, and never had an escort with him. And every time I wrote him up, he made snide remarks, and said the admiral said he didn't have to do those things. I didn't know it at the time, but every time I wrote him up, Admiral Ballentine called Commander Bartel and chewed his tail. Anyone who works with classified material will find this hard to believe, but it is true.

One day, Mike came in with a large, clearly marked, top-secret chart, which everyone in the lobby could read. I not only wrote him up, I wouldn't let him in the building. Mike was enraged.

"You stupid little shit," he roared, "I'm going to teach you not to fuck with the admiral."

Mike walked behind the security desk, picked up the phone, called Admiral Ballentine, and said, "That little weasel I've been telling you about won't let me in the building with your chart."

Mike handed me the phone. "Good morning, Admiral. Petty Officer Russell Quigley speaking."

"Listen, Russell, I don't have time for your petty bullshit, and I am not going to tolerate it anymore. I want to speak to your boss, and I want to speak to him right now."

I summoned Commander Bartel and handed him the phone. I could hear the admiral screaming into the phone, and I could see the commander's face getting redder and redder. When he hung up the phone he said, "Let him in."

I let him in and escorted him to the studio where they would copy his chart. It was not like the commander to back down, and I could tell he was pissed, but I didn't know how pissed until he called me and Petty Officer Mason, our guard mail petty officer, into his office later in the day.

"Mason, tell me again everything this Mike character does that violates security regs."

"Well, the thing I see him do that is most wrong is leave his truck open and unguarded, and you know he is carrying classified material."

"That is outrageous. Are you sure about that?"

"Yes sir," Mason replied.

"Okay guys, this is what we're going to do. We're going to wait for him in the Pentagon parking lot near where you say he always parks, and if his truck is open, and if it contains classified material, we are going to empty his truck into our truck. I've been on the phone all day, and I'm sure I can get all of the material we pick up back to where it belongs. In any case, I will take full responsibility for the classified material. Are you with me?"

The next day, the three of us waited for Petty Officer Mike Mullens in the Pentagon parking lot. He pulled in right on schedule and parked his truck. Mike retrieved a few packages and headed inside the building. We waited until he was out of sight and went over to his truck. Sure enough, it was full of classified information and it was unlocked. It was incredibly stupid; it was the sort of thing people went to jail for.

We emptied his truck into ours, and drove back to the Naval Photographic Center. The security officer helped us carry everything inside. We never saw the classified material or Petty Officer Mike Mullens again.

Fat Pat

To her face, we called her Patty. Patty was six feet, two inches tall and weighed 267 pounds. She had the foulest mouth I ever heard and all she ever talked about was sex. Fat Pat didn't like the Navy from the start, and she wanted to get out any way she could. She had been trying to get pregnant for about six months. Now she was concentrating on getting a "morals discharge." "Whichever comes first," she would say.

The Navy has trouble dealing with women today, but back in 1956, it was simple. A man wasn't a "man" unless he could brag about his exploits, but if a woman had sex with two different men in the same century, she was eligible for a "morals discharge."

Anyway, Fat Pat was willing to fuck anyone, anytime, anywhere, and we all did our best to accommodate her. I nailed her a dozen times in the cleaning gear locker and once in a darkened hallway between darkrooms. The last time it happened, she asked me if I could hang around and do it again.

"Why?" I asked, figuring she already had enough sperm to get pregnant, and if it didn't work, a bunch more wouldn't help.

"Because I didn't make it," she replied.

"Didn't make what?" I asked.

"You know, I didn't cum. It wasn't your fault; I always have trouble cuming."

Well, this was all very embarrassing. I always just banged away until I got mine because I knew that's how it was done; I never thought nothing about whether a woman ever made it or not.

Well I didn't mind trying again, so I said, "Sure." Well, I tried again, and she didn't make it again, and she told me so. Well now, she was putting me on the spot again, and I was real embarrassed, so I blurted out, "I bet I could make you cum with my vibrator." Well, I don't know where that came from because I didn't even own a vibrator.

Anyway, she got all excited and asked me what kind of vibrator I had, and how did it work, and did I really think it would work on her. I just mumbled, "You'll see; you'll see." We made a date to meet in the film editing room at 1700. She said she used that big green table back there a lot. The Photo Center secured at 1600 so even the dedicated lifers would all be gone by 1700 and there would just be her and me.

I considered just standing her up, but I was kind of intrigued myself. I remembered seeing vibrators over at the exchange, but the exchange was all the way around to the other side of the airfield. I knew I would have to run all the way over and back if I didn't want to be missed. I found a two-speed Swedish hand massager, you know, the kind that straps on to the back of your hand. It had a huge motor that sure looked like it ought to do something, but there was a problem; it cost $15.95 and I only had $12.00. There was nothing to do but to run back to the Photo Center, borrow the money, run back over to the exchange, buy the vibrator, and then run back to the Photo Center again.

I approached the film editing room with caution, and was alarmed when I heard voices and giggling and laughing. I was about to turn around when someone spotted me and said, "Here he is." I walked into a room full of people standing around a large green table that had been pulled to the middle of the room. An extension cord was ready and waiting. Fat Pat had told everyone what was happening and they were all, including some of the girls, waiting to see the show.

Fat Pat was already naked and lying spread-eagle on the table. "She said, "I've been drinking a little to help me relax. You wanna do it first? I already did everyone else."

There was no way I could do it in front of everyone, so I strapped on the vibrator and turned it on low. I held it over her face, so that she could see it; she turned crimson all over and started panting. I moved my hand down toward her crotch and she started moaning before I even touched her.

I pushed my index finger into her wide-open hole and she yelped. I bent my wrist toward her clit and put as much pressure there as I could. She began moaning. "Harder. Faster. Deeper. More," she sputtered. I inserted all my fingers at once, pushed down hard, and turned it on high. She really started groaning. Sometimes it was shrill and high pitched and at other times, it was low and throaty. The smell emanating from her crotch was powerful and people started crowding around the table as if they couldn't get enough of it.

"What the hell is going on here?" shouted a voice from behind me.

I froze. I would have pissed my pants if I hadn't had an erection. As it is, I managed to dribble all over myself as it came back to parade rest. I knew the voice. It was Lieutenant Burton, a no-nonsense line officer, who did not consider the Photo Center a career-enhancing billet, and he despised "photo pussies" as he called us.

Fat Pat was doubled up and convulsing on my fingers. She had both of her hands clamped on my wrist holding my vibrating hand in place. She was oblivious to the lieutenant and kept saying, "Oh God, oh God, oh God."

"You're on report, all of you," he said. The crowd had diminished from about 30 to 5 as people disappeared through the many entrances to the editing room.

Fat Pat got her morals discharge. I got 30 days restriction, 20 hours extra duty, a $75.00 fine, and a reduction in rate, suspended for six months.

Married with Family

It was not a good time to get married. I was getting out of the Navy in two months. The girl I gave up the apartment for, Carla Brewer, was in the Navy and had a year to go on her enlistment. I would have to get a job, stay in the area, and postpone going to college for a year.

Well, there was no way that I could go back to South Dakota without her, so I would just have to find a job. We got married in the base chapel and moved into a small apartment in Anacostia. Married life was wonderful, and to my surprise, I did not miss my apartment. We decided not to plan for or against having a baby, and soon learned that if you weren't planning against, you were planning for.

CDR Bartel knew I wasn't fond of the Navy, but couldn't help pointing out the benefits of extending for a year rather than getting out and looking for a job.

"Russell, you passed the first class test, so if you stay in the Navy you will get a promotion and a good pay raise that would be hard to match on the outside. And, you would only need one car because you would both be working at the same place."

Well, it just made too much sense. I agreed with him, and told him I would extend for a year. I went to the Personnel Office and asked to speak to Lieutenant Commander Hutchinson.

"Mr. Hutchinson, I would like to extend for a year so that I can stay here and be with my wife."

"Now wait just a cotton-picking minute young man, you don't come in here and tell me what you're going to do. You can't extend unless I say you can, and I won't know if I even want you in my Navy until I examine your record. Furthermore, you'll go wherever the Navy needs you."

I knew Mr. Hutchinson was a cantankerous old fart, but I was not prepared for his bullshit, and I knew I didn't want him examining my record. The more he talked, the angrier I got until finally I said, "Never mind, Mr. Hutchinson, I don't think I want to stay in your Navy."

CDR Bartel couldn't wait to ask me how it went.

"I'd suck elephant dicks at ten cents a herd before I would extend in this outfit."

I was instantly sorry. I saw the pain and disgust on Commander Bartel's face before he turned and left. I offended the only officer I ever liked.

I was honorably discharged from the United States Navy on October 23, 1957.

A CIVILIAN AGAIN

All I wanted was a job for one year while my wife finished her tour at the Naval Photo Center, and then I was going back to South Dakota to go to school. I had accepted a job for $1.10 an hour, but just before I was discharged from the Navy, I saw this ad for meat cutters for a major grocery chain. They were paying $1.75 an hour while you were in meat cutting school and $1.85 an hour when you started work.

A Meat Cutter

The school was difficult. We studied the anatomy of cows, pigs, chickens, and fish before we even learned the different cuts of meat. We learned how to grade meat by its appearance, and how to tell when it was going bad. We even learned the best way to cook every cut of meat in case a customer were to ask. I was surprised at how much I enjoyed it.

I was assigned to a small corner store in a poor black neighborhood in the Southeast section of Washington, D.C. I parked right across the street. My fellow meat cutters told me that was a grave mistake, that neighborhood gangs would trash my car before I got off work. They said they would show me their parking lot about nine blocks from the store. "It's only $2.00 a week."

I worried about my car all day, but when I returned that evening, my car was fine. There was an 11-year old boy leaning up against it. "It's fifty cents," he said.

"What is?" I asked.

"For your car. I been watchin' it. I'm Jackie." He put out his hand.

"Aren't you a little young to be in the protection racket?" I asked. "How can you protect my car? Besides, aren't you supposed to be in school?"

"Size doesn't matter as long as someone is being paid to watch your car, they'll leave it alone, and I can't go to school because my mom can't watch this space and take care of her customers too. That's her in the window."

I looked up at the brownstone and saw the woman in the window.

She hollered, "You hire my son, Jack. He's a good boy; he won't ever leave your car. I'll see to it. We need the money."

I hired her son. I thought it was a good deal, but the others seemed to resent it. They said it was the principle of the thing.

Another thing they resented was my loaning money to the women that came into the store. It did seem to get out of hand, but when a woman told me that her kids were hungry and hadn't eaten in two days, I couldn't say no. In no time at all I was loaning money, a few dollars at a time, to 15 or 20 regulars. I couldn't keep track because my boss would get angry if I stopped to write it down, but I don't believe I ever lost a dime.

Our two best sellers were "filla fish" and pork neck bones. "Filla fish" was whatever filet of fish was on special, which was usually haddock or perch at 9 cents a pound. The pork neck bones were boned at the warehouse, so there was precious little meat left on them, but they made great soup, and were popular at 19 cents a piece. My boss was always bitching because he was paid a commission on what we sold out of the meat case. He dreamed of moving uptown where people bought steaks.

One day a woman asked me for one neck bone and would I please chop it up. "I want one with plenty of meat on it," she said. Well, I did, and she rejected it. I was a little embarrassed because there really wasn't any meat on any of them, but I tried again. And she rejected it again. When she rejected it a third time, I expressed my frustration.

She said, "Mister, if you only had 25 cents to buy your family's supper, you would find some meat on those bones."

My boss came to my rescue by going to the freezer and getting a neck bone and showing it to the customer.

She said, "Yeah, that's the one. See, your boss knows what he's doing."

When she left, my boss said, "The frozen ones are redder, so they look like they have more meat on them."

Jack's mother was watching my car when I got off work. "Jackie's sick, so I watched your car today." I wondered if she really stood outside all day for 50 cents. She looked at me and said, "I can take care of your other needs for another 50 cents." She made at least a dollar that day.

The year went by fast.

A Student

There is nothing like a cup of hot chocolate at 20 degrees below zero, and the cafeteria at Northern State College in Aberdeen, South Dakota, makes the best hot chocolate in the world. I chose "Northern State" because it was cheap, and I thought I could get by on the GI Bill.

I was wrong. My wife couldn't find a job, and our new son had unexpected medical expenses. I was already taking 21 hours of classes when I found a job clerking at a hotel for 44 hours a week at $1.10 an hour. It wasn't as bad as it might sound because I could study on the job.

I wanted to join the veteran's group and the Young Republicans, but I decided to concentrate on my grades because I really needed a scholarship. I made the dean's list with straight A's, but I didn't get a scholarship because I didn't participate in any extracurricular activities.

The school would not give a student a second loan until the first one was paid off, so I borrowed from a bank for the second quarter. I borrowed enough to pay for tuition and books and make payments on the first loan. Neither loan was paid off in time, so I borrowed the third quarter from a small loan company. The stress was more than my wife could handle, so she took my son and went home to her mother.

I lasted several more quarters until the stupid college ran a credit check and refused to loan me any more money and also said I couldn't work full time anymore even though I had all A's. So I quit and joined my wife in Panama City, Florida, and started looking for work.

A Sailor Again

My goal was to be a teacher, and as luck would have it, Florida was desperate for teachers. I answered an ad for elementary teachers, and went for an interview at a local high school gym. Picnic tables had been set up for the interviews.

Once they established my eligibility—two years of college and the willingness to attend classes during the summer—they sent me to a distinguished looking woman for an interview. The interview went well until I asked about the salary.

"Damn," I said, "$75.00 dollars a week? I could make that much as a seaman in the Navy."

She leaned back, turned her head away, punched her nose up a notch, and then, turning back towards me, said, "Well, why don't you, then."

I was a little miffed, so I said, "I think I will." I thanked her and left.

I couldn't believe I had said that. I stopped at the first bar and bought a beer. I couldn't stop thinking about what I had said. I didn't really want to go back in the Navy, did I? I knew I missed the excitement, and I did long to experience the flight deck of a carrier. I remembered all those stories Silas used to tell me. I also remembered all the trouble I got into.

I had another beer. It would have to be different. I would have to swallow my pride. I have responsibilities now. I couldn't be getting into trouble all the time. I had another beer. The Navy has a career path; that's more than you can say for teachers. And it does have benefits. And I like being a photographer; it's just that you can't find a job on the outside, and if you could it wouldn't pay anything.

I had another beer. Outside? What do I mean on the outside? I'm talking like I'm already back in the Navy. I had another beer, and then I went and joined the Navy. I felt pretty good until I realized that I hadn't even discussed it with Carla. There would be hell to pay.

Carla smelled my breath, and said, "I wondered why your interview took so long."

"I have news for you," I replied.

"You're going to be a teacher?"

"No, I joined the Navy."

"Thank God. No more worrying about Donald's medical bills, and something else I couldn't tell you while you didn't have a job, we have another baby on the way."

For once there was peace in the Quigley household. It didn't happen very often. I was aware that I had the same problems at home that I had in the Navy. I vowed to work on both areas. Carla decided not to come with me until after our second child was born. She wanted her mother's help and I could understand that. I would be on my own again. I could live with that.

I went by bus to Charlotte, North Carolina, where I was sworn in. I was provided with a complete sea bag, and everything fit this time around. I retook the GCT test. After a few days of indoctrination classes, I received orders for the USS *Wasp*.

THE USS *WASP*

The *Wasp* (CV-18) was an Essex class aircraft carrier, 872 feet in length and a beam of 93 feet at the waterline. It was my first duty station after I reenlisted. Fully loaded, it displaced 34,881 tons. Four Westinghouse turbines powered the *Wasp*. It had a crew of 2,700 and could carry nearly a hundred aircraft. It was a mighty warship with a distinguished war record. I arrived on June 27, 1960, and I was proud to be onboard.

The *Wasp* had a 12-man photo lab. When I walked in, I saw a photograph of a large table piled high with money hanging on the finishing room wall. I pointed at it and said, "You guys have a thing for money, huh?"

"No," Petty Officer Second Class Ray Simmons said, "that picture is there to remind us why we don't have any work to do. A couple of months ago, we were asked to photograph all the ship's money in the disbursing office. It was some kind of publicity stunt, but apparently it was too much for the disbursing officer. He's down in South America with that table full of money, and somehow, the captain thinks it's our fault. You can't even get an ID photo shot without the OPS officer's signature on a request chit."

"Wow, I guess we don't have a lot of work, then?"

"We keep one man on the flight deck and one man on the 07 level during flight ops. Beyond that, three people could handle the rest of it. However, we do seem to be catching more than our share of working parties and shit details."

"How is Boston?"

"Boston is fabulous. More girls than you know what to do with, and there is a lot going on here. We go on antisubmarine patrols for two weeks at a time, and then we're in port for two weeks, so we have a lot of time to do stuff."

"Sounds great."

It was true. There wasn't much to do in the lab; however, we figured that was about to change when the ship announced an all hands working party at 2300 hours, and some of the boxes we carried aboard had KOTEX® printed on them.

We were ordered to the South Atlantic where we were standing by to evacuate civilians when civil strife broke out in the newly independent Congo. Our boss, Chief Photographer's Mate Al Pruit, was set to go in with the Marines to photograph the evacuation, but he was never tasked to leave the ship. Apparently, the crisis cooled off and was over in a few days. We off loaded our avgas, except enough for our planes to fly off when we got back to the States. Even though it was a bit of an anti-climax, it felt good to be where the action was, and to be doing something important. I was beginning to understand what Silas was always talking about. I realized that I, too, liked being where the action is.

Flu Shots

I received my first flu shot aboard the Wasp, and I actually stood in line to get it. A corpsman used a stun gun to deliver the shots as we marched by. I was sick for three weeks. It reminded me of when my whole family caught the flu at once. I was quite young, but I remember it to this day. It was a strain called Virus X. I have been terrified of the flu ever since. I swore I would never receive another flu shot.

A year later, when it was announced in the plan-of-the-day that it was time to get a flu shot again, I simply ignored it. A week later, our division officer, Ensign Sweeny, ordered everyone to report to sickbay to get a flu shot. I ignored his request.

Apparently, there were a lot of stragglers because when I went to get paid, there were corpsmen standing at the end of the pay line with their stun guns. I ducked out of the pay line. I could go without pay for two weeks if I had to. It was preferable to getting another flu shot.

Imagine my surprise when I saw those same gangsters with their stun guns at the end of the pay line again two weeks later. Whoa! How long are they going to keep this up? How long can I go without getting paid? I wrote home to Carla for a loan. She was on a tight budget and not sympathetic. I borrowed money from shipmates who were braver than I was.

I was deep in debt by the time the gangsters gave up, but I never got another flu shot. I am weakening, though; my doctor says they're safe now. I'm not so sure.

What is it With Redheads?

Petty Officer Tom Kelly had a freckled face, curly red-orange hair, and a smile that could melt the Arctic in mid December. He was disarmingly friendly and had a wonderful sense of humor. Tom was unusually perceptive, and could analyze newcomers instantly into lists of strengths and weaknesses. If he accepted you, he never missed an opportunity to praise you for your good points, and if he rejected you, he never missed a chance to plant barbs on your weaknesses.

I was instantly rejected. He reminded me of Chief Warrant Officer Butz. Tom seemed to be neutral towards Chief Pruit; however, the division officer, Ensign Sweeny, was one of his greatest fans.

Tom was the leader of a clique that followed him wherever he went. They all hung out in the film development room at the far end of the lab. My favorite spot to read or write letters was in the print room. The two rooms were next to each other, but the doors were at right angles. When I looked out the door of the print room, I could see the coffee mess on the other side of the hall. Whenever I stepped out to get a refill, I was right outside their door. I could hear everything they said from the coffeepot, and nearly everything they said from inside the print room.

Tom slept with a chipping hammer under his pillow. We both had top bunks that were directly across from each other. At night he would show me the chipping hammer and say, "Don't ever fuck with me, Quigley, because I will kill you."

One day Tom got into an argument with Petty Officer Richard Mackentire. It escalated into threats of physical violence, and we started trying to calm them down. Without warning, Tom grabbed a large glass ashtray off the counter and used it to smack Richard across his temple. Richard sank to the floor out cold. We took him to sick bay and told the corpsman what happened. The word got back to Ensign Sweeny.

"Kelly, what the hell did you do to Mackentire?"

"I didn't do nothing to Mackentire, sir. We got into an argument and he hit me. He's a lot bigger than I am, so I hit him back with everything I have, and he fell down the ladder into the bunkroom. Go ahead and ask him. He'll tell you."

"You got anything against Quigley?"

"Not really. He's a little prissy and too bookish for me, but he's alright."

Ensign Sweeny went to sick bay and talked to Richard. When he came back, he called me into the print room and closed the door.

"Quigley, you lied to the corpsman about what happened to Mackentire."

"No, sir, I saw what happened to Mackentire, and I haven't lied to anyone."

"Mackentire just told me himself that he fell down a ladder. I should write you up for this."

"Go ahead. I'll be glad to tell the captain what I saw. And if the captain will promise to get rid of that psycho Kelly, Mackentire will tell him the truth fast enough."

Ensign Sweeny glared at me, "Don't ever use that word again, Quigley. You are not a psychiatrist." He glared at me and left.

Tom came in. "Quigley, you better watch your step. I'm going to tell you the same thing I told Mackentire. I can crack your skull any night of the week and dump you over the side. Nobody would ever know the difference."

"Tom, there's a big difference between me and Mackentire. I will not back down no matter how afraid I am. Everybody knows what happened here today. If I disappear, it wouldn't take people long to figure out what happened. I don't like you, but I know you ain't stupid."

I was afraid. I slept in the print room with the door locked for a week. When Richard returned to the lab, I cussed him out for not telling the truth. Richard told Tom that if anything happened to me he would tell Ensign Sweeny the truth.

Tom said, "That's okay. I can do you both."

We worked five days a week in port and six days at sea. Most of the divisions slept in on Sundays at sea. Chief Pruit mustered us at 0800. He was like a mother hen keeping track of her chicks. Tom used his influence with Ensign Sweeny to make an end run around the chief.

"Why do we have to muster on Sundays? Nobody else does."

"I don't know why you guys have to muster, Tom. I don't. I'll talk to Chief Pruit."

I could hear Ensign Sweeny and Chief Pruit arguing all the way back to the print room, and I could tell by how pissed Chief Pruit was after the ensign left that he had lost. Chief Pruit spent Friday evening at his desk. We did not disturb him.

Chief Pruit finally got up from his desk and came back for a cup of coffee. I knew he had been pouring over the ship's regulations hoping to find one that required the ship to muster on Sundays. The print room door was open. It was the first time I ever saw the chief smile. When he saw me, he said, "OP Division is supposed to air mattresses at 0800 on the first Sunday of the month. That is this coming Sunday."

Sure enough, Chief Pruit woke us up at 0800 Sunday morning, and we all had to carry our mattresses up to the hanger deck and tie them to the side rails. I was tickled, but when Ensign Sweeny heard about it, he was not. They had a big argument again, and Chief Pruit lost again. Chief Pruit spent very little time in the lab after that.

Ensign Sweeny invited Tom Kelly and his gang to his apartment for a party. Very few officers would make such a blunder, but he was a boot ensign, and I think he was genuinely fond of Tom.

To hear them tell it, the party was a big success. Ensign Sweeny had offered to drive them back to the ship, but they said they would rather catch a bus since they had all been drinking. They did a little bar hopping before catching a bus, but they all made it back okay.

I was in the print room with the door closed when they returned. They were drunk and talking loud.

"Did you see the expression on her face when I hit her in the gut? How old do you think she was?"

I recognized Tom's voice. He was talking to Petty Officer Third Class Ed Reily, one of his lackeys.

"She must have been 65 or 70 years old. I can't believe she stood up so long. You must have hit her 50 times before she went down. Must have been the booze. She was so drunk she could hardly walk."

I couldn't believe what I was hearing, and all the time they're laughing and whooping it up. I will have to tell Chief Pruit because I know Ensign Sweeny ain't gonna believe me. Anyway, it'll keep until morning. I slipped out of the lab and went to bed.

After a restless night, I went to the chief's quarters and talked to Chief Pruit.

"You'll have to talk to Ensign Sweeny. He's running the lab. I told him if he ever gets tired of playing chief, he knows where to find me."

"Okay. What do you do all day, Chief? I'd go nuts down here."

"I used to be an aviation ordnanceman. They're short handed, so I'm helping out. I may have made a mistake when I switched to photography."

I went back to the lab to wait for Ensign Sweeny.

"Quigley, I don't care what you have to say to me, you're going to have to say it right here in front of everybody."

"No sir. It's a private matter, and if you don't want to handle it, I'll take it to the department head."

"You wise ass son-of-a-bitch, Quigley. Okay, back in the print room, but it better be good."

I told him what I heard.

"Quigley, I'm going to get rid of you. Maybe the galley can use another mess deck master-at-arms. And if I hear a word of this from anybody, I'll take you to mast."

"Mr. Sweeny, I'm not going to be intimidated. I know what I heard. You ought to at least call—"

"Shut up, Quigley. You just shut up, and don't you ever presume to tell me what to do. You hear me?"

"Yes, sir."

A voice from the hallway shouted, "Hey, Russell, you've got a phone call."

Ensign Sweeny turned and left. I went out and answered the phone.

"Russell, this is Chief Pruit. It really happened. It's in this morning's paper. You tell Ensign Sweeny?"

"I told him. He said he is going to send me to the mess decks, and told me not to tell anyone else."

"Don't worry, Russell. I won't let that happen. Just play it cool while I do some checking."

Later that night I was in the print room reading *Self Analysis* by Karen Horney. Chief Pruit stopped by the coffee pot just outside my door.

"I thought I would find you here."

I put my finger to my lips, and said, "The gang is in the film room next door."

"Okay," he said, lowering his voice, "I've been asking around. Seems a lot of people are aware of Kelly's Dr. Jekyll and Mr. Hyde personality. Also, Mackentire told me what really happened. I'm not quite ready to go to Commander Sully, but I will—"

It was Ensign Sweeny getting a cup of coffee. He turned to knock on the film developing room door, but stopped when he saw us. It was obvious he was not pleased to see us together, but before he could say anything, it happened. Their voices became louder and louder, but Kelly's voice topped them all.

"Don't worry about that fucking Quigley. I have Mr. Sweeny eating out of the palm of my hand. He ain't never going to believe that fuckhead. We have nothing to worry about."

I guess Ensign Sweeny was as red as a human being can get without exploding. He did an about face and rushed out of the photo lab.

"Well, Russell, I think it's over. I'll talk to the ensign in the morning. While I'm at it, I'll take back my photo lab.

The Texas Tower

We were sitting in a semi-circle in the finishing room just shooting the breeze when Petty Officer Ray Simmons, our leading petty officer, asked for some help in the print room. Ray listened to a bunch of silly excuses as to why they couldn't help without challenging them, so when he got to me I said, "I can't. I have a bent eyelash."

"Screw you guys," he said as he went storming off to print the job himself. He stopped just short of the print room door. "What did you say to me, Quigley? Get your ass over here and print this job."

I suspect there is nothing worse than a lab full of people with nothing to do. It became unbearably boring. My friend Bill Davenport and I got into the habit of staying up and talking all night. One day, Bill said, "Do you think it would help if we brought a bottle of booze aboard?"

"No way." I was afraid of being caught. The punishment would be too severe. "It sure would beat just sitting around all the time." Before the night was over, we agreed to smuggle a bottle onboard before we went out to sea again.

Several months went by and we forgot all about our booze masquerading as a bottle of uric acid in the chem-mix room. Our workload had not picked up, and we were as bored as we could be. Late one night when Bill and I were the only ones left in the lab, Bill asked, "Russell, have you ever checked on our booze?"

"No." I replied. "Who would mess with a bottle of uric acid?"

"Well, you never know. Somebody might dump it out or turn it in."

"Well, let's go check." It was right where we left it.

"Let's check it out." Bill said.

"Okay," I said, pulling the stopper out. I gave it a sniff first. It smelled like fine whiskey, so I took a slug and passed it to Bill. "Ain't nobody been messing with our whiskey, Bill."

The more we drank, the more the ship started pitching and rolling. We were having a ball rolling around the finishing room on two office chairs. Bill realized it first. The bottle was nearly empty when he said, "Hey, Russell, it ain't just the booze, we're in one hell of a storm here."

"By god you're right. Let's go check out the expansion bracelet."

The expansion bracelet consisted of two overlapping deck plates that moved back and forth in a storm enabling the ship to absorb some of the force large waves had on the bow.

"No thanks," Bill said, "that thing gives me the creeps."

Undeterred, and too drunk to realize that this storm was much worse than any we had ever been in before, I headed by myself to the expansion bracelet. I put one foot on each of the overlapping deck plates. It was a real kick. I could hear and feel the waves crashing against the bow. The rolling and pitching was getting more and more pronounced.

My legs were moving in and out with the deck plates. At one point, the deck plates actually separated a few inches, and I could see into the compartment below. They separated again, about 12 inches this time, letting in enough light for me to see piles of rope about 30 feet below. Then suddenly my legs were spread wide apart. I even had to go up on my tiptoes. I looked around for something to hold on to, but there was nothing.

I knew I couldn't maintain my balance very long while the ship was rocking back and forth and side to side. The expansion bracelet seemed to hang open forever. I had visions of falling to my death or being cut in half when the bracelet closed. I had just begun praying when my feet were slammed together, and I heard the grinding of metal. Drunk as I was, I knew this was not the place to be. I headed back to the photo lab.

"Thanks for getting here so quickly, Russ." It was Chief Pruit. "Bill is already setting up the print room. Give him a hand."

I nodded and went on back without a word. "What the hell is going on, Bill?"

"Some oil rig called the Texas Tower collapsed in this storm, and we're trying to get there in time to pick up survivors. You picked a hell of night to decide to get drunk."

"Me? You're the one that asked about the booze."

"Russell, you were the one that took the first drink, and handed it to me."

The door flew open. It was the chief. "Can you guys print?"

Oh, oh, he must know we're drunk. "Yes, sir," I said.

"Stay out of sight," he said as he left.

"Chief Pruit's alright ain't he Bill?"

"He sure is. Did you know that he picked up a 500 pound bomb that came bouncing down the flight deck and threw it over the side?"

"No way. When did he do that?"

"On his last ship before he converted from ordnanceman to photographer's mate."

The lab was soon full of people. Divers, equipped with underwater cameras, were flown out to the ship, and made the lab their headquarters. We were up all night expecting to process and print their film, but their first concern was rescuing the 27 people who were on the tower. They searched for hours, but there was no sign of survivors.

The divers were back onboard when the chief told us to go to breakfast. Afterwards, he thanked us for our help, and told us to sleep in.

Lost and Found

"Russell, you know how to use an OBA?"

"Yes I do, Chief Pruit. What's up?"

"They found something in one of the voids, but they can't get in to see it without OBAs. They want a photographer to go in with them. You better change into old clothes."

I had never been in a void before. This one was surprisingly deep. My knees ached by the time I got to the bottom. They had already tested the air and were rigging lights. My vision through the goggles was not good, and even while I was breathing oxygen from the OBA, I could tell the atmosphere was extremely foul.

I got my bearings and proceeded to the far end where everyone was huddled. I've had to photograph a number of bodies, but nothing like this. You couldn't even tell it was human. An officer was trying to remove his billfold. Finally he said, "It's Wieser, Boatswain's Mate Wieser. We thought he went over the hill six months ago."

Now and then there is a fellow human being that is just plain mean beyond all reason. When such a fellow is in a position of authority, he can make life miserable for many people. Boatswain's Mate First Class (BM1) Thomas Wieser was such a person. Many people knew of his abuses, but they didn't do anything because the deck force functioned like a well-oiled machine.

They'll have a devil of a time figuring out who done it. Everyone on the deck force hated his guts. I took pictures of the body and a bloody pipe wrench. They would not let me in the photo lab when I returned. They took the film, but they left the camera on the sponson to air out. They brought me a towel and told me to throw all my clothes over the side. I went straight to the shower and scrubbed for an hour. I didn't even think about water rations.

Solving the murder was not as difficult as I thought it would be. Seaman Kurtz had gone over-the-hill the same time as BM1 Wieser, and his fingerprints were all over the pipe wrench.

The Great Coffee Caper

Petty Officer Third Class Jack Bennard was a genuine card-carrying kleptomaniac. He would go to the ship's store during their busiest time of the day and ask to see three or four cameras one after the other. One of them would always wind up in his pocket. The same procedure worked for watches and any other small, high priced items.

But he was at his best on the hangar deck when the ship was taking on stores. He walked around with a clipboard and pencil as if he was in charge of the whole shebang. He would spot something he wanted and say to the nearest working party personnel, "Take a case of these knives through that hatch to the photo lab, and be sure to come right back."

One day Jack outdid himself. He had a whole pallet of 20-pound cans of coffee delivered to the photo lab. I don't know what he was thinking of because we could never use that much coffee. The missing pallet of 20-pound cans of coffee did not go unnoticed.

"NOW HEAR THIS. NOW HEAR THIS. THE MASTER-AT-ARMS HAVE BEEN DIRECTED TO SEARCH THE SHIP UNTIL THEY FIND THE MISSING COFFEE. WHOEVER HAS IT WILL BE DEALT WITH SEVERELY. DO NOT ATTEMPT TO THROW IT OVERBOARD. WE HAVE PEOPLE WATCHING EVERYWHERE. YOU ARE GOING TO BE CAUGHT, AND YOU ARE GOING TO BE PUNISHED."

If we knew anything about Jack, it was that he would not own up to his part in this fiasco. We were all in trouble and we knew it. What could we do?

ABH3 Lewis, who was in the lab to ask for a picture of the ship, came up with the answer.

"Why don't you stack them up against this wall, and use that roll of brown wrapping paper to cover them up. You could even paint it if you wanted to. Look at all that green paint setting over there."

By the time I said, "That will never work," they had all those cans of coffee neatly stacked up against the wall and were busy taping the cans to each other and to the wall with duct tape. The cans were about a half row short of the ceiling. They started measuring and cutting the heavy brown wrapping paper and attaching it to the cans using duct tape again.

Airman Jones was taking the pallet apart with a chipping hammer. When he was finished, he slid all the lumber into the cabinets under the counter. I have to admit that I was no help. I just stood there amazed, and watched it all happen. ABH3 Lewis opened the cans of paint and prepared a couple of rollers. They had it painted in a matter of minutes, and by golly it looked like a wall.

"Hey Russell, give us a hand. We might as well paint the rest of the room. That's what we got the paint for. I got a brush and busied myself painting the trim around the hatches. It wasn't more than two minutes tops when we heard them come in.

"Attention on deck!" The inspection party consisted of one master-at-arms and a young officer.

"What are you doing here, Lewis?" The officer was a pilot who recognized Lewis.

"Just helping out, sir. Thought I might get some pictures of the ship."

"Way to go, Lewis. See if you can get one for me while you're at it. How many rooms do you guys have here anyway?"

We proceeded to show them around the lab. The ship was gently pitching and rolling, and the wall of coffee was swaying slightly, but it went unnoticed.

"Sorry about the interruption, guys. Carry on."

Icicles

All of us except the chief and the LPO rotated duty on the flight deck and the 07 level during flight ops. Since we had no work in the lab, I much preferred to be outside and volunteered every chance I got. The only difficulty I had was standing between two propeller-driven planes when we were in the North Atlantic. The prop wash would freeze and then be blown into your face leaving little cuts that wouldn't bleed until you got inside where it was warm.

And the wind was strong enough sometimes to blow you down and slide you around on the frozen deck.

My friend, Danny Straight, who, believe it or not, was a member of the Boston Ballet, showed me how to stand on the flight deck. You point your left foot forward, move your right foot back, and point your right foot 90 degrees to the right. This allowed you to lean into the wind while maintaining sideways stability.

Danny and I were great friends until one day Ray asked me to do something and I said, "Might as well; can't dance." I never could convince Danny that it wasn't a slam.

The weather deck, just outside the aerographer's shop on the 07 level, was my favorite place to hang out even when I wasn't working. Not only do you get a perfect view of flight ops but you could also see for miles in any direction. You had to be on your toes constantly when you were on the flight deck, but it was much less hectic seven stories up. You tracked all the take-offs and landings, kept an eye on the angel, and took an action photo now and then. The crew loved action pictures, and they could be traded for almost anything.

The aerographers were great. You could always count on them for a hot cup of coffee when it was really cold and even when it wasn't. One day, after a week of high winds and freezing cold, it suddenly turned warm. The ice on the deck and railings began to melt and, except for the wind, the weather was quite pleasant. I set my camera on the deck and was enjoying a cup of coffee when there was a loud noise and my feet exploded out from under me. I shot across the steel deck at 90 miles an hour and slammed into the steel bulkhead that surrounded the weather deck. I just knew a plane had crashed into us.

"Russell! Are you alright?"

"I think so. What the hell happened?"

A huge icicle missed you by inches and crashed at your feet. It would have killed you for sure. It must have weighed 80 pounds. Your camera is smashed to smithereens. I looked up at the superstructure. There were several more large icicles hanging from the yardarms. You would think a boy from South Dakota would have thought of icicles. You can bet I never went up there again without checking.

Tea Leaves

I've had some of the best food I've ever eaten in the Navy. The *Wasp* was no exception. They had the largest and the best tasting scallops I had ever seen.

There was this day we had T-bone steaks. They looked fantastic. My mouth was watering all the time I stood in the chow line. Then the word came rippling through the chow line, "The scullery broke down; there are no more knives."

No reason to panic. I can probably cut it with a spoon. I was given a huge steak that appeared to be cooked perfectly. I tried to cut it with a spoon. No way. I tried to tear it apart with my hands. No way. I tried holding it in my hands and biting off a piece. No way. I left the table in disgust, and by the time I got back to the lab I was furious.

I decided to have a cup of tea. I banged my cup on the counter, poured some hot water, and snatched a tea bag out of its packet. Then I saw it. A little saying on the small card to which the string was attached, "A man is as emotionally stable as what it takes to make him angry."

I immediately translated, "A man is as stable as what it takes to piss him off." So what pissed me off? The absence of a knife? All that food and I came unglued just because I didn't have a knife. I couldn't believe I was that unstable. I vowed never to lose my temper again without asking myself, "Why?"

It became a very positive ritual. I learned that my shaky ego was behind most of my temper tantrums, and I was able to substantially reduce their occurrence. Thank you, Tender Leaf.®

Together Again, Again

Reporting to any new duty station can be a little overwhelming, especially when you don't know anyone, but reporting to your first ship is like stepping into a new world. I sure wished Silas had been there to help me over the rough spots, but I had already been onboard about six months when I saw him bouncing up the gangway grinning from ear to ear.

Silas knew we were going on a three-month Mediterranean cruise in a few months, and he was excited. "Just think," he said, "you and me and all that ocean and all that liberty. It'll be great, man, just great."

Silas had stopped drinking and spent most of his time onboard ship. He still loved to read about the Navy, and now and then he would tell me about what the two *Wasps* did during the war. I wondered what he did with his money because I seldom saw him leave the ship, and every now and then he would ask to borrow ten or fifteen dollars, which he never paid back. Maybe he was sending it to his mother. I worried because it really wasn't like him not to pay me back; he was always so conscientious.

I worried, too, because my friend was becoming depressed again even as the Med cruise was getting closer. One day after being onboard for about two months, Silas asked me if he could borrow fifty dollars. I hesitated for a second, remembering he still owed me, but then I thought, what the heck, after all we've been through, who cares if he pays me back.

He thanked me, and said it was really important; said he really needed to talk to his mother. We said goodbye, and he mentioned he would be gone all weekend, but that he would see me Monday.

I was doing a little reading myself the following Sunday when one of the new guys came back from liberty. "Hey, Russell," he said, "did you hear about Silas? He dropped himself in the East River. He's been an unauthorized absentee for the last two months. The shore patrol has been looking everywhere for him."

Touch and Go

The *Wasp* spent most of its time on anti-submarine patrols in the North Atlantic, but there came a time when Castro was threatening Latin America and our presence was required to calm him down. It was a pleasant change from the ravages of the North Atlantic. The weather was warm and balmy. We practiced general quarters and other drills, but for the most part, it was uneventful.

We had flight ops, of course, and we had photographers on the flight deck and on the 07 level. Planes were landing and taking off as usual, and no one noticed anything different about the larger than usual plane coming in for a landing. I wasn't on watch, but I couldn't honestly say that I would have spotted it for a B-17, or that I would have realized that it didn't belong on our flight deck. Well, be that as it may, a B-17 did do a touch and go on our flight deck, and not one of the photographers took a picture.

Again, I can't tell you that I would have recognized the Cuban markings; I might have noticed that they weren't our markings, and I might have taken a picture.

The captain said it was an act of war for an enemy plane to do a touch and go on our flight deck, and that we should have taken pictures, so that we could prove that an act of war had taken place. That's what the captain said, and if you will recall, he was already pissed at the photographers for photographing all that money, which tempted the disbursing officer to run off with it.

It was unfair, of course. It was the public affairs officer who wanted a picture of all that money. The photographer was just doing as he was told. And it wasn't our fault that the admiral cut the captain's operating money to the bone.

"NOW HEAR THIS. NOW HEAR THIS. THIS IS THE CAPTAIN SPEAKING. A CUBAN B-17 HAS JUST COMPLETED A TOUCH AND GO ON OUR FLIGHT DECK. IT WAS AN ACT OF AGGRESSION. IT WAS AN ACT OF WAR.

"THERE WERE TWO PHOTOGRAPHERS ON THE FLIGHT DECK. THEY SHOULD HAVE TAKEN PICTURES, BUT THEY DID NOT TAKE PICTURES. THERE WAS A PHOTOGRAPHER ON THE 07 LEVEL. HE SHOULD HAVE TAKEN PICTURES, BUT HE DID NOT TAKE PICTURES. THE PHOTOGRAPHERS NEED OUR HELP. THE PHOTOGRAPHERS NEED TRAINING. WE ARE GOING TO SOUND GENERAL QUARTERS, AND WE ARE GOING TO REMAIN AT GENERAL QUARTERS UNTIL THE PHOTOGRAPHERS UNDERSTAND WHY THEY ARE ONBOARD. THEY ARE GOING TO PHOTOGRAPH EVERY PLANE THAT TAKES OFF, LANDS, OR FLIES OVERHEAD FOR THE NEXT TWO WEEKS AT THE VERY LEAST."

"BONG, BONG, BONG, BONG. NOW HEAR THIS. NOW HEAR THIS. THIS IS A DRILL. THIS IS A DRILL. GENERAL QUARTERS. GENERAL QUARTERS. ALL HANDS MAN YOUR BATTLE STATIONS. ALL HANDS MAN YOUR BATTLE STATIONS. THIS IS A DRILL. THIS IS A DRILL. GENERAL QUARTERS. GENERAL QUARTERS. BONG, BONG, BONG, BONG.

Except for the flight deck photographers and our station on the 07 level, our battle stations were in the photo lab, which consisted of five small rooms: an office, a finishing room, a washing and drying room, a print processing room and a film developing room. Two weeks was a long time to be cooped up in such a small place with nine other photo mates, and nothing but cold sandwiches to eat three times a day.

The captain repeated his comments every two hours. I was amazed at how fast his attitude towards photographers became the crew's attitude towards photographers. It was not that the captain didn't have a right to be pissed. It was, after all, our job to track every plane that took off or landed on the flight deck. And it was our job to photograph everything that happened on the flight deck that was unusual or out of the ordinary, and a B-17 doing a touch and go on our flight deck did qualify as an unusual event. We really should have taken pictures.

However, it was a good thing we already had a ham in the refrigerator, because all the pictures in the world could not have bought us another one.

Collision at Sea

I think it was the loudest noise I have ever heard, metal crushing against metal and reverberating throughout the ship. I awoke to a high-pitched voice shrieking into the loud speakers, "COLLISION! COLLISION! WE HIT A SHIP. WE HIT A DAMN SHIP."

Sheer terror shook my bones. I jumped out of my rack and into my clothes and was in the photo lab in less than a minute. I grabbed an empty five-gallon jug figuring it would keep me afloat for a long time if I had to jump overboard before we got to the lifeboats.
"GENERAL QUARTERS! GENERAL QUARTERS! ALL HANDS MAN YOUR BATTLE STATIONS. ALL HANDS MAN YOUR BATTLE STATIONS. THIS IS NOT A DRILL. THIS IS NOT—WAIT A MINUTE. STANDBY."

"NOW HEAR THIS. THIS IS YOUR CAPTAIN SPEAKING. WE ARE NOT IN ANY DANGER. I REPEAT.

WE ARE NOT IN ANY DANGER. A CRANE SWUNG INTO ONE OF THE STARBOARD ELEVATORS AS IT WAS BEING RAISED. I DID NOT EVEN KNOW THIS WAS POSSIBLE. THERE IS SOME DAMAGE, BUT NOTHING SEVERE. SECURE FROM GENERAL QUARTERS."

Another Emergency Draft

I don't know how the Navy selects people for these emergency drafts, but I seem to have caught more than my share of them. My friend, Bill Davenport, Jack "the kleptomaniac" Bennard, and I were transferred to the USS *Enterprise* to be part of the pre-commissioning crew. We would be plank owners. The ship was in Newport News, where they were putting on the finishing touches. I hadn't seen my wife and son in over a year, and I had a new daughter. I took leave and went to Panama City where they were staying with my in-laws.

It was a joyous reunion, and we made plans for them to join me when the ship moved from Newport News to Norfolk in about six months. For once I was sorry to leave. You could find a woman anywhere if you wanted one, but it was different with little children. They come with families, and for the first time in my life, I felt like I was a member of a family.

THE USS *ENTERPRISE*

The most famous *Enterprise* was CV 6, commissioned in May of 1938. During WWII she participated in almost every major battle, and was the only U.S. aircraft carrier operating in the Pacific at times.

Her first action of the war came on the first day of U.S. involvement, when her aircraft dueled with the Japanese attackers over Pearl Harbor. Early in 1942 she escorted the Hornet on the famous Doolittle raid on Tokyo, and was rushing south to the Battle of the Coral Sea when she was recalled to Pearl to prepare for the Battle of Midway.

At Midway her aircraft participated in the sinking of three carriers, ending the Japanese offensive in the Pacific. She fought with distinction through the rest of the war, sinking 71 ships and shooting down 911 aircraft. She was the most decorated ship of the war. Silas told me once that he didn't understand how anyone could serve aboard one of these great warships and not know these things.

The up and coming *Enterprise* (CVAN 65) would not be commissioned until 25 November 1961. She was to be the first nuclear powered aircraft carrier as well as the longest warship ever. She was 25 stories high, enclosed 3,500 compartments, and had 4.5 acres of flight deck. She used four of eight nuclear reactors to turn four propeller shafts—about 4 feet in diameter and 127 feet long—which turned four 3.5-story-high propellers. It was, I believed, the most awesome ship in the world. Silas should have been there.

CDR Bunch

The photo lab was run by Commander Bunch. The 53-year-old warhorse was a big man, about 280 pounds, sort of a pudgy John Wayne. Commander Bunch already had his 30 years in, but he knew the *Enterprise* was going to make history, and he wanted to be a part of it.

CDR Bunch joined the Navy a year before I was born. He had apprenticed at both Life and Look, and he was a master photographer. He worked for Edward Steichen during the war. He had several commendations, but never talked about them. One of his buddies, the ship's boatswain's mate, told me that Mr. Bunch had received several medals during the war including the Purple Heart, but that he wouldn't talk about any of it.

CDR Bunch became a limited duty officer (LDO) back when LDOs had to qualify to do everything that line officers did. He knew more about ships and being an officer than any man I ever met. He was, however, an enlisted man at heart, a rather rough one at that. He could not stand an officer who did not know his job, and he bedeviled junior officers every chance he got.

CDR Bunch's abrasiveness was rewarded with every shit detail they could pile on. He was the permanent sea and anchor detail officer. He always had the first watch in port. And he always ran the small boats overseas. It didn't bother him because he loved doing all these things.

His flash temper reminded me of my father, but Commander Bunch never hit anyone, although he was always threatening to. And unlike my father, he got over it quickly, and he never held a grudge. Commander Bunch liked men that knew what they were doing, worked hard, and who were not afraid to assert themselves. He loved to tell me about all the hard working seamen and junior petty officers he met while setting the sea and anchor detail.

On the other side of the ledger was Master Chief Blair, the chief-master-at-arms, whom Commander Bunch thought was a blowhard, and he ragged him every chance he got. Commander Bunch was not popular among the officers, but he was the most respected officer aboard the *Enterprise* as far as the enlisted men were concerned.

Commander Bunch was the epitome of patriotism, the definition of dedication, and the personification of loyalty to his men as well as to the chain of command.

Psychology 101

I learned to hypnotize myself when I was at Northern State College. My goal was to develop better study habits. I was impressed with myself, and soon started practicing on my friends. I developed a reputation, and people began expecting me to entertain them at parties.

One time I hypnotized a young newlywed and told her that she would not be able to remember her husband's name. She never said a word when she woke up, but you could see the desperation in her face. She rubbed her wedding ring furiously as if doing so would produce his name. We asked her questions designed to elicit his name. She reddened, and then she turned purple. I had to tell her what it was all about.

My favorite technique was to use a hypnotic wheel with swirling colors that would literally draw you into a light trance. Aboard ship, I found that if I mounted it on the film supply wheel of our movie-printing machine, it would turn at just the right speed.

"Hey Russell! Can you hypnotize me so that I can get up in the morning? I sleep right through reveille every morning. One of these days I'm going to get into real trouble."

"I can try, Charlie. Step into my office and have a seat. Take a deep breath, relax, and just watch the wheel go around. You will begin to feel like you are moving into the wheel. Just relax and let it happen. Breathe deeply. Feel the relaxation flowing through your body."

Charlie's eyes closed. I had him tense and relax all the muscles in his body.

When he was ready, I said, "You will hear reveille in the morning, and you will sit right up. While the bugle plays the notes you will say the following words to yourself in synch with the music: I can do get up. I can do get up. I can do get up in the morning."

The next morning, I couldn't wait for quarters, so I could ask Charlie what happened, but he didn't show. When he came in two hours later, he had a large bandage on his forehead.

"I guess I should have told you; I sleep on the top bunk and there's this pipe just over my head."

One day John Wayne came to me for help. No, not THE John Wayne, Petty Officer Third Class John Wayne. John had a serious problem. The problem was made worse by his new girlfriend, Emily Hutchinson. He was real fond of Emily, but Emily was going to dump him if he couldn't solve his problem.

You see, Petty Officer John Wayne couldn't finish a sentence without the word "fuck," or some variation of it. It was fucking this and fucking that, fuck you and even fuck me. It was a word we heard often at sea, but never in such quantity from one man. We had all gotten used to it, but Emily refused to, and she really liked John.

Well, you know me; I thought I could do anything, so I said, "Sure, John, I can fix it." We planned to meet late at night. John didn't want an audience, but he brought two of his friends, and he said it was okay if my friend Bill watched.

It went well. John was an excellent subject; he quickly went into a deep trance.

"John, you won't use the words "fuck" or "fucking" anymore. You won't even think of them. Emily will be proud of you. On the count of five, you will wake up feeling fine. How do you feel, John?"

"I fe fe fa fu fu fe fu eeee eeee eeeg eeeg oh ah ah I fe fe fu fu fu EEEE EEEE EEEG EEEG. EEEEG. EEEG. EEEG. OOH. EEE EEE OH OH AG. AG. AG. AG. EIEIEIG."

John could not talk, and he was becoming extremely agitated. He stood up, arms flaying. "AAAHG! AAAHG! EEEEEG! AAAAHG!" He did manage to point at me even while his arms were flaying around. "AAAHG! AAAHG! AAAHG!"

I put my arms around him and captured his arms. He was struggling to get free, but I held him as still as I could, and started talking softly into his ear.

"Relax John. Don't try to talk. We'll fix it, John. Take a deep breath, John. We'll put it back the way it was."

"NG NNNG NNG NNG."

"We don't have any choice, John. It isn't working. We have to put it back the way it was."

John started crying, "ANGANGANGANGANG."

I put my right hand over his eyes and massaged the back of his neck with my left hand. "Relax John. It's going to be okay. You'll be alright." I put my foul weather jacket on the floor for a pillow and got John to lie down. I kept my hand over his eyes.

"Relax, John. Don't try to talk. Take a deep breath. Remember how you felt when you were under? You feel that same way now, John. You feel very, very relaxed."

It took an hour to get John under again. I told him he could say fuck and fucking as often as he wanted to, and that he could talk clearly and fluently. I asked him how he felt when I woke him up.

"What the fuck did you do to me? I don't feel so fucking good. That's the last fucking time I'll ever ask you for help."

I grinned from ear to ear. That was my old friend John. Fuck never sounded so good.

Emily dumped him.

I hadn't done John any good, but I was still impressed with my success at getting John in and out of a trance and myself in and out of trouble. Everyone went to bed except my friend Bill and me.

"Bill," I said, still full of myself, "You know who would make a good subject? Joe, Joe Foss. He talks in his sleep all the time. Have you ever heard him talk in his sleep? People who talk in their sleep are supposed to be very good subjects for hypnosis."

"How can you hypnotize them if they are asleep?"

"Supposedly, you just talk to them as if they were already in a trance."

"This I've got to see."

I slept in a middle bunk. Joe Foss had a top bunk across from me. That's how come I knew he talked in his sleep. I heard him jabbering all the time. Joe Foss was sound asleep when we arrived.

"Joe," I said, "give me your billfold."

Joe reached up, turned on his bunk light, rolled over, dialed in his combination, opened his locker, handed me his billfold, closed his locker, turned out his light, and lay back down.

I was flabbergasted. I had read about it, but I didn't expect it to work that well. I was a bit embarrassed, standing there in the middle of the night holding Joe's billfold.

"Joe, put your billfold away."

Joe went through the motions again, tucking his billfold safely away in the process. Bill was duly impressed, and said so as he said good night.

The stories were already zooming around the lab when I arrived in the morning.

"Did you hear what Russell Quigley did to John Wayne? He hypnotized him and screwed him up so bad he couldn't talk."

"And I heard he goes around the compartment at night getting people's billfolds. How does he do that?"

About an hour after quarters, Commander Bunch came back to the movie room. "Hey, Russell, I hear you've got quite a setup back here. He stepped around the movie printer to where he could see my hypnotic wheel. He pulled it off the film supply wheel.

"Those your psychology books?"

"I, um, yes, sir."

"Pick them up. Come with me."

The photo lab was one deck below the hangar bay on the starboard side. It was a long walk back to the fantail. When we got there, Commander Bunch threw the hypnotic wheel over the railing and into the sea, and then he just looked at me in silence. I hesitated, but then I threw my books over the railing and into the sea. You can't fight people like Commander Bunch. He was big like the real John Wayne, but he was nothing like him. I mean the real John Wayne played a hero; in my book, Commander Bunch was one.

Admiral's Mast

Petty Officer First Class Pete Karnas was unbelievably hyper. He was forever giving us more work than we could do, but we soon learned that he couldn't remember whom he told to do what. He was always so excited that he was a pain to be around. We avoided him whenever we could except when his mother died. He was hurting, but surprisingly, he was calm. We thought he was all right until we realized that he was leaving in a few hours and had not packed.

"How much time do I have to get tickets?" he asked.

"Pete, you should have done that yesterday," I said. We all pitched in and helped him pack, but we had to enlist Commander Bunch's help to get him on his way.

Since Pete was going to be gone for a full month, I put in for flight skins, so I could shoot the aerial assignments while Pete was gone. They turned me down. The department head, Commander Burton, said it wasn't worth the trouble to do the paperwork for only one month.

He said that we could surely do without an aerial photographer for one month.

However, hardly a week had gone by when the XO called and told Commander Burton to prepare for a very important aerial assignment. "I want your best people on this," the XO said.

"Quigley," said Commander Bunch, "You've got an aerial assignment to shoot tomorrow. You better check your equipment because it sounds pretty hot. Something about a new task force coming here just to have their picture taken.

"No, sir, Mr. Bunch. You'll have to get someone else. I put in for flight skins and they turned me down. I don't have to fly if I don't want to, and I ain't going to."

"Where the hell did you get an idea like that?"

I could see the pink on the back of Mr. Bunch's neck, but I was determined to stand my ground. "They told us in school that if we weren't on flight skins, we didn't have to fly."

"Well, they were dead wrong. You'd better get your ass in gear and check out some equipment."

"No, sir, Mr. Bunch. I ain't flying and that's final," I said as I walked back to the finishing room.

"Quigley, you're going to be one sorry son-of-a-bitch if you ain't ready for that job tomorrow."

About an hour went by before Commander Bunch came back to see me. His neck was normal. I knew I was going to have to shoot this job, but I wanted everybody to know that I wasn't happy about not getting paid for it.

"Quigley, I don't know how he found out, but Admiral Cortez already knows you don't want to fly. He wants to see you in his quarters. Chief, get everybody out here right now. I want to talk to them. You people should know that what you hear down here stays down here."

Admiral "Chip" Cortez was standing behind a podium waiting for me when the marines let me in. A yeoman read me my rights.

"Is this a captain's mast?" I asked.

"No, but it may be an admiral's mast, Quigley, if what I hear is true. I understand you are refusing to fly."

"Yes, sir. I thought it was my privilege to refuse. That's what they told me in school."

"Quigley, I'm sorry you were misinformed, but you were. I can get you the instruction if I have to, but the bottom line is, if I say you have to fly, you have to fly. Now what's it going to be?"

"Well, sir, I guess I was wrong. You know, when push comes to shove, I would never refuse an order."

"That's good news, Quigley, because this is a very important picture you're going to take tomorrow. You're going to be proud to have your name on it."

The admiral was right about the picture being important. The caption read, "Nuclear Task Force One." However, I could only be half proud. The office crew was so used to putting Pete Karnas' name on all aerial pictures, they put his name on everything I shot while he was on leave.

Something Old, Something New

I thought Nuclear Task Force One was just a publicity stunt. The ships were together for all of 30 minutes. I was sure the picture would make a splash in all the papers and magazines, and then fade away. I was wrong. Nuclear Task Force One came together again and sailed around the world. The picture hung in every office in the Navy for years.

A week after I shot Nuclear Task Force One, I was called upon to shoot what I thought would be the most published picture in naval history. One of the oldest forms of transportation was about to meet and pass the first nuclear aircraft carrier. A replica of the *Santa Maria* was about to pass the USS *Enterprise.* The ship was a trimaster with glorious colors in her sails. It was a beautiful day; the sun was shining; the lighting was perfect and there were white billowy clouds in the background. I shot 30 7 X 7-inch color transparencies in the time it took the *Santa Maria* to approach the fantail and clear the bow.

I never saw the picture in print.

A Letter to the City of Norfolk
Dear Norfolk,

Let me commend you for all that you are doing to make Norfolk more attractive to the Navy. I have a few suggestions:

1. I understand our old honky-tonk area is in ruins and that you're planning to build a new civic center in its place. Never mind the civic center. Keep the ruins. We don't get off the ship in Norfolk until 2000, but liberty starts at 0800 in cities that have old ruins. Think of all the business you would get from sailors roaming around your city all day photographing the ruins of honky-tonk. The Europeans love it.

2. You should invite the prostitutes to Norfolk when we are in port. The girls follow us from port to port over here. I know some of them better than I know my wife because I get to spend more time with them. It would be good for business, too. I drink a lot of beer when I'm with the ladies.

3. You need to get rid of your communists. This is really important. When we are in Norfolk, we are surrounded by the world's largest naval base, and we still have to post guards at the end of the pier to protect our ship. But when we are in Cannes, Rome, Athens, Salonika, or Barcelona, we not only don't have any guards, we have open house every day, and our guests can even take pictures.

If you do these things, we could spend more time in the city of Norfolk, and with all these things going on, no one will even notice if we see our wives now and then.

PH2 Russell Quigley
USS *Enterprise* CVAN 65
Somewhere in the Mediterranean

NOTE: The city of Norfolk took these suggestions very seriously. They sent my letter to Admiral Chip Cortez for resolution.

The Blockade of Cuba

My son Donald has the most amazing built-in alarm clock. He would be playing in the yard with his friends when suddenly he would stop, race into the house, and turn on the television just in time to watch a commercial he called "Being Close." It featured a lion strolling through a train station without anyone taking notice. An announcer would say, "Take the worry out of being close." When it was over, Don would run back into the yard and continue playing with his friends.

One day I went to work and never came back for five months. It was the blockade of Cuba. All the VIPs and visiting press were scooted off the ship. Half of the photo lab crew became a bomb-handling working party, and I went to the flash lab to process and print aerial film.

The flash lab had two new Kodak Versamat® aerial roll film processors and two new MD-11 aerial roll print processors. The Versamat® would process a 100-foot roll of 9-inch wide aerial film in a matter of minutes. The print processors had built in print dryers and automatic paper cutters. That's why it was called the flash lab. It was fast. We could process a photo run and deliver dry prints in 25 to 30 minutes.

Of course, wet prints took a little longer. We had to dip them individually into a tray of water, squeegee them, and then put them into another tray to deliver them to Commander Robert S. Bingham, the photo-intelligence officer. Commander Bingham was a dedicated naval officer. He was a millionaire from a wealthy southern family and was in the Navy solely to demonstrate his patriotism.

CDR Bingham insisted on wet prints. He had previous experience and knew he could trim 10 to 11 minutes off the delivery time by looking at wet prints. He refused to listen to how our new equipment worked and threatened to place us on report if we ever delivered dry prints to him again. "This is real," he would say. "This is war." "Every second counts." So, for five months we processed and printed hundreds of prints each day in record time and then dipped them into a tray of water one by one.

The flash lab was next to Admiral Chip Cortez's quarters. The practical dark green tile that covered the passageways throughout the ship stopped just a few feet from the flash lab and was replaced by the pure white tiles that marked the admiral's territory. Dogs do it differently. A marine guard stood at the admiral's door from 0600 to 2300 every day. The marines polished the deck with shoe polish and kept it buffed to an unbelievably high gloss.

The ladder to and from the flight deck was located about 10 feet aft of the flash lab in the middle of the gleaming white passageway. We were not allowed to go through admiral's country to get to the ladder because we would track gunk from the flight deck all over the glow. Consequently, we went forward about 60 feet, turned left and went all the way across the ship to the port side, turned left again and went aft about 60 feet and then up a ladder to the flight deck, and then went all the way back across the flight deck to get next to the island where they parked the photo planes so that they would be close to the flash lab. We unloaded the film from the plane's cameras and then retraced our steps back to the flash lab.

CDR Bingham wasn't convinced that we were as dedicated as he was, so he decided to follow us every step of the way to discover where we were wasting time. He met us at the door to the flash lab—he never came inside; he knew we did everything in the dark—and followed us on our crazy path to the flight deck. He was unaware of the prohibition against traversing admiral's country and thought we were giving him the run around. He went into a rage and put us all on report.

Running a couple of blocks carrying 9-inch film canisters to get to a destination 30 feet away was not fun. I'm not sure whose idea it was, but we all jumped on it. Since we were at general quarters permanently and everyone was so serious, we actually thought it would work. If we painted the white tiles a dark green to match the rest of the ship, surely they would leave it that way at least for the duration of the blockade.

We only had 25 feet of passageway to paint, but the smallest can of dark green paint we could find was 5 gallons. We started at 0200 and were finished by 0235. We put up ribbons to block traffic and to keep anyone from seeing us. We tossed the paint, brushes, and rags over the side. We were not environmentally astute at the time.

It was a lot of noise for 0600. I looked outside and down the hall to see what was going on. A marine working party had already removed half of our freshly painted tile and was feverishly working on the rest of it. They had new white tile laid and spit polished by noon.

Meanwhile, the Cubans were doing everything they could to harass us. Every night they would run a bunch of old cars and trucks up to the fence around the base at Guantanamo Bay, and the base would respond by sounding general quarters, and the Marines would meet the advancing hordes in full battle gear. The Navy quickly tired of playing this game and soon asked the USS *Enterprise* to photograph this nightly episode so that they could expose the Cubans before the United Nations. This was a serious request. The only way to light such a large area at night was with a flash bomb. Dropping a flash bomb on a foreign country was an act of war and would require President Kennedy's permission.

I wanted to fly the mission, but there was only one man drawing flight skins (getting paid) to fly aerial missions and that was Petty Officer Pete Karnas. Pete was a truly nice guy, but he was the most disorganized, nervous, and forgetful man on planet Earth. The photo officer, Commander Bunch, knew he would have to send someone more dependable than Petty Officer Karnas, but before he could make up his mind, the XO called and demanded that the senior qualified man shoot the pictures. That meant Petty Officer Karnas. An hour later the XO called again and demanded that the senior qualified man also process the film. Again, that meant Petty Officer Karnas. We all felt like we were being forced to march into an ambush.

Permission to drop a flash bomb was granted by President Kennedy. It was a difficult decision because a flash bomb could elevate the tension between the United States and Russia even further. The XO started calling every few minutes with questions and orders. Every time he called, Pete Karnas was elevated to a new level of anxiety. He begged the photo officer to let someone else do the job, but to no avail. Commander Bunch was an old and experienced warhorse, and if there was anything he understood, it was an order from the executive officer.

The flight went off without a hitch. The flash bomb was dropped and exploded at just the right altitude; the pictures were taken. The Cubans fled. And then they filed a protest with the United Nations. Petty Officer Karnas, beaming from ear to ear, arrived in the main photo lab with film in hand. The XO had decided that film would be processed by hand because he didn't trust our new automatic processors. Pete took the film canister into the darkroom, removed the film, and wound it onto a double spooled cassette that would be used to crank the film back and forth in the developer, the rinse water, and then the hypo.

Pete then did the unthinkable. He went against 20 years of training and experience. He dropped the cassette into the chemical tank on the right, the hypo tank. Photochemistry is always set up left to right: developer, rinse, hypo. The latent images were aborted before they were born.

The ship requested permission to drop a second flash bomb. Permission was denied. In anger, the CO of Guantanamo secured the water that the base was still supplying to a few small communities around the base. The Cuban newspapers said we cut off our hose to spite our base.

CDR Bunch put Petty Officer First Class Peter Karnas on report for technical incompetence and asked that he be reduced to petty officer second class. Commander Bunch was a bulldozer, but a wily and crafty bulldozer; however, this was a blunder. Commander Bunch had just recommended Petty Officer Karnas for chief, and in the process, had commended him for his fine work. Petty Officer Karnas skated free. Commander Bunch, however, was confined to quarters for 30 days for assigning the wrong man to the job.

CDR Bunch completed his 30 days in hock before submitting his request to retire. Strangely enough, I was the only one he would let into his room. He never came back to the photo lab.

When I returned home, I enjoyed a 10-minute hug from my wife Carla, but my five-year-old son, Donald, wouldn't let me come near him. When I tried to approach him, he would turn and run. He burst into tears and started shaking whenever I cornered him. This went on for several weeks; although, he was slowly coming closer and closer. He was up every morning at 0500 to watch me shave and watch me eat and stand by the door until I left, but he would never speak or get close enough for a hug. Finally, after three weeks, as I was going out the door, Donald spoke, "Dad, are you coming back?"

Shore Patrol

I thought the *Enterprise* had a permanent parking permit for pier 12 at the Norfolk Naval Base, so I was surprised when it was announced that we would be anchoring out along with the *Constellation*. It was distressing because I had shore patrol. I figured I wouldn't be getting any sleep tonight.

It is ridiculous to wear dress whites when your primary job is to shepherd drunken sailors safely back from liberty, but that is what sailors assigned to shore patrol wear.

I arrived at Fleet Landing at about 2000. I was happy to see a first class gunner's mate wearing a shore patrol armband. I didn't want to be in charge, as I was sure there was going to be trouble what with sailors from rival carriers meeting at the same place.

The boardwalk was parallel to the shoreline and about a hundred feet long. About half of the boardwalk was bordered by a one-story building with lots of antennas on the roof, undoubtedly used for communicating with the ships anchored out. A ten-foot-high chain link fence prevented entry onto the boardwalk without going through the building. There was a small gate about 20 feet from the building, but it was secured with a chain and a padlock.

It started drizzling as we were introducing ourselves. My partner's name was Jim Baker and he was from the *Constellation*. He said we were supposed to check in with the shore patrol officer, Ensign Eldridge, so we went inside. We spotted Mr. Eldridge by his armband talking with someone on the radio.

Mr. Eldridge posted us on the boardwalk opposite the chain link fence, and stated that one of us had to be there at all times. The weather had taken a turn for the worse while we were inside. The wind was up and the seas were choppy at about five feet.

The storm continued to worsen, and the drizzle turned into steady rain. My fellow watchstander, GM1 Jim Baker, excused himself and went inside. He said he would be back in a bit. I didn't see him or the ensign again for six hours.

Meanwhile, the longboats quit running, but the officer gigs continued to ferry officers to and from the ship. Sailors from both carriers began to gather at the fence. I guess there wasn't enough room inside where the officers were waiting. Apparently the rain took all the fight out of them because they were really quite calm except for a few epitaphs being hurled at the officers as they boarded their gigs and headed back to their ships.

I began to worry, as the crowd grew ever bigger. They were pushing against the fence, and it was beginning to lean towards me. I visually measured the height of the fence and the width of the boardwalk; they seemed to match. If that fence came down, I would either be crushed underneath it or forced into the water. I couldn't swim and I sure as hell wouldn't be able to hold onto the shell-encrusted pilings.

A first class cook—his nametag read "P. W. Waternik"—from the *Constellation* started jerking the gate back and forth in an apparent effort to break through the fence.

"That lock's not going to break, but if it does, and you come through the gate, I'm going to col' conk you right up side of your head," I said, as I pulled my nightstick out of its holster.

He never said a word; he just kept jerking the gate back and forth. I figured he'd get tired of it soon enough, but time wore on and he kept jerking on that gate. I was not about to leave my post, but I couldn't help but think the ensign would move me if he saw what I was up against.

Long about midnight I was getting steamed because I hadn't been offered a single break in four hours. I was dying for a cup of coffee. Meanwhile the cook was still jerking that damn gate back and forth and the crowd had swelled to somewhere around five hundred people.

The rain never let up. The sailors began taking their misery out on me.

"Hey, fuckhead, how come those officers can run back and forth all night, and we can't get back onboard and get some sleep?"

"Go ask them to put us in a barracks if they can't get us back to the ship."

"Hey you, shore patrol, if I get through this gate, I'm going to dump you in the water."

"Yeah, fuckhead, I hope you can swim because you're going in."

I was afraid, but I sympathized with them. The guys next to the fence couldn't leave if they wanted to. They were being squashed against the fence. I wanted to talk to Ensign Eldridge, but I couldn't bring myself to leave my post. I still remembered my general orders. You just don't leave your post when you're on watch, but they should be out here checking now and then.

By 0200, I was angry, and I was soaked; I was exhausted from six hours of rain. And I was scared. The fence was at a 45-degree angle. The cook was down on one knee, but he was still jerking the gate back and forth. And then it happened. The gate was wide open, and the cook was standing square in front of me. All my anger and all my fear poured into my nightstick as I slammed it into the man's temple. It made a sickening sound, and I was instantly sorry. He dropped lifeless to the deck. The crowd froze and became silent.

A drunken commander staggered over to the man and said, "Get out of the way; I'm a doctor." He felt for a pulse, found none. "My god, you killed him! You dumb bastard you killed him. You had no cause to do that. You don't ever hit a man in the head with a nightstick."

I can't describe how bad I felt. There are times in life when you just want to disappear and never be seen again. Gunner's Mate Jim Baker hit me on the shoulder so hard it knocked me backwards.

"What the hell did you do? What the hell have you done? You killed a man? What were you thinking?"

"You'll be court martialed for sure." It was Ensign Eldridge. "You should never hit anyone in the head. Why didn't you tell me you were in trouble out here?"

Ensign Eldridge made arrangements for the mob to be bussed to the transient barracks. They were gone in twenty minutes. The cook's body was gone too, but I didn't remember seeing them take it away.

"You'd better get back to your ship. Ride in the officer's gig," said Ensign Eldridge, "and tell the officer-of-the-deck what happened. Tell him I'll send a report. They may want to put you under arrest."

I usually hear reveille even if I don't have to get up, but I slept until 1000 when Commander Bunch woke me up. "Get dressed, Quigley. The captain wants to talk to you about last night. You really screwed up good this time, Quigley. That man you hit still hasn't woken up. I'm going to back you up, but I don't—"

"What do you mean, he still hasn't woke up? They told me last night he was dead."

"He ain't dead, but it doesn't look good. What ever possessed you to hit him in the head?"

"I thought that was where I was supposed to hit him. I didn't even think about it. All I know is, I wanted to knock him out. There were 500 people behind him ready to kill me. I wanted them to know I meant business."

"I'll call King and King and get you a lawyer. They practically wrote the Uniform Code of Military Justice."

"Quigley," said Captain Peror, "I don't understand why you would strike a man on the head after all the training you've had."

"What training, Captain?"

"Training on how to stand shore patrol, on how to use a nightstick."

"I've never had any training like that, sir. I've never even heard of it."

"Nonsense, it's in your record. Have you found it yet, lieutenant?"

"No sir. I've gone through his record three times now. There is nothing in his record."

"How can that be?" asked the captain. "Surely everyone gets trained on a nightstick before they stand shore patrol."

"I'm not aware of it, Captain," said the lieutenant.

"Quigley, *Constellation* is insisting that you be court marshaled. We'll probably have a hearing next week. You'll need a lawyer. That'll be all, Quigley."

"Yes, sir."

CDR Bunch got me a cracker-jack lawyer. He asked for and received permission to visit the ship for a few days before the hearing. That meant he was eating in the wardroom and hanging around with the officers. They were accustomed to civilians in the wardroom. Since the *Enterprise* was the first nuclear powered warship, we had between 50 and 100 VIPs aboard at all times.

His name was Skip Curtiss. I didn't know it at the time, but the legal staff in the area knew him as "Killer Curtiss." Commander Cox, the engineering officer, was in charge of the hearing. After Commander Cox introduced everyone and explained the purpose of the hearing, Mr. Curtiss, with his elbow resting on the table, waved his hand and received a nod from the commander.

"Commander Cox, gentlemen, I would like to say a few words before we begin, if I may."

"Permission granted," said Commander Cox.

"If this were a court instead of a hearing," began Mr. Curtiss, "I would ask that all of you be disqualified. I have tape recordings of each of you declaring Petty Officer Quigley's guilt and that there is no excuse for what he did."

Several of the officers blushed with embarrassment. Commander Cox, the reddest of them all, was not embarrassed; he was pure mad. "Sir, taking advantage of our hospitality is unconscionable; you should be—"

"Commander, I was duty bound to take advantage of your hospitality because that is the only way to expose your prejudice and make it a part of the record. I do not expect this hearing to be fair, but I am here, and I want to be heard, so I am willing to hear you out. However, I want to make it clear that I have no illusions. In addition to your prejudice, you have probably been directed by Captain Peror to find cause for court martialing my client, but let me war—"

"Sir, you are out of line. This hearing is adjourned until 1300."

"Well, fine, I guess you have to confer with Captain Peror. Let me know what he has to say. I'll be in my stateroom with my client if you want to confer with me."

Mr. Curtiss asked me if I thought we could eat in his room. I told him I was pretty sure that they didn't do that for anyone. He called anyway and explained that this was his only chance to confer with his client in private, and that if they couldn't bring us anything we would have to go hungry. To my surprise, they did it.

Commander Cox kept us waiting for some time. When he finally returned, he was redder than when he left. He took his time getting settled. When he spoke, he did so without making eye contact.

"Captain Peror has requested that I apologize for our careless gossip about this matter. The wardroom is usually a sanctuary where we can let down our guard, but we were wrong to do so in this case. The captain has also assured me that we are all free to vote our conscience. He said we should take a fresh look at the evidence and keep an open mind.

Without further delay, I will present the evidence against Petty Officer Quigley, and perhaps, when I am finished, Mr. Curtiss, you can tell us why we should not press charges against him."

At that point, Commander Cox looked at Mr. Curtiss for the first time. Commander Cox was really quite brief, and when he was finished, he looked at Mr. Curtiss again and said, "Okay, Mr. Curtiss, it's your turn."

"Commander Cox, you have said that you believe that Petty Officer Quigley has had training on a nightstick, and that you know that he knew better than to strike a man on his head. I am here to tell you that if you use the words, "we believe," or "we know," in your recommendation to the admiral, I will have the charges dropped before your recommendation leaves the ship. You also said that all sailors get training on the proper use of a nightstick. I didn't have much time, but I managed to survey 37 petty officers, and not one of them has had training on a nightstick. These are not sailors off the street, Commander; these are all sailors aboard your ship.

"You asked me to tell you why you should not press charges, and I'm going to do just that. The main villain in this tragedy is the United States Navy because it did not train Quigley or anyone else on the proper use of a nightstick. You can say you believe and you know 'til hell freezes over, but I can't find one man aboard your ship that has received training on a nightstick.

"If you don't believe the Navy is a guilty party, consider this: my firm is preparing an offer to represent Commissaryman First Class Peter Waternik in a lawsuit against the Navy as we speak. We can't move in that direction until I have cleared my client, but I think we will clear that hurdle today.

"There is a guilty party in this affair, but it is not Petty Officer Quigley. It is Petty Officer Jim Baker. He was absent from his post for six hours and you haven't even said a word about it. That constitutes dereliction of duty. Furthermore, it was his absence that prevented any communication between the field and the command center. And finally, Ensign Eldridge, did not have control over all that he surveyed or was supposed to survey."

"Well," said Commander Cox, "you really have given us a lot to think about. I believe you have opened our eyes and hopefully our minds. But I have to tell you, Quigley, I really have trouble believing that you are so stupid that you would hit a man over the head with a club. I think it has been made clear that we don't have a case against you; however, we do not owe you an apology. We may have overreacted against you, but we did so because we were horrified by what you did, and I think it was a proper reaction. I would like to formally state that the Navy will not press charges against Petty Officer Quigley. Are we all in agreement?"

There was no opposition; it was over. Commissaryman First Class Waternik recovered without any permanent damage. I am not so sure about myself.

The Valley

I did not get off scot-free. The recommendations of the hearing were accepted; however, it was determined somewhere along the line that I should receive training on a nightstick, and that this training should be provided by Gunnery Sergeant Guzman.

I did some snooping. Gunnery Sergeant Guzman is an expert at hand-to-hand combat. He loves to drink and fight. The shore patrol brings him back to the ship more often than not, and he is fond of saying, "There is no such thing as a fair fight." He has been married and divorced three times.

The sign on his door said, "Knock, Sound Off, and Wait. I wasn't sure what "Sound Off" meant, but I knocked, and said, "Petty Officer Second Class Russell Quigley to see Gunnery Sergeant Guzman."

"Come in, maggot mouth."

Oh oh, I wasn't prepared for this. I decided not to respond.

"Hey! Maggot mouth, I said come in."

I stood pat. The door opened. He was an inch shorter than me, but he was a yard wide at the shoulders, and he didn't have any neck.

"What is the matter, maggot mouth? Are you hard of hearing?"

"There is nobody here by that name."

"Listen up, maggot mouth, if I say your name is maggot mouth, then by God it's maggot mouth."

"What ever you say, Daddeo." I knew that would get him. I mean, if he wasn't going to address me properly, well, I could play that game too.

He stepped forward, chest to chest, raised himself up eyeball to eyeball, and said, "Daddeo? That's cute, Quigley. I don't remember fucking your mother. Was she a whore?" He stepped back into his office and sat at his desk. "Come on in, Petty Officer Quigley." He was grinning from ear to ear. "I was told to teach you a lesson, but I wasn't told how much fun I was going to have."

The walls of his office were full of certificates and commendations. I was going to ask him what Filipino stick fighting was, but I thought better of it. Then I saw the sign on his desk: "YEA THOUGH I WALK THROUGH THE

VALLEY OF DEATH, I SHALL FEAR NO EVIL FOR I AM THE TOUGHEST MOTHER IN THE VALLEY." I thought of Abel Leahman, and wondered if I was going to survive another walk through the valley.

My training would take place in a small clearing in the Marine compartment next to his office. There was nearly always someone else present, which I thought was good for my sake.

"I'm going to begin by showing you how you should have struck that man. Stand in front of me the same way Petty Officer Waternik stood in front of you."

I stood about two feet in front of him. He was holding the nightstick in the middle down at his side. It came forward so fast I couldn't even begin to move. The end of the stick sank into my solar plexus.

"AAAAAAAHG!" I sucked long and hard, but I couldn't get any air. When I came to, I asked the compartment cleaner how long I had been out. "About 20 minutes." That's all I remember of my first lesson.

My second lesson began with a question. "Quigley, now that you know how to put a man down without hurting him, are you sorry you hit Petty Officer Waternik up side the head?"

"No, sir," I said without hesitation. I really was, you know, but I wasn't about to admit it.

Gunny Guzman was surprised, and seemed genuinely concerned. "Why not, Quigley? You put him in a coma for 11 hours. You cracked his skull, for God's sakes. You could've killed him."

"Well, first of all, I just plain didn't know any better, and second, when I cracked his skull, it made a sickening noise that stopped that whole crowd. I don't know what hitting him in the stomach would have done as far as that angry mob was concerned.

"You know it wasn't my fault. The Navy shouldn't have left me there alone, and they should have put those men in a barracks instead of leaving them out in the rain all night. If they would've done their job, I wouldn't have had to hit anybody anywhere."

"Quigley, I'm disappointed in you. I guess it's going to be my job to make you sorry." Every lesson after that began and ended with the short version, "Are you sorry yet?" I never gave in. I always said, "No."

My persistence paid off and eventually he started teaching me how to use a nightstick instead of just beating me to a pulp. I was never afraid to stand shore patrol again. In fact, I was the cock of the walk.

Top Secret

CDR Bunch said, "Quigley, we have a top secret job to shoot this afternoon. Meet me in front of my office at 1300, and bring at least 50 film holders. The lights will already be set up."

"Yes, sir."

We descended into the bowels of the ship and stopped on the platform that surrounded the reduction gears. Several civilian engineers were in a huddle with the engineer and the XO. Apparently this job was a big deal.

Adolf Dengler, a large bald man in a khaki jump suit, left the huddle and came over to us.

"The largest gear is full of hairline cracks. I need a series of close-up pictures that can be overlaid like a map. In other words, I need to see every little crack in relation to the others. Can you do that?"

I was about to explain that there was no room to mount the camera on a tripod and that we couldn't take hand-held close-ups when Commander Bunch said, "Certainly, we can do that."

"Mr. Bunch, there ain't no way I can shoot this job. I can't hold a speed graphic still enough to shoot close ups, and besides, I would have to scoot out along that I-beam to even get close en—"

"You're going to need a safety harness."

"I what?"

"You're going to need a safety harness in order to sit on that I-beam and take your pictures."

"You want me to sit on that I-beam and take hand-held close-ups of that reduction gear with a speed graphic?"

"You got it. Think you can do it?"

"Well, of course I can do it. I just don't think we will get anything useful. I ain't never shot hand-held close-ups of anything. The depth of field is too narrow."

"We'll do just fine, Quigley. I'll be right here to help you every step of the way. If I wasn't so big I'd crawl out on that beam myself."

I knew Mr. Bunch well enough to know that he wasn't kidding. He loved photography more than any man I ever knew, and he loved a challenge. They turned the reduction gear a couple of inches between each picture. Hours passed and we had to send for more film. Every bone in my body hurt.

"Why all the secrecy, Mr. Bunch? Are we afraid the Russians will find out we're down hard and welded to the pier?"

The old German overheard me and repeated what I said to the others in a heavy accent, but apparently they understood because they all laughed.

"What's so funny, Mr. Bunch?"

"No one is afraid of the Russians, Quigley. They are afraid of what Congress would do if they knew their billion-dollar warship couldn't get underway."

Candy in Cannes

Having just finished the 2000 to 2400 quarterdeck watch, I decided to drop into the photo lab for a snack before hitting the sack. To my surprise, the lab was empty except for Commander Bunch who was in his office giggling up a storm.

"What's so funny?" I asked.

He waved a piece of paper at me and said, "It's a message from the Senior Officer Present Ashore to our skipper. Here, you read it. I can't; my eyes are full of tears."

    1. Congratulations! You have completed two weeks of liberty without a single man being placed on report. I believe you have set a record that will stand for a long time.

    2. I sure hope we don't ever have to go to war with your bunch of candy asses.

In the Eye of the Beholder

We had this well-known TV producer, Bert Ups, onboard, and the photo lab was bending over backwards to help. We were also kept busy photographing Bert and his crew at work aboard the *Enterprise.* I was called to the flight deck to photograph a bevy of beautiful models in swimsuits resting on a yellow tow tractor with our distinctive island (air tower) in the background.

Bert was very friendly, but his grips (two hundred and fifty-pound gorillas that do all the heavy work on a sound stage or on location) were running interference. Part of their job was to keep still photographers like me from popping flashbulbs or strobe lights while they were shooting movies, because it caused "white frames" on their motion picture film. I understood this so I waited until they were done before attempting to shoot; however, these guys weren't going to let me shoot at all, and stepped in front of me every time I raised my camera.

It was more than a little irritating. I mean, after all, it was my ship, and they were the guests, not the other way around. I tried walking around them, but they stopped me in my tracks. Then I got this brilliant idea. Bert was using a big hand-held spot meter to determine the precise exposure. I flipped my strobe down and flashed it directly into the lens of his spot meter. He screamed and stepped back about two feet. His grips stepped back to see what was wrong, and I raised my camera and shot my picture.

The models saw it all and were grinning from ear to ear; it was a great picture. I was about to apologize to Bert when I heard a deep roar from across the flight deck.

"QUIGLEY! I saw that, you dumb son-of-a-bitch. You get your ass over here on the double." It was Commander Bunch. He was standing next to our skipper, Captain Peror, who was glaring at me. I trotted over to where they were and got my ass chewed royally, but I could see a twinkle in Commander Bunch's eyes. At that moment, he reminded me of my father.

Admirals Mast II

"Quigley, I have a letter here that you wrote to the city of Norfolk. You said some terrible things, Quigley. What would your wife say if she knew that you invited prostitutes to Norfolk? You shouldn't even be talking about those prostitutes. Many wives would get the wrong idea if stuff like this got out. What have you got to say for yourself, Quigley?"

"Well, sir, it was really my wife's idea. I mean I told her how things were over here, and she got real mad. I mean, she couldn't understand why I could get off at 0800 to see the Parthenon, but I had to wait until 2000 to see her."

"Quigley, I don't think I like your attitude. You know you are responsible for your wife's actions."

"Admiral, if I'm responsible for my wife's actions, I'm in a world of trouble, and I need to get out of the Navy fast. My wife is talking about divorcing me and naming the Navy as co-respondent. She says the Navy is coming between us. Do you know that I've only seen her 28 times since I came aboard a year ago?"

"Quigley, that's impossible unless you're just not going home when you get off."

"No, sir, I couldn't afford the bridge toll, especially since we didn't get off until late anyway, so most of the time, I just went home on weekends."

"Quigley, I don't want you writing any more letters to public officials, and I don't want to hear you talking to anyone about whores or communists. Do you understand?"

"Yes, sir."

"Dismissed."

Admiral's Mast III

The USS *Enterprise* sucked and everybody knew it sucked. It was bad duty. The USS *Enterprise* was built in Newport News. Those of us on the precommissioning crew were in three-section duty, worked until 2000 every night, and then had to pay several dollars to cross the bridge to get home. Those of us who could not afford to pay the toll every day only went home on weekends.

Our morale was so low our mantra was, "*Enterprise* sucks." It was said so often that Captain Mike Peror promised to take two stripes from anyone caught saying it. People risked their careers by getting up in the middle of the night and sneaking onto a sponson to whisper, "*Enterprise* sucks," over the loudspeaker system.

The ship moved to Norfolk after it was commissioned. We went on a three-month shake-down cruise, blockaded Cuba for five months, and then went on a nine-month Med cruise, which was extended to eleven months. I rarely saw my family. We had two small children, and my wife worked full time to make ends meet.

Imagine her chagrin when she opened a newspaper and saw a double page spread about how great the morale was aboard the USS *Enterprise*. It seems the Navy had a unique way of determining morale that had nothing to do with how the sailors felt. Morale was measured by the percentage of the crew that reenlists. This method of measuring morale did not take into consideration the fact that the population of the *Enterprise* was seriously skewed.

The *Enterprise*'s eight nuclear reactors and its Navy Tactical Data System required nearly 1,500 more senior petty officers than previous carriers. Since these senior petty officers were already on their second or third or fourth enlistment, they could be expected to reenlist again when their current enlistment expired no matter how bad the duty was.

My wife, Carla, wrote a five-page letter to the paper telling what it was really like to be stationed aboard the *Enterprise*, and what it was like to be a working mother of two small children and not being able to count on any help or support from her husband because he was never home.

The paper published Carla's letter. It seemed to piss off the entire Navy, and the entire Navy seemed to feel that I was to blame. Navy men were expected to keep their wives in line.

"It seems to me that we've had this conversation before, Quigley. I thought you were going to keep that wife of yours under control. Didn't you tell me that, Quigley?"

"No, sir, Admiral, that's what you said. What I said was that I did not have any control over my wife, and that she was considering filing for a divorce and naming the Navy as corespondent."

"Corespondent? Tell me, Quigley, just what the hell do you think that means?"

"Well, sir, it means she thinks the Navy is responsible for our marriage falling apart."

"Nonsense, Quigley. A good marriage can stand a few separations. She's the only one complaining, and the only one writing letters and the only one embarrassing the Navy. I'm putting you on notice right now that I'm not going to tolerate her behavior any longer. Either you keep her in line or you're going to have a very short career. Do you understand? I don't ever want to see you here again. Dismissed."

"But sir, I—"

"No 'buts,' Quigley, you are dismissed."

C.A.R.E.

Dear Admiral Cortez,

We have a letter from one of your sailors asking for a C.A.R.E. package. Says he doesn't get enough to eat. We would have passed it off as a joke, but he included a picture of a chow line that concerns us. The picture shows a line of men several blocks long winding through a "hangar bay." Mr. Quigley says the line continues, "below decks for several more blocks and takes several hours to get through." He also says that he is on a shooting crew and never has enough time between jobs to go through the chow line. He goes on to say that you have thousands of extra people on board to take care of your reactors, and that you can't feed them all.

We are concerned because it certainly looks that way in the picture. We can't really help you because we are a charity organization with limited resources. However, if this is not a joke, and it really is a serious situation, we are prepared to send you as many C.A.R.E. packages as you need on a temporary basis. We cannot support you for any length of time.

Respectfully,
William Gunderson

"QUIGLEY!"

"Yes, Mr. Bunch."

"Admiral Cortez wants to see you in his quarters, on the double."

"Yes, sir."

Admiral's Mast IV

"Quigley, what is it with you and your damn letters? You must lay awake at night thinking of new ways to embarrass the Navy. I can't believe you told Mr. Gunderson that this is a chow line," he said, showing me the picture I sent to C.A.R.E.

"But Admiral, it is a chow line. It's like that every day. The noon line is the worst, but I can't get through any of them. One reason I joined the Navy was so that I would never be hungry again, and now I'm hungry all the time."

"You can't be serious, Quigley."

"Yes, sir, I am serious. You can see for yourself any day of the week."

"Quigley, I think you are exaggerating. How do you survive if you can't get through the chow lines?"

"Every now and then I get up at 0430 for breakfast, or I stay up for midrats. They're both hard to do because of the hours we're working."

"Quigley, you should have told your division officer. You should not be writing letters to people who can't help. Your letters only wind up embarrassing the Navy."

"Admiral, everybody on board this ship knows how hard it is to get something to eat, and what malarkey all that publicity about having six galleys is. We're only using four of them and a lot of people are going hungry, not just me."

"If the problem is really that serious, I can't believe I haven't heard about it. I'll look into it. I'll show your picture to the captain. In the meantime, you can eat out of my galley when you get in a bind. But stop writing these damn letters. You hear me?"

"Yes, sir. Thank you, sir."

President Kennedy

The military plans everything down to the last minute detail. President Kennedy's visit to the *Enterprise* was no exception. Elaborate plans were published weeks in advance. I studied the plans in order to uncover every picture possibility. It paid off because I got more pictures published than anyone else onboard did, including 50 or so civilian photographers who were there to photograph the president.

I was on the flight deck with a movie camera when he arrived. The ship rolled out a red carpet from the island out to his helicopter. I got great coverage of the president greeting our senior officers and waving at the crew. As soon as he disappeared into the island, I ran back to the photo lab and switched to a still camera. He was going to tour the ship in one hour and I wanted to be ready.

The ship was going to present the president with a Navy flight jacket to wear while he toured the ship. I studied his itinerary and found the perfect spot for a close-up of the president with his new jacket on. The chief-master-at-arms was going to walk 15 feet ahead of the president and there would be nobody in between. I would wait in the admiral's galley and when the chief-master-at-arms came by, I would step out and take his picture. I prefocused at 10 feet, determined the correct exposure, and set my f/stop and shutter speed.

"You must be Quigley. The admiral told me to give you something to eat when I see you. You want a sandwich?"

It was Miguel Ramos, Admiral Cortez's cook. "Not right now, Miguel. The president's coming by here any minute and I want to get his picture. I picked this spot because everything is painted white and I'm shooting color. I will come back later, though."

It went as planned. The Chief-Master-at-Arms sailed by and I stepped into the passageway and shot my picture. A mountain of a man came from out of nowhere and knocked me ass-end-over-tea kettle and back into the admiral's galley where I hit my head on a steel sink. I was woozy but I could tell that the man on top of me had lost all color from his face.

"Don't do that. Don't ever do that. Son, you just can't step in front of the president and pop a flashbulb. You just can't do that."

The president's party rushed on by. I realized I had done something really stupid and mumbled an apology.

"Quigley, you want that sandwich now?"

"I'd like one," said the Secret Service man. I haven't eaten in two days.

"Sure, why not? Make it two, Miguel."

Apparently, Admiral Cortez was serious about my grabbing a bite to eat in his galley. I was impressed. I was also impressed with my picture of President Kennedy. It was the best picture taken during his visit.

Naval Intelligence

We were anchored out in the bay while visiting Salonica, Greece. Bill Davenport and I were assigned to shoot an admiral's party one Friday evening. It was inappropriate to shoot private parties, so they always presented someone with an award, so that it could be called an official ceremony. We knew we would be working late because the party didn't start until 2000, and it was being held in a hotel downtown.

We wore dress whites, took 35-mm cameras, strobes, and plenty of film. We rode in one of the ship's longboats to fleet landing where a civilian driver picked us up and took us to the hotel. A chubby civilian in casual clothes met us at the door. There was a female lieutenant watching television in the next room.

"Where is everybody? We're supposed to photograph a party."

"You're at the right place. This is just a cover. You're going to shoot ships coming in and out of the harbor. There are two Russian ships in port we've never seen before. They are loaded with antennas, and we have just got to get pictures of them."

"Why did they tell us it was a party?"

"Because nobody can know what you're doing. You can't talk to anyone about this. If you get caught, you will be in big trouble. If they spot you, they will probably send divers out to get you."

"What do you mean, they will send divers out to get us? Aren't we going to shoot from here?"

"Oh, no. We are going to take you to an abandoned ship in the harbor. It sunk several years ago, but the top two decks stick out of the water."

"But we're in dress whites, and there's not enough light for pictures now. We'll go back to the ship, change clothes, and pick up a telephoto lens."

"Oh, no, I can't let you do that. You might tell someone. We can't take that chance. The Navy will reimburse you for any uniforms ruined on the job. All you have to do is route a request chit through supply."

"Why would the Navy give us top secret clearances if they don't trust us? What kind of pictures do you think we will get with normal lenses? And if we shoot from sea level, we'll be shooting through sea spray. We won't get anything usable even if they pass within a hundred yards. And who are you to be telling us what to do, anyway?"

The lady lieutenant stepped forward and explained that they were intelligence specialists working out of the embassy. They showed us their credentials. The lady was Karen Foster and the man was David Shoemaker.

"We really should have thought about telephoto lenses, said David, but it's too late now. The frogmen are going to be here any minute to take you out to your station. You're the only hope we've got."

"When are they going to bring us back?" I asked.

"They will pick you up Monday evening as soon as it is dark."

Bill, who had been silent up to this point, spoke up, "Three days! Are you crazy? How are we going to eat? How can we go to the bathroom? What if we get sick?"

"Easy, Davenport," said Karen. "Just because it is a difficult assignment doesn't mean you can be disrespectful."

"Lieutenant," Bill said, "it is not a difficult assignment; it is an impossible assignment. You are risking our lives, and there is no way we can get anything that will be of any use to you."

"You have to try," Karen said.

There was a loud knock at the door, but it was not the frogmen. It was the same civilian driver who brought us here. He said he would take us to a small boat landing where the frogmen would be waiting.

There were four of them, but only two of them rode out to the sunken ship with us. They brought all kinds of supplies, including guard belts with huge knives and holsters.

"What are you doing in dress whites? They will be ruined."

"I know," I said. "This operation was planned by naval intelligence officers. Why are you guys in black? Are those wet suits? You must not have any naval intelligence officers in your organization. Are you guys going to stay with us?" I was hoping out loud.

"Nope. We're just supposed to get you settled in and pick you up when you're finished. Don't worry. You have a radio in case you really need us. We'll be in the area. We aren't going to let anything happen to you. Don't worry about your whites, either. They'll be black by morning."

We stepped into their rubber boat and purred out into the darkness. The more we penetrated the bay, the more we became aware of the smell of it. Ships have their own digestive systems that spew sewage into the sea. Our nostrils were treated to a cocktail of raw sewage, garbage, oil, dead sea creatures, and salt air.

As we approached, we could see by the moonlight that it was a small cargo ship sitting on the bottom of the bay. It had about a 30-degree list. We boarded on the high side, which was about four feet out of the water. There was enough light to see an identical opening on the low side of the ship straight across from us. If we slipped, we could slide right into the ocean.

They helped us get all our gear and ourselves topside and then they disappeared. We had K-Rations, bottled water, shaving gear, toilet paper, a makeshift potty, blankets, pillows, a map, a raft they forgot to tell us how to inflate, a radio, and our oversized knives that we had to remove because they kept getting in our way. We also had two large tarps, which we used to build our nests.

The frogmen said one of us should be awake at all times to listen for strange noises that might indicate intruders. Obviously, they hadn't spent a lot of time aboard a sunken vessel. There was a constant stream of strange noises. It took us about five minutes to decide that we would both try to sleep at night.

Bill and I were both second-class petty officers, but there was a difference. Bill was on the tail end of his first enlistment and I was in the middle of my second enlistment.

"Russell, whatever possessed you to reenlist? I wouldn't reenlist for all the gold in Fort Knox. I just can't believe that anyone on this Earth would be stupid enough to put us on a sunken ship in the middle of the night with no warning, no training, in dress whites, and with cameras that won't do the job."

His anger increased as he talked and it seemed to be aimed at me as much as the Navy. Well, I couldn't blame him. It was the stupidest mess I'd ever been in. Every time we touched the ship, its skin came off in our hands. The sweet smell of rotting onions was playing king of the hill with the smell of raw sewage. To my surprise, I went right to sleep.

The sun woke us up early the next morning. The sun caused the colors of the rainbow to dance on the oil slicks. The frogman was right. Our whites were already black. Bill looked worse than I did. He had a heavy black beard that matched his whites. And he was angry, angrier than I had ever seen him. I didn't try to talk to him.

We were nested safely on a sponson, a kind of protected weather deck. It was perfect. We had a great view of the harbor; we wouldn't have any trouble photographing ships as they came and went. Neither of us tried to shave. No one told us that the ship would be moving all the time. Most of the time it was a gentle rocking, but every now and then it would lurch and really give us a scare.

By 1000 I was wondering why sun tan lotion and sunglasses weren't included in our supplies. By 1200 I knew my forehead, eyelids, cheeks, and forearms were seriously burned. I photographed a large ferryboat as it left the harbor just to see what kind of an image size I would get. I could barely see it in the viewfinder.

Bill wasn't having any trouble with the sun because he remained in a fetal position in the shade. He hardly spoke except when he had to use the makeshift can, and then he cussed a blue streak. It was awkward, but I couldn't imagine what we would have done without it. I don't think we smelled as bad as we looked, but I was sure we would by the time we got back to the *Enterprise*.

I have been on all kinds of ships without getting seasick, but the constant rocking and occasional lurching was making me nauseous. I started throwing up about 1600. I looked over at Bill to warn him not to ever tell anyone I got seasick on a ship that wasn't underway, but he was sound asleep. I felt better when the sun went down, and was soon fast asleep myself.

I felt rotten when I woke up. I wasn't sick, but my stomach hurt. My face felt so bad that I decided to stay out of the sun myself. I was going to raise hell with Bill, and tell him it was his turn, but he refused to wake up. I decided to join him. We both slept through the next two days. I figured we would be put on report if the Russian ships left and we didn't get pictures, but I just didn't care. I was beat.

"They here yet?"

I was startled to hear Bill's voice.

"I can't believe it's over," he said.

The frogmen showed up on schedule. They couldn't believe how bad we looked and were still apologizing for not being more helpful when they dropped us off at fleet landing.

"I thought we were supposed to go back to the hotel," I said.

"No need," came the answer. "The Russian ships never left the pier."

Everyone was staring at us. A shore patrolman came over and said the shore patrol officer wanted to know what happened to us. We told him we were on an official assignment, and that it didn't go to well. A few minutes later a really sharp-looking ensign in dress whites and a shore patrol armband came over and said, "I radioed the officer-of-the-deck on the *Enterprise,* and told him two totally fucked-up smart asses were coming his way. He's waiting for you. He says he's heard them all, but he's anxiously waiting to hear your story."

I wanted to tell my story too, but not to the OOD. I wanted to talk to Commander Bunch and let him take it up the chain of command.

My stomach still hurt and I was getting sick again. The long boat would take about 30 minutes. I was anxious to get back, but I dreaded the trip. I sat next to the rail for the fresh air and in case I got sick. Halfway back I had to lean over the side and heave. I dragged my neckerchief in the water and used it to wash my face, and then I let it go.

I didn't realize how sore I was until I climbed up the ladder to the quarterdeck. Bill was right behind me. The others were giving us plenty of room. I saluted Lieutenant Blackmon, the officer-of-the-day.

"Alright, you two scumbags, over here. What division are you from?"

"OP Division, sir," I said.

"Stand at attention. Watch, call the chief-master-at-arms. I want these scumbags on report right now. And while you're at it, call Mr. Bunch and tell him were holding two of his finest. Tell him to send somebody for their cameras because they're going to be a while."

"Sir, I need to go to sickbay. I think I'm—"

"Shut up, sailor; you're at attention."

"But sir, I'm—"

He spun around and stepped towards me. He was about to say something, but I upchucked all over him.

"IEEE! You son-of-a-bitch! You did that on purpose. If you weren't so filthy I'd break every bone in your body."

"I'm not filthy. You want to take a swing at me?"

It was Commander Bunch. All 280 pounds of him, and the back of his neck was as red as I've ever seen it. You didn't want to mess with Mr. Bunch when the back of his neck was red.

"Mr. Bunch, this man puked on me on purpose."

"Bullshit! Nobody pukes on purpose. Let me see you puke on purpose, Lieutenant."

The Chief-Master-at-Arms walked right past Mr. Bunch and asked us to go with him. "How long have you guys been UA?"

"Wait a damn minute, Chief," said Mr. Bunch.

"Master Chief, Mr. Bunch, Master Chief."

"You're not taking my men anywhere, Chief Blair. You don't even know where they've been or what they've been doing, either of you. They were on a classified mission and they ran into trouble. You should be helping them, not giving them a ration of crap."

Lieutenant Blackmon was not buying it. He thought Mr. Bunch was just trying to save a couple of his men. "Mr. Bunch, these scumbags aren't going anywhere. They're on report, and they are going to spend the night in the brig."

The lieutenant should have checked the color of Mr. Bunch's neck before he talked to him that way. Mr. Bunch walked right up to Lieutenant Blackmon. "Listen, peckerhead. If you call my men scumbags again, I'm going to pick you up and throw you over the fantail. I mean it. Now, get off the quarterdeck and get cleaned up.

Chief Blair, assume the watch until the lieutenant is presentable.

"No sir, Mr. Bunch. I called the XO. He's on his way."

The XO was Captain Harshbarger. The crew called him "god Harshbarger" behind his back. The senior medical officer, Captain Shackel, called him "god Harshbarger" to his face.

"What's going on here? Mr. Bunch, are these the photographers you've been so worried about. You better take them below and get them cleaned up. That man looks like he needs to go to sick bay."

"But, sir, that man puked on me. He did it on purpose."

"Nonsense. Go below and get cleaned up. Master Chief, locate the standby OOD and tell him he has the remainder of this watch." The XO turned and left without another word.

"Quigley, you need to go to sick bay?"

"No, sir, Mr. Bunch; I just want to take a shower and sleep for a week."

"I'll give you until noon tomorrow," said Mr. Bunch as he walked off towards his stateroom.

We couldn't get paid for our uniforms because we never officially left the ship.

Pineal Cyst

I was climbing 11 flights of stairs to shoot a routine assignment on the bridge when it felt like every ounce of fluid in my body drained into my tailbone. It was a pineal cyst.

I was scheduled for an operation in a couple of days, but a crash on the flight deck tied up every doctor onboard, so it was postponed until we got back to Norfolk. I soaked in a sitz bath eight hours a day for two weeks.

I was detached from the USS *Enterprise* upon our arrival in Norfolk, and sent TAD to the Norfolk Naval Hospital only to discover that I had soaked the pineal cyst away. Since I was on TAD orders and detached from the *Enterprise*, the hospital was forced to send me to my new duty station with only 12 hours traveling time.

I screamed bloody murder, but there was nothing the hospital staff could do. I should not have been detached from the *Enterprise*. The hospital had no choice, but to transfer me to the Naval Photographic Interpretation Center. Normally, I would have been given several days travel time and up to 30 days leave to move my family from Norfolk to Washington D.C.

So, after an 11 month Med cruise, I had 12 hours to say hello and goodbye to my wife and two children and to travel from Norfolk to Washington D.C.

THE NAVAL PHOTOGRAPHIC INTERPRETATION CENTER

The Naval Photographic Interpretation Center (NPIC) was located in Suitland, Maryland, next to the Census Bureau. The building, especially designed for photo interpretation work, had 135,000 square feet of office, lab, and vault space. NPIC had a proud history. Navy photographers and photo interpreters, working around the clock, produced the photo mosaics for Operation Overlord—the invasion of Europe.

NPIC also was instrumental in determining the reason the nuclear submarine, *Thresher*, was lost off the coast of New England in April 1963. Using an array of cameras towed behind a surface ship, technicians from NPIC located the wreckage at a depth of over 5,000 feet. Subsequent interpretation of the photography revealed that a defective valve was the cause of the disaster.

It was sprinkling when I got there, and there was the smell of damp dust in the air. The parking lot that NPIC shared with the Census Bureau was huge. I circled for an hour, but there wasn't a spot to be had.

I had already checked into the transient barracks in Anacostia, D.C. where I would be staying until I could move my family up from Norfolk. All I needed to do now was to get a signature from the officer-of-the-deck to let them know that I had arrived and that I would be back the next day ready for work.

I decided to use the chief-master-at-arms' parking spot since I would only be a minute, and then I would be going back to the personnel office in Anacostia to finish checking in. They signed my check-in card and logged me in at the desk, and I was back outside in a matter of minutes.

My car was gone. I thought maybe the chief-master-at-arms had it moved, so I looked around the building, but I couldn't find it. I went back inside to tell the duty officer that my car was gone. He ignored me; he pretended not to hear me. I spoke to the duty petty officer; he ignored me also. I walked out.

I was fuming. I circled the building in ever widening circles until I wound up at a Census Bureau building. I went into what I thought was a hallway, but instead, walked right into someone's office.

"Can I help you?" asked a lady in a brown suit.

"I need to report a missing car," I said.

"That happens all the time out here," she said as she dialed the phone and handed it to me.

"Brady, FBI,"

I put my hand over the phone, "Why do I need the FBI?"

"Because you're on federal property, honey. It's okay; they're used to it."

"Mr. Brady, sir, my car is missing from the parking lot near the Naval Photographic Interpretation Center. I parked in the chief master-at-arms' parking spot. I think they moved it, but they won't talk to me, and I need my car."

After getting a complete description of my car, Mr. Brady said he would get back to me.

The lady in the brown suit asked me to call her Carol after I "mam'd her one time too many.

"Where did you say you have to go?" Carol asked.

"I have to get back to the Receiving Station in Anacostia, and then I'm gonna have to come back here in the morning."

"Not a problem," Carol said. "They run a shuttle bus back and forth between the Receiving Station and your building about four times a day. It comes right by us; that's how come we know."

"Thank you," I said, and headed back to NPIC to wait for the shuttle.

I reported for work the next morning. It was the chilliest reception I ever received. It didn't help to hand Chief Maslow, the leading chief, a leave request while I was checking in.

Chief Maslow was short, dark, and stocky. He also was very good looking, but his clothes didn't fit all that well. Chief Maslow said, "So you're the kid who likes to park in the chief master-at-arms' parking spot. If you have a problem with authority, you're at the right place, because we know how to fix it."

"I don't have a problem," I said, "I just couldn't find a—"

"You see, kid, that's just what I'm talking about. There is no excuse for what you did, and if you don't understand that, you're in a lot of trouble," he said as he tore up my leave request, without looking at it, and dropped it in the wastebasket.

"You can't do that," I said. "Regulations say you have to forward it."

"What did you say?" said a voice from the side of the room. I turned to see Warrant Officer Minchke glaring at me.

I stood my ground. I said, "You can't just tear up my request chit. You have to forward it."

"Chief," Mr. Minchke said, "he's got you there. He knows his regulations. Have him make out a new chit and you sign it properly."

I made out a new chit and Chief Maslow marked it disapproved, signed it, and handed it to Mr. Minchke. Mr. Minchke printed in two-inch high letters diagonally across the chit:

DISAPPROVED.

"Here," he said, "take it to the personnel office." I was discouraged. I wanted my family with me. I had just come off an eleven month Med cruise. No one on the USS *Enterprise* had been allowed to take leave. There was something about it in my personnel record.

I was called to the lobby where a young woman asked me if I was Mr. Quigley. I told her I was. She introduced herself. "We found your car. We came over after everyone had gone home, so it was easy to pick your car out of the few that were left. It was broken into; the window vent was broken out, otherwise it looks okay. We took prints. C'mon, I'll show you where it is."

It was only about a half block from the building. I wondered how I missed it, and how they found a parking spot when I couldn't. I checked to see if the car would start; it did.

"Okay," she said, "we'll be in touch when we find out something."

I went back inside. I had to get some time off and find a place to live and bring Carla and the kids up here. I remembered my record again. There is something in my record about my leave. I'd better check it out.

I found it. I had 108 days of leave on the books, and until I got under the legal limit of 60 days, the only way to disapprove my leave was to go through the Bureau of Personnel. I showed my leave request and the letter to the Personnel Officer. She took it and the letter to the captain. It came back approved.

I found an apartment across the street from NPIC. I liked the area and it was convenient. When I returned, I went to work for First Class Petty Officer Michelle Hamburg. She was a real hard-ass. She said the leading chief and the warrant were really pissed at me, and that I had two hours extra duty every day for a week.

Well, now, I knew they couldn't do that. I hadn't even been to mast. I told her no way, and after she dressed me down, she hauled in to see Chief Maslow, and told him I refused to do extra duty without a captain's mast, so did he want her to write me up or what? Chief Maslow asked her to leave us alone and he chewed my ass so well that I figured he was aspiring to be an officer. He assured me I would be placed on report if I failed to work the two extra hours a day for a week.

I was demoralized. Never had I ever gotten off to such a bad start. Then I remembered I still had 88 days of leave on the books. I never said another word to Chief Maslow. I just let him rant and rave. When he finished, I went to the Personnel Office and said I would like to take another 30 days leave.

"Would you like me to run a chit through the chain of command?" I asked.

"Of course," was her automatic reply, "Why wouldn't I?"

Then she remembered the letter in my record and the war going on between the chain of command and me. She said, "Wait a minute," and stepped in to see the captain. When she returned she said, "Just give me a leave request with the dates on it and it will be approved."

I made out a request for 30 days starting the next day and returned it to the personnel officer.

"Quigley, is that you? I hadn't met the captain yet, but the voice coming from his office sounded familiar. A big man stepped out and looked me straight in the eye. "Do you remember me?" he asked.

"Yes, sir," I said, "You're Commander Bartel from the Photo Center."

"Captain Bartel," he corrected, "I just want to know one thing before you go on leave." He paused, and then he said, "How did they taste?" He turned and went back into his office before I realized what he was talking about, but it came to me.

I was home for two days when the phone rang. They wanted me to come to work for a couple of hours. Something about the chief master-at-arms being arrested by the FBI for breaking and entering. It wasn't car theft because the car never left the parking lot.

Everyone wanted me to drop the charges. I didn't even know if I could, but I refused anyway. After what these bastards put me through, I wasn't giving anyone an inch. He went to court and was fined $200.00 and put on probation for a year.

I was afraid to go back to work when my leave expired, but of course, I had to. There was no mention of extra duty when I returned, but I got the cold shoulder from everyone except Chief Blackwell whom I met the next day at General Military Training (GMT).

More time has probably been wasted under the guise of General Military Training with the possible exception of mustering for quarters, than anything else the military does. I did think, however, that a session on communism might be more interesting than most GMT lectures.

The Communist Manifesto is a deceptive little book. It contains some of the most destructive concepts ever known to man, such as, "from each according to his ability, to each according to their need," and "government ownership of all production and property." But unknown to many, it contains some perfectly acceptable gems, such as, "the abolition of child labor and free public education for all children." I doubted that anyone in attendance had ever read it, which is why I thought it might be fun.

The instructor was Chief Blackwell, who hadn't spoken to me; however, he hadn't gone out of his way to give me a hard time as most of the senior people had. He passed out several pamphlets and fliers. To my surprise, they were not printed by the Navy or the government; they were printed by the John Birch Society. The literature dwelled on the harshness of communist dictatorships and their quest for world domination. It also named prominent Americans, such as Dwight D. Eisenhower, that were supposedly more than just a little pink. This didn't seem to bother anyone besides me.

"Chief Blackwell?"

"Yes, Quigley."

"Do you believe Dwight D. Eisenhower was a communist?" I asked.

"He is not the subject of our training," replied Chief Blackwell.

"But wasn't Eisenhower our commander in chief?"

"Quigley, I told you, Eisenhower is not the subject of this training."

"But Chief, it's in this literature you handed out. If our commander in chief was—"

"Quigley, shut the fuck up."

Chief Blackwell went on and on about the evils of communism. "We won't be safe until every last one of them is dead and gone because they're not going to stop until they rule the world."

"Chief, what you said about getting paid what you need instead of what you earn, doesn't that apply to the Navy? I mean, don't we get paid more if we have kids?"

"Quigley, there's no comparison. Now how about paying attention to the real issues?"

"Well, Chief, did you know that the communists wanted to put a stop to child labor?"

Chief Blackwell stared at me. He seemed speechless, so I went on.

"They also believed that every child should receive a free public education."

"Okay, Quigley, that's enough. Class, take five. Get a cup of coffee. Except you, Quigley; you stay put."

Chief Blackwell waited for the room to clear before lighting in to me. "Quigley, I heard about you, but I was willing to give you the benefit of the doubt. What the hell is the matter with you? Are you deliberately baiting me with those outlandish lies? If you are trying to bust up my class, it isn't going to work, because you're out of here. Get yourself a cup of coffee, but don't come back here. Go back to work."

As much trouble as I was already in, I should have known better. I guess I was just as irritated with the people in the command as they were with me. I went back to work sorry to miss what could have been a stimulating discussion.

Chief Maslow was in an excellent mood at quarters the next day. He even said hello to me when I came in. It wasn't long before I understood why.

"Listen up, guys and girls. I have news. Some of you are being transferred to the Defense Intelligence Agency (DIA): Petty Officer Overstreet, Petty Officer Singletary, and Petty Officer Quigley."

They were trying to put one over on me and they weren't going to get away with it. They couldn't transfer me until I had been there at least a year. I went to see Captain Bartel.

"Quigley," he said, "no one is trying to put one over on you. I put your name on that list myself, and I did it to get you out of a jam. I don't think you realize how angry these people are at you. If you stay here, they're going to get you. I strongly advise you to go to DIA and make a fresh start."

I took his advice.

THE DEFENSE INTELLIGENCE AGENCY

The move from Suitland, Maryland, to somewhere in Alexandria, Virginia, qualified for a dislocation allowance because it involved moving to the other side of the Potomac River. The thought of a daily drive from Suitland over the bridges and into Alexandria did not appeal to me, so we moved.

The location of the DIA photo lab was a secret. It was listed on my orders as the receiving station in Anacostia, which was also the official address of NPIC where I was already stationed. My orders did not qualify me for a dislocation allowance, nor did they constitute authorization for breaking the lease on our apartment. The apartment manager filed a lawsuit for $1200.00. The move from Norfolk to D.C. had already cost me about $2000.00 out of my pocket; I simply could not afford a double whammy.

I went to see the colonel in charge of the photo lab. No help there. I went to see the admiral in charge of DIA. No help there. When I asked to see the comptroller of the Navy, my supervisor said I had had enough time off and that I would have to see him on my own time. I took leave. I saw the comptroller of the Navy. I told him that I wasn't going to pay $1200.00 to keep the Navy's secret.

The comptroller agreed with me; although, he let me know he didn't appreciate my attitude. He signed the paperwork and gave me a letter of explanation that stopped the lawsuit and got me my dislocation allowance.

The following day, I received a phone call from my neighbor in Suitland, Mr. Gunter Eisenbein. He was a UPI reporter from Germany who had White House clearance and was an expert at wrestling information out of bureaucracies. He was fascinated by my situation, and told me he was going to investigate.

"Russ," he said, "You know that address you've been trying so hard to protect? It's in the phone book, Russ. It's in the phone book."

The DIA Photo Lab

DIA is the military equivalent of the CIA. Officially, it is the Defense Intelligence Agency. DIA had taken over a large NASA photo lab with a backlog of over a million jobs. It was a huge lab with all kinds of equipment that I hadn't seen before. The lab was run by an Air Force colonel, Mr. Mitchell, who chewed me out the first time I saw him.

"Sailor! Come back here. You didn't salute me."

"We don't salute indoors or uncovered, sir. Er. . . In the Navy, sir."

"You will while you're here," he said.

"Yes sir," I said. There are some things you would think the services could agree on. When to salute should be one of them.

Most of the civilians were from an area called Vint Hill Farms. They did not have any formal training, but they were good at their jobs. We got along great. One of the supervisors was a tall, trim black lady with a superstructure that would embarrass a battleship. She was always asking the sailors to take her measurements. They all copped a feel in the process, but she loved the attention.

I was the only one that had declined, and she started ragging me something fierce until I finally gave in. I took the tape measure, walked up to her, dropped to my knees, put one end of the tape next to her ankle, ran the other end up her dress and smacked her pussy with my right hand. "Inseam, 28 inches," I said. It was the only time I ever saw her flustered.

DIA laid off all the janitors because they didn't have high enough security clearances. They could not get replacements. It is not easy to get top-secret clearances for anyone; apparently, it is impossible to get top-secret clearances for janitors. Sailors are used to cleaning up at the end of the day, but the colonel wouldn't allow it. "We are too far behind in our work," he would say.

The lab went downhill in a hurry. You don't realize how much work janitors do until they stop doing it. It did not seem to bother the civilians, but it did not set well with the eleven sailors. Cleanliness aboard ship is an absolute necessity. You only have to visit one unclean ship to understand why.

The leading chief went along with the colonel; however, our senior first class rebelled. He announced at quarters that we were going to secure the lab and hold a field day. And hold a field day we did. We scrubbed that place from top to bottom. The civilians refused to help, so they just stood around. We finished about 1300 and Petty Officer Second Class Bill Porter said, "The Colonel said to secure and go home." We didn't think anything of it because that is what we normally do after a field day. I mean, who wants to go back to work all grimy and sweaty.

The next morning we were all lined up before the Colonel. He didn't understand our behavior and he was furious. He started with Petty Officer Bishop.

"Bishop, what the hell were you thinking of? We lost a whole day's work."

"Well, sir, I ain't working in no pig sty," came the reply.

"Bishop, it is not going to happen again."

"Not 'til next week," Bishop said defiantly. "I don't care if I have to go all the way to the admiral, I ain't working in a filthy lab." Bishop's reminder that there was a sailor at the top seemed to soften the colonel.

"Once a month at the most, and it doesn't start until 1300," the Colonel retorted. "Now then, who the hell said you could go home in the middle of the day?"

"I did, sir," came the prompt reply. It was Petty Officer Second Class Bill Porter.

"And who authorized you to dismiss the troops?" demanded the colonel.

"Nobody, sir, I lied, sir," replied Petty Officer Bill Porter.

We were all stunned by his frankness, but none more so than the colonel, who stood there staring at him, apparently at a loss for words. Finally, he said, "go back to work." So we did, and we held field day on the first Friday of every month after that, and we secured when we were finished.

The addition of 11 sailors and computerized job control eliminated the backlog in one year. We expected the workload to drop off; however, it got bigger, and we started working overtime. Soon we were working seven days a week. Most of the civilians loved it because they were taking home unbelievable paychecks. The sailors, however, were unhappy. They expected 12- to 14-hour workdays at sea, but on shore, they expected to get a break.

After several months without a break, the guys turned on me and said, "Hey, Russell, how about calling that brother you're always bragging about and ask him why we're working like slaves? You know, the commander."

I was really on the spot. I had his Autovon number, but we hadn't spoken in years. He was a submariner working for Admiral Rickover and putting in a lot of hours himself.

I rubbed my chin. What the hell, it wouldn't hurt to ask, so I called. I told him where I was working, and what happened to our workload. He was not at all enthused, but he said he would look into it. I didn't expect anything to come from it, but the guys were satisfied. I really had a brother, and I really did talk to him.

I had called on a Friday. The following Sunday at 1000, the colonel came in and told everyone to go home, and apologized to the civilians. He said he wouldn't be able to pay them for coming in that day because his funds had been cut off as of the day before. We never worked another hour of overtime.

Admiral Rickover was opposed to the very concept of a military intelligence agency. He felt the CIA already went too far, and given the military's propensity for following orders no matter what, he was sure DIA would also go overboard.

It seems someone was redirecting all of the photo intelligence jobs from other labs to this one. Someone was trying to grow an empire. The workload was being used as an excuse for new hires as well as the overtime. There was a big investigation. The command was audited and we were all interviewed. The Command never knew what hit them, but on my level, I was the hero of the day.

The Ladies Love a Hero

I think Evelyn was the prettiest girl I ever made love to. She had shoulder-length blonde hair, light brown eyes, lovely curves, and the most photogenic face I ever photographed.

Evelyn was a bit of a groupie. I was the hero of the day, so I got to be the boyfriend of the day. I was so excited the first time we made love, I exploded in the middle of the first down stroke. I didn't know girls could be so cruel.

While we were waiting for the resurrection, she said, "Come, I'll show you something." She turned out the lights and we walked over to a window on the backside of her second story apartment. "Look down there. See that man standing there. That's Ensign Newman. I used to date him. He's the security officer where we work. He's there every night."

We tried again. I did better, but she wasn't impressed. We never dated again. She was always doing something with her hair.

The next day I was called into the Security Office.

"Quigley, you are a married man, right?"

"Yes, sir," I said.

"I understand you're having an affair with Evelyn Foley. That's adultery. We can't have that. You're leaving yourself wide open for blackmail. I'll have to pull your clearance if you continue to see her."

"What makes you think I'm having an affair?" I asked.

"Don't play games with me, Quigley. It's my job to keep track of you people. Either you stop seeing her, or I'll call your wife."

Obviously, he didn't know how bad things were between my wife and me. I decided to call his bluff. I picked up his phone and called my wife. "Carla," I said, "there's a man here who wants to talk to you." I handed him the phone. The color left his face, and he hung up the phone.

"Quigley, you're on report for adultery. It's an offense, you know," he stammered.

"Well, that would give me a chance to tell the colonel you're stalking one of his secretaries, hanging around her backyard like a lost puppy."

His color came back with abundance. He stiffened, and took on a mean look. In a stone cold voice, he said, "you'd better leave."

For once in my life, I knew I was not on report.

An Inquisition

I was called out from work one day and told to report to an Army office in the Pentagon. I was familiar with the building from my days in the mailroom at the Photo Center, so I didn't have any trouble finding the right office. I wasn't familiar with the organization, but the name implied that it had something to do with security.

I was directed to sit at a large round table across from an Army master sergeant. Two civilians and an Army major joined us. The civilians wore suits and ties. One was a redhead; the other had brown hair. There were no introductions.

"What do you think of communism? Did you ever tell anyone that communists have it better than we do?" asked the master sergeant.

"I don't have a clue what you are talking about. Capitalism will out-produce communism every time, so I can't imagine communists as a whole having more than we do. I know I never said anything that stupid."

"What do you think about communism?"

Before I could answer the master sergeant, one of the civilians, the redhead, said, "You know a lot of communists don't you?"

"Where are you getting all this bullshit? I don't know any communists."

"Ah ha, you are a liar. You know the First Secretary of the Russian Embassy," said the redhead.

"I was introduced. That doesn't mean I know him. My friend Gunter Eisenbein asked me to go to a reception at the Russian Embassy. Gunter is a well respected press agent with White House clearance, so I thought it would be alright."

"Your friend is from Germany, right?" It was the man with brown hair.

"Yes."

"Is he a communist?" asked the man with brown hair.

"No. He is from West Germany. He has a White House clearance."

"He spent three years in Israel before coming to the U.S., right?" asked Brown Hair.

"That's what he told me. Is Israel a communist country?"

"Did you tell anyone you were associating with a foreign national?" asked the master sergeant.

"Yes I did. He is my next-door neighbor. It's hard not to associate with your next-door neighbor. Besides, he is a great chess player, and he is teaching me a lot about the game."

"You didn't notify anyone that you were going to the Russian Embassy," said the major. "We could jerk your clearance."

"Bullshit! It was all I talked about for two weeks. I was excited. I told my division officer, Captain Malard; I told my chief, Chief Springer; I told all my friends at work."

"Please watch your language, Petty Officer Quigley," the major requested.

"I'm sorry, Major, but you people are telling a lot of untruths that in my book qualify as bullshit."

"So you say, Quigley," said the major, "but our job is to determine what the truth is. That's why we're here."

"You mean, the truth is not the truth; the truth is whatever you determine it to be."

"Quigley," said the Major, "our job is to determine whether you have the character to maintain a top secret clearance. Character speaks to a lot of things, and you're not coming across as well as you could."

"Well, sir, I haven't called you a liar, and I haven't told you any lies. That's more than I can say for you. What does that say about your character?"

One of the civilians, the one with brown hair, left the table and went into another room. The redhead asked, "Why would the Russians think you were a spy? Have you ever told anyone you were a spy?"

"No, but Gunter Eisenbein introduced me to the First Secretary as an 'agent for the Defense Intelligence Agency.' I told him it was a mistake and that it could cause me problems at work. He apologized. He said he thought it would be fun to send them on a wild goose chase."

"You have an alibi for everything don't you, Quigley?" said the master sergeant.

"I don't know, sergeant. I'm telling you the truth. If that qualifies as an alibi, so be it."

"Quigley," the major spoke more slowly than the others, "I don't think you're taking this seriously."

"Well, sir, let me tell you what a top secret clearance means to me, seriously. It means working longer hours than anyone else in the Navy, overtime without pay, time away from the wife and kids. It means working in the middle of the night when everyone else has gone home. It means knowing things I don't want to know, things that keep me awake at night. It means not being able to go on leave because there is no one else with the right clearance to do a job.

"Losing my clearance would mean having to leave Washington, D.C., the most expensive city I have ever lived in. I had $2000.00 in the bank when I moved here, and now I'm $2000.00 in debt. If I hadn't made first class, I'd probably be drawing welfare."

"I thought I was making worthwhile sacrifices for my country, but if you don't think I have the character to maintain a top-secret clearance, then by all means take it away from me. What I lose in self-satisfaction I will more than make up for in shorter working hours and less hassle. And best of all, I won't have to take any more crap from people like you."

They told me to go back to work, and that I would be hearing from them, but I never did. I needed my clearance for my next tour of duty aboard the USS *Observation Island*, a missile test ship. Carla did not accompany me. She was going to Pensacola Junior College, and did not want to interrupt her education. I became what the Navy calls a geographic bachelor.

THE USS *OBSERVATION ISLAND*

The USS *Observation Island* (EAG 154) began her career in 1952 as a merchant vessel, the SS *Empire State Mariner*. The ship was transferred to the Navy in 1956 for use as the seagoing facility for test and evaluation of the Fleet Ballistic Missile Weapons System. The ship was commissioned as the USS *Observation Island* in December 1958.

The USS *Observation Island's* primary mission was to test new missiles for submarines, but it also supported submarines by tracking missiles fired by submarines, often when they were qualifying.

I am a Chief Petty Officer

All armed forces have two classes of service, enlisted and commissioned; however, the United States Navy and the Coast Guard have the distinction of also having bureau-appointed chief petty officers and bureau-appointed warrant officers. The United States Naval Bureau of Personnel appointed me a chief petty officer in the United States Navy on 16 September 1969.

Worthy or not, I am now in elite company. No longer can I claim that this isn't really my Navy, and that I'm getting out at the end of my next enlistment. This is my Navy, and I am in it for the long haul.

I am a duly initiated chief petty officer. I am Chief Buckley, who didn't know me, but defended me from the feds as if I were his son. I am Chief Pointer who defended me at a hearing for a court martial, not because he had to, but because I was in trouble. I am Chief Clark who told the division officer I was present when I was not. I am all of the chiefs who gave me better evaluations than I deserved, and I am all the chiefs who taught me my job, and then trusted me to do it.

I am Chief Petty Officer Russell Quigley, but you can call me "chief."

I am on the lookout for young Quigleys who need help with their self-esteem. They are easy to spot. They carry large chips and are loaded with attitude. I wonder how many of my peers began their careers as military misfits.

A Family Reunion, of Sorts

I knew my older brother, Roger, had made captain, but I didn't know that he had his own boat, so I was pleasantly surprised when I got a call from him asking me to dinner. His boat, the Sea Wolf, was in port to qualify. ADM Rickover would be the inspecting officer.

I arrived early and was disappointed when he said he couldn't make it. "The worst thing that could possibly happen the night before qualifying has happened. I had a new man report on board. He's been through sub school, but he's never been stationed on a boat. He's going to be mess cooking for the next three months, but he still has to know when and how to operate all of the systems in his area."

"Can't you get someone else to teach him?"

"I could if there was anyone on board who was free. My policy is simple. If you're qualified and your system is up, you go home or on liberty until I need you. If you're not qualified, or your station is down, you can't leave the ship. I got a lot of static from the wives until everyone was qualified and got their systems up. But right now, as a result of my own policy, I am the only one available to help Seaman George Applebee get ready for tomorrow. But stick around; we can talk."

I was impressed with his patience and his thoroughness. He spent the next four hours teaching George everything he needed to know. He also put a number of cheat sheets in strategic places. We really didn't get to talk much because he spent most of his time speaking to George.

I did get the impression that Roger was worried, not about the big inspection, but about whether or not his men would heed his warning to not paint the boat's hull number on the local water tower. It was a tradition of long standing that every boat that came here to qualify had to paint its hull number on the water tower; however, the city of Cocoa Beach had had enough, and had let the Navy know it. ADM Rickover had issued a direct order, but Roger knew how much the crew did not want to be the first boat to break tradition.

I got up early the next morning to look at the tower.

There it was, big as life: SSN 575. Roger thought it was the chief-of-the-boat, but I heard it was one of his officers.

I wasn't allowed on board until after the inspection and all the debriefing. "Well, how did it go?" I asked, sensing his anger and frustration. I was afraid he had failed.

"The Sea Wolf was the first boat to ever get a perfect score. One of my petty officers threatened Rickover with a wrench when he tried to go into the reactor spaces without showing his ID card. 'You know damn well who I am,' Rickover bellowed, but the man would not let him pass. 'At last, someone who understands security,' said Rickover. But he chastised me because of that damn water tower."

"Yes, but the first sub to get a 4.0. You've got to be proud of that."

"I am, but that isn't all that happened. He doubled back to congratulate me—he was too angry when he left—and saw all my people pouring off the boat. He made me call them back, and then he chastised me again for my liberty policy."

"Oh."

Petty Officer Third Class Bristol

Most Navy photographers are excellent craftsmen, but few are artists. Petty Officer Robert Bristol was an artist. Every picture he took was not only well exposed, but also well composed. His pictures were on display throughout the lab indicating that others also had recognized his talent. His photos reminded me of Commander Bunch's. Nearly every center of interest had a dramatic frame around it. I was anxious to meet him.

We exchanged pleasantries. He was tall, dark haired, and good looking. He had a warm if not impish smile; you just knew he was up to something he shouldn't be. And his uniform had a strange appearance, but I couldn't put my finger on anything wrong. I complimented him on his work.

Then I noticed a sweet, but foul smell. I was puzzled. I was certain that I had never smelled anything like it before. It seemed to be emanating from Bristol. I was about to say something when I noticed that his collar seemed to be coming apart at the seam. Reflexively, I reached up and took hold of it, and it came off in my hand.

"What is this? And what is that odor?"

"Thank God, thank you chief, five months, twenty-three days, and six hours."

"What are you talking about?"

"I bet the guys that I could go six months without a shower and without washing my clothes, and that no one would notice. You cost me a hundred bucks, but I sure am anxious to get cleaned up."

I turned to go into the finishing room and was met with a round of applause. "At last we have someone who is aware that we exist."

"He really hasn't had a shower in five months?"

"We offered to call it off, but he wanted our money."

A Qualified Swimmer, At Last

I normally didn't go to sick bay for a cold; however, this one had hung on for three weeks. Dr. Odell seemed to be giving me a complete physical and was asking the same questions over and over again.

"Are you running around at night? Are you getting enough sleep?"

"No, sir, I'm not running around at night. Yes, sir, I am getting enough sleep."

"You must be doing something wrong. You must be tired all the time. Do you know that you have had a temperature of 99 degrees ever since you have been in the Navy?"

"I was not aware of that. Is that little bit of temperature serious?"

"You're damn right it's serious. It is like carrying a 50-pound weight on your shoulders 24 hours a day. It means something is wrong."

With that, he seemed to start checking me out all over again. After another 20 minutes, he said, "Well, I can't find it. There is something wrong with you, but I can't find it."

He didn't seem to be interested in my cold at all. He studied the information he had gathered. Finally he said, "Damn! I should have thought of it sooner. It's your teeth. There is something wrong with your teeth. Has to be." He darted into the dental office.

"Get dressed and go next door. They are going to x-ray your teeth."

Well, there must have been something because the dentist who took the pictures called all the other dentists in to look at them, then I heard him say, "Call Dr. Odell."

"Wow! I didn't expect it to be that serious," said Dr. Odell.

"We'll have to pull all his teeth. We won't even be able to save any anchor teeth," said the dentist.

"Chief, come over here and look at these x-rays. The roots of your teeth have grown into your sinuses, and everything is infected, even your jawbone. We're not going to be able to save anything."

"Is that why my teeth are loose and move around?" I asked.

"I'm sure it is," said the dentist.

"Do you know Navy dentists have been chewing me out for not brushing my teeth for years. I have been avoiding dentists because even though I brush my teeth three times a day until they bleed, I know that one of them is going to chew me out."

"Well, there is no way—"

"You're right to be irritated, Chief Quigley," Dr. Odell interrupted. "A dentist should have recognized your problem a long time ago." Dr. Odell turned and left before anyone could respond.

"Do I need to make an appointment?"

"No, Chief, this needs to be done right now. We will pull your molars today and your front teeth tomorrow. You should notice the difference right away."

He was right; I did notice a difference. I gained 30 pounds in 30 days. Most of it was evenly distributed; however, there was a slight concentration in the middle.

Carla didn't see the new me until I went home on leave again. She couldn't stop giggling, and she teased me unmercifully, especially about my new little potbelly.

"Well at least you can swim now," she said.

"Swim? What do you mean swim?"

"Isn't it that you couldn't swim because you were so skinny?"

"No. I couldn't swim because I had negative buoyancy."

"Same difference. Well, you aren't skinny—I mean you don't have negative buoyancy anymore."

"You know, you're right. With all the lessons I've had, I should be able to swim around the world nonstop. I'm going to the chief's pool at NAS and see what I can do. Want to come?"

"No, thanks. I've already started dinner. Don't be too long."

I swam four lengths of the pool. I was a qualified swimmer at long last.

Naval Education and Training

The Navy distinguishes between education and training. Education is for a lifetime. Training is for the here and now. The Navy believes strongly in both of these pursuits. I tried hard to get into one of the Navy's educational programs, but I never made it. It took me thirty years to finish a BS degree. I was, however, very fortunate on the training side of the ledger.

In addition to basic and advanced photography schools, the Navy sent me to the Rochester Institute of Technology to study photographic quality control. The Navy also sent me to Motion Picture School and Camera Repair School. I had nearly two years of training in photography and countless other schools in countless other subjects.

My tour aboard the USS *Observation Island* was especially fruitful. I studied motion picture photography for two weeks in "A" School and for four weeks in "B" School. I knew how to load, operate, and unload all of the Navy's motion picture cameras, and how to shoot most basic assignments.

The mission of the *Observation Island* was to test missiles for the submarine service. My part of that mission was to take high-speed motion pictures of all missile launches. It was an important job, but it was an easy job. We loaded the cameras before each launch, set the f/stops and shutter speeds, and unloaded and processed the film after each launch. All cameras operated automatically in concert with the missile launch. No one was allowed on the missile deck during a launch.

Lieutenant Copeland, the electronics officer, was also the photographic officer. "Quigley, I'm sending you to Motion Picture School to learn how to operate the ship's movie cameras."

"But, Mr. Copeland, I already know all I need to know to do my job. I will not learn anything in mopic school that will help me with my present assignment."

Mr. Copeland was not convinced and sent me anyway. It was a fabulous school, and I enjoyed every minute of it, especially since the school was in Pensacola, Florida, where my wife and children were living. Carla was going to the University of West Florida, and did not accompany me to Cocoa Beach, Florida, where the *Observation Island* was stationed.

All of the cameras had electronic timing devices consisting of pulsating miniature lights that put a series of fogged dashes along the border of the film. Whenever anything happened, the pulses could be counted and the exact time the incident occurred could be determined.

I had been aboard about a year when Mr. Copeland said, "Quigley, I'm sending you to Camera Repair School. We have new timing devices. The old ones will have to be removed and the new ones will have to be soldered in place."

"Sir, Camera Repair School is not going to teach me how to do that. Besides, can't your people do that?"

"Quigley, my people aren't going to do your work. Get that idea out of your head."

I enjoyed another three months in Pensacola with my wife and children. The school was not so enjoyable; I am not mechanically inclined, but I struggled through it. I did not learn anything about reading schematics or soldering, and I still did not know how to replace the timing devices.

"Quigley, I don't believe you. I'm giving you ten days to replace those timing devices, and don't bother asking my people for help. I've told them that anyone caught helping you will be placed on report."

Fortunately, I knew most of the missile technicians, since I had a station in the missile control room during launches. They were happy to show me how to remove and replace the timing devices. I was amazed at how simple it was. The devices were the size of a triple A battery and had five color-coded connections. We heated the contacts to remove the old devices, put the new ones in place, and put a drop of solder on each contact. We were done with all of them in thirty minutes.

I received three months per diem for each school. I got a pleasant surprise when I got to the ship. Unknown to me, the school's barracks had been declared substandard, so I also received a substantial check for three month's lodging even though I had lived at home. Mr. Copeland was rather strange, but it was hard not to like him.

Ribbons

I was home on leave when I received an invitation to a party at a friend's house. She thought I would add spice to her party. She warned me that the professors were opposed to the war in Vietnam. Well, if it's spice she wants, I thought, why don't I wear my dress blues with ribbons? Carla, being more perceptive than I, took this as reason enough to stay home.

I know professors can be a pompous lot, but I was not prepared to be totally ignored. When I spoke to them, they not only didn't respond, they didn't even look at me, so I retreated to the bar and had a few drinks. The bar, built in a den, was really quite lavish for a home bar, and even came with a bartender. I was impressed and envious.

A woman sat next to me, and I thought she might be coming on to me as there was plenty of room, in fact, I was the only one sitting at the bar when she arrived. She was staring at my ribbons. My chest swelled. She leaned forward so that she could see them better. She studied my ribbons. I smiled, bursting with pride.

I realized in that moment that it was no longer me against them, no longer me against the Navy. I had become one of them. I knew every one of my ribbons and why it rated a spot on my chest.

She looked a little awkward, and I realized that she might be drunk, but I could tell she was fascinated with my ribbons. I wondered if she knew what any of the ribbons meant.

"SPLAAAT!"

I jumped backwards off the stool, my arms flying straight out beside me. I had no idea I felt so strongly about my ribbons. I stood there shaking with my arms still stretched out. I saw the spittle move slowly down across my ribbons.

"Don't move," I heard someone say.

"We're making a citizens' arrest," said another as their arms folded around mine. "Call 911," somebody said.

"Yes, a drunken sailor has assaulted a female college professor. We want him arrested. Please hurry."

I finally looked down past my ribbons, and understood what they were talking about. The woman who was sitting beside me was lying on the floor with her arms straight out forming a cross. I realized that I must have hit her when my arms flew out.

The deputy must have been in the area. He was a big man, late thirties or early forties. They all began talking at once. "She was just sitting there having a quiet drink and he up and knocked her out."

The deputy ignored them and went to the woman on the floor. He kneeled down and smelled her breath. "Are you sure she isn't just drunk?"

"Oh, no. He col' conked her. I saw it. He knocked her clean off her stool."

The deputy waved something across her face and she began coming to. He looked back at us; "You can let go of him now." He helped her to her feet. "What happened?" he asked, looking at her.

"What do you mean, what happened?" she asked.

He turned to me. "Suppose you tell me what happened."

"She spit on my ribbons," I stammered, still shaking.

"Is that right?" he said turning back to her.

"No, that isn't right. I didn't spit on anyone. I wouldn't do—"

"It's still there," I said defiantly.

The deputy looked down at my ribbons. "Oh my," he said, and reached behind him for a napkin from the bar. To my embarrassment, he cleaned my ribbons. He was meticulous. "You can have these dry cleaned," he said. I realized then that he must have ribbons of his own.

"Folks," he said, "it's against the law in the state of Florida to spit on another person. It is an assault just the same as if you hit someone with your fist. The chief was within his rights to hit her back."

"But she's a woman."

"Doesn't matter. The law applies equally to men and women. C'mon chief, I'll walk you to your car. We're not wanted here."

Don't Fence Me In

One way to avoid surprises is to read all the letters in a photo lab's incoming and outgoing letter files soon after checking aboard. I discovered a gem in the *Observation Island's* files. It seems that my photo mates, or some previous photo mates, had thrown some safety fences over the side. And apparently, it was not the first time. There was a letter on file from the captain stating that there was no way that he was going to pay for more fences.

I asked my crew if they knew anything about the missing fences. To a man they denied being involved in throwing the safety fences over the side; however, they all were anxious to explain the problem to me.

The safety fences were supposed to surround a camera platform that was on top of a 35-foot steel column. The problem was that the fence was not allowed to remain in place when we were not launching a missile. Each time we had a launch, the photo mates had to carry heavy sections of the steel fence straight up the 35-foot steel ladder. They strapped a section of the fence to their backs and used two safety harnesses, so that one would be latched to one rung of the ladder while the other one was being moved up a rung. Once they were up on the platform, they had to slip the sections of fence into their holding brackets. Once the launch was completed and the cameras were returned to the photo lab, the fences had to be brought back down again.

If it had been my job, I might have thrown the fences over the side myself; however, it left me with a safety problem that I could not overlook. I wrote the captain a letter requesting that the safety fences be replaced. He sent a one-word memo back denying my request. I assumed that that was the end of the matter; however, I did warn my photo mates that if I ever saw them on that platform without a safety harness attached to the ladder or the pole, I would take them to mast. Petty Officer Second Class Billy Joe Ledbetter took exception to my warning.

"Chief, I don't think we should have to go up there without safety fences. In fact, I ain't going up there again until we get safety fences."

Now, Billy Joe wasn't one of my favorite people. Billy Joe was the best looking, most successful ladies' man I had ever met. He would proposition your wife right in front of you, and I was amazed at how often that worked. I supposed I envied him at one level, but I can tell you that having a man like that in your work center does not make for harmonious relationships. I took a 12-inch blade away from one of my photo mates who was waiting to ambush the man.

And as if that wasn't enough, our captain's name was also Ledbetter, and he seemed to be fascinated by the exploits of his namesake. They became good friends and started hitting the beach together. I don't recall the Navy making a fuss over fraternization at the time, but you knew this relationship was wrong. However, they were both single, and no one on my level was going to tell the captain he shouldn't be running around with a second class petty officer.

All of this came to mind when Billy Joe challenged me in front of the crew. I stared into Billy Joe's eyes, but I spoke to Airman Robert Valesillio. "Val, can you take care of Billy Joe's camera station?"

"Sure thing, Chief."

Val was motivated. The passageway outside the photo lab became a wind tunnel whenever the hatches were open, which was nearly all the time. We flunked inspection every Friday, until the XO ordered me to put someone in the passageway eight hours a day every day to ensure it was clean for our many visitors. Airman Valesillio was a striker and the junior man in the photo lab, so the job fell to him.

"Good," I said. "Billy Joe, you can take Val's place cleaning the passageway."

Billy Joe kept the passageway spotless for two weeks, and then he came to me and said, "Chief, this isn't right. I should not have to do an airman's job for refusing to work on a camera station without a safety fence. Even if I deserved to be punished, which I don't, it is inappropriate to humiliate me in front of the others."

I knew I was on thin ice, but I refused to back down. "Billy Joe, that fence disappeared before you came aboard, so I know you were not responsible, but everyone who has worked on that camera station says it's more dangerous to haul sections of fence up and down that vertical ladder than it is to work without the fence in place. You know the captain isn't going to buy another fence and that the job has to be done. You also know that as long as you keep a safety harness attached to the ladder or the pole, you will not fall off."

"Chief, it's not right to make me clean the passageway in front of junior troops. If you have to punish me, you're going to have to think of something else. If you don't, I'm going to request an audience with the captain."

"Billy Joe, I think the junior troops know what's going on here. It didn't bother you to challenge my authority in front of the junior troops, and it doesn't bother me to have the junior troops see the consequences. You're going to stay in the passageway until you resume your assigned duties."

Billy Joe requested and was granted an audience with the captain. I don't mind telling you, I was a little worried. Most of my peers thought the punishment was inappropriate even when I explained that the man was continually challenging my authority. Lieutenant Copeland thought I was making a serious mistake and said if I didn't change the punishment, he was going to reconsider his decision to let me run the photo lab without any interference from him.

The XO greeted us and made it clear that he wanted to settle our dispute without disturbing the captain. "Chief Quigley, I've read Petty Officer Ledbetter's complaint, and quite frankly, I agree with him. You know the rules, praise in public, punish in private. Put someone else in the passageway. You've punished this man more than enough already."

"No, sir, I can't do that. You see—"

"Damn it, Quigley, you insist on infuriating me every time I talk to you. What the hell is wrong with you?"

"Well, sir, Petty Officer Led—"

"Never mind, Quigley." The XO stepped into the captain's office. "Skipper, these men still want to see you."

"Okay, send them in. Petty Officer Ledbetter, I've read your complaint. Is there anything you want to add?"

"No, sir. I think I said it all."

"Well, Chief, I haven't heard your side yet. Suppose you tell me why you think this is an appropriate punishment."

"Captain, I have thirteen men and twelve launch stations. Since the XO said I have to keep one man cleaning the passageway, I don't have anyone to spare. Airman Valesillio offered to take Petty Officer Ledbetter's launch station, so I thought it would only be fitting if Petty Officer Ledbetter took his passageway. I only have one airman, so if a petty officer has to clean the passageway eight hours a day, why shouldn't it be the petty officer that refused to man his launch station?"

"Petty Officer Ledbetter," said the captain, "that sounds fair to me."

Hanging Around

The photo lab had twelve missile stations that had to be manned during a missile launch, so when the photo lab got down to eleven men, we had a problem. We had a man, Airman Randy Knutson, coming from PH "A" School, but he would be on leave for two weeks, and he was entitled to some travel time. That meant we were going to be one man short for an upcoming missile launch.

The XO cancelled Randy's leave and ordered him to report aboard immediately. Randy was one very unhappy camper when he arrived. He was trying to talk his fiancé out of breaking up with him, and having to come directly to the ship, he felt, really hurt his chances. He felt a little better when we explained what was at stake. "They won't fire a missile unless every watch station is manned."

Randy was a pleasant young man with a ready smile and a friendly hello for everyone he met. He quickly made friends with everyone in the photo lab. He had a coin collection he was proud of, and he enjoyed explaining the significance of some of his rare coins. I sent him on a practice assignment—I didn't tell him it was just for practice—and he did an outstanding job, and he was real proud of his work. It was always nice to have new blood.

The XO was having difficulty with another policy that had nothing to do with missiles. We had a disproportionate number of junior troops on board, so not everyone had to go mess cooking. The XO thought that the policy was unfair and set a new policy that every seaman that reported onboard would have to do a tour of mess cooking, even if it was a shortened tour. He didn't realize how that would affect Airman Randy Knutson, the man whose leave he had cancelled.

Randy had only been onboard a week when he got the word that he would be going mess cooking. It was the same day he got his Dear John letter. "I guess I'm not really needed to man a missile station after all," he was heard to say. He seemed to take it okay and was making more friends outside of the photo lab than most of us did. He was hanging out with the boatswain's mates as often as he was with the photographers.

He said he wanted to learn how to tie some knots and asked for some rope. BM2 Coats thought it was kind of odd that he wanted exactly 11 feet of rope, but hey, there's no shortage of rope on a ship. Petty Officer Bristol was young and inexperienced, but I couldn't help but blame him a little. I mean, if someone offered you a valuable coin collection that you knew he was proud of, you ought to know something was wrong.

One of our cameras was mounted on a weather deck located right over the bridge. It was one of Randy's favorite hangouts, so no one thought anything about seeing him up there that night. Randy tied the rope to the railing right above where Captain Ledbetter always stood. He took all the knots into consideration when he requested his 11-foot rope. He calculated he would break his neck right in front of the captain's eyes. He was right.

A SHIPALT

I toured the missile deck once a week in port and once a day at sea looking for problems with my spaces or camera stations. Keeping everything clean and free from corrosion was a constant battle.

One day, while touring my spaces in port, I noticed two civilians welding a four by five foot metal plate between the camera mount closest to the missile tube and the missile tube itself. I was stunned. It was one of my most important cameras because it showed whether or not the missile had any trouble coming out of the tube.

"Hey! What are you guys doing?" They didn't even look up. They just kept on working.

"That plate is blocking the view of my camera."

"Don't look at the light; it'll burn your eyes."

"Who asked you to put a metal plate here?" Still no answer.

I went below and found the missile officer, Lieutenant Baker. "Mr. Baker, some men are welding a plate between my cameras and the missile tube."

"I don't have time for that now, Chief."

"But, sir—"

"Not now, I said."

I went back to the photo lab thoroughly frustrated. That has always been the first film the engineers and scientists looked at. Somebody doesn't realize what they're doing. I called my division officer, Lieutenant Copeland, and explained the problem to him.

"Quigley, it was okay for me to bail you out of hock when you were a first class, but now that you're a chief petty officer, you have to solve your own problems."

I decided to take a picture of the plate to show to Lieutenant Baker; then he could tell at a glance that we had a serious problem. I wouldn't take up any more of his time than I had to. The picture came out perfect; I ran over to show it to Lieutenant Baker.

"Quigley, I said I didn't have time for your problems. Whatever it is, put in a damn job order and have it fixed."

A job order? How can I put in a job order to undo his job order? What is he going to do then, put in a job order to undo my job order? I might as well put in a SHIPALT to weld the missile tube shut. Now there's an idea.

I went to my friends in engineering and told them what I wanted to do. They helped me with the paperwork and suggested I retake the picture with cameras on the camera mount to make the problem even more evident. The engineering officer got wind of it and created a line drawing on a clear acetate overlay to further illustrate the problem.

I submitted the SHIPALT through the chain of command beginning with my division officer. The purpose read: To weld the hatch shut on the number one missile tube. The justification read: Since our mission is to collect photo-graphic data on all missile launches, and since the metal plate mounted in front of our cameras prevents the accomplish-ment of our mission, the missile tube should be welded shut to improve watertight integrity.

I knew the minute Mr. Copeland saw it, he would phone Lieutenant Baker, and the whole mess would be taken care of.

A few days went by without a word. I was not concerned because I knew everyone was busy, but by the end of the week, I wondered if Lieutenant Copeland hadn't just thrown it in the trash. I don't think he has a sense of humor. I began to worry because if Mr. Copeland threw it away, then I still had a problem.

I was summoned to the XO's office the following Monday. The Operations Department head, Commander Martin, the missile officer, Lieutenant Baker, and the electronics officer and photo officer, Lieutenant Copeland, were already there. The XO pointed to the spot where I was to stand.

"Chief Quigley, I assume you think this SHIPALT to weld our missile tube shut is funny. Well, I'm here to tell you that it is not, and if you so much as smile, I'll bust you down to a seaman recruit. It is also not funny that all of these dumb shits in front of me approved it, apparently without even reading it, and then gave it to me to send to BUSHIPS. And they didn't think it was important enough to send it through the engineering officer. God only knows if the engineering officer would have read it."

I smiled to myself on that one.

"Quigley! I warned you."

Damn! The man can read minds. I have mentioned before that I believe senior officers get schooled in ass chewing because they are universally good at it. The man kept us there for 45 minutes going from one to the other. He did mention that the steel plate that obscured the view of my cameras was gone. I felt like I was really coming up in the world because there I was getting my ass chewed with two lieutenants and a commander.

I requested instructor duty at the Photo School in Pensacola, Florida. I really needed to get back with Carla and the kids. My daughter was already nine years old and the joy of my life. Much to my surprise, my request was granted. I was really looking forward to being with my family again.

PHOTO SCHOOL, AGAIN

The Photo School had not changed much since I was a student. I was assigned to teach the third and fourth weeks of PH "A" school. My classrooms and darkrooms were in the west basement of the school building, an area that was always cold and damp. I really looked forward to being an instructor.

The command believed that all incoming chiefs should attend the Chief Petty Officer's Academy, which was located right behind the school. The school did not have a good reputation; I did not look forward to going.

The CPO Academy

It was a silly school with a serious curriculum. The staff was more chicken shit than anyone at boot camp. We polished the decks with shoe polish and wore marine shirts with pointy collars because Commander Basil thought they looked more military than regular navy issue. We marched and drilled until we almost knew what we were doing. The 16-hour workday included classes, drills, and volleyball. We went to bed exhausted every night. The worst part was no liberty. I had been separated from my family for three years; I didn't need to be in the same city and not allowed to see them for another 30 days.

For all the silliness, I was exposed to a lot of useful information. My favorite courses were strategic geography and geopolitics, which opened my eyes to what was happening in the world. Time went by quickly and before I knew it I was taking final exams and participating in a speech contest. I gave my speech on brainwashing and compared the procedures used at the academy to those used by the North Koreans. I drew a laugh when I said the academy blew it by feeding us so well. Commander Basil stood up, paused until everyone saw him, and then walked out of the auditorium.

Commander Basil was annoyed again the next day when he had to present me with the plaque for honor man.

Zombies

Navy instructors are among the best in the world. They develop objectives that keep lessons focused on what's relevant to the job. They are far better presenters than the average high school teacher or college professor. One of the ways they remain sharp is through frequent evaluations by master training specialists.

I was scheduled to be evaluated by Master Chief Langford. I was fully prepared. I had a mastery of the material. I knew all of my students by name. I was ready to go.

I looked out at my class. I had never seen students look so out of it. I introduced Master Chief Langford, and explained his purpose in the classroom. Only one student turned around to look at the master chief.

I gave the name of the lesson, and stated the objectives. I told a story that told of the consequences of not knowing the material. I asked a question. No response. Even when I called on a student by name, I got no response. Nothing. I moved on and covered the first objective. I asked a few questions. Nobody moved; nobody responded. I wanted to scream at them, but I calmly moved on.

The lesson was scheduled for an hour, but it was timed to include a lot of interactivity. I was done in 15 minutes. I panicked. I slowly repeated the lesson in its entirety. I still had 15 minutes to go. I gave up. I gave the class a 20-minute break.

The review was a killer. "Quigley, you have no rapport with these people. You didn't establish eye contact with anyone. Is that all there is to this lesson? I'm not sure you are cut out to be an instructor."

On and on it went. I finally realized there was a student waiting to see me. I was embarrassed to have a student within earshot of my evaluation. When the Master Chief finally left, I turned to the student and asked, "Well, what is it?"

"Chief Quigley, the whole class went to Fort Barrancas at lunch time and had a pot party. They all got bombed. I don't do pot, and I don't approve of it. I wasn't going to tell anyone though, but then I saw what you just went through."

"Thank you, Airman Hauley. I won't let on I know what happened."

When classes reconvened, I said, "Class, I just failed my instructor evaluation. I failed it because of your unresponsive-ness. Not one of you answered a single question that I asked. You acted like a bunch of zombies. I can't teach zombies. I'm not that good. I'm not going to waste my time even trying. We might as well go outside and get some exercise."

Before I came to Florida, I did not know you could have 100 percent humidity without rain. The temperature was 98 degrees, a perfect day for marching. My students were drenched by the time they had marched 100 feet. I stood in the shade of a tree, and barked commands, "Left flank, march. Right flank, march. To the rear, march."

After about an hour I got bored and started marching with them. I passed under Captain Nolte's window just in time to hear him say, "What is Quigley trying to do, kill his students? They are supposed to be in class. It is just a matter of time until one of them has a heat stroke. Get that asshole in here on the double."

I marched them over to the shade tree, put them at ease, and awaited my summons. It wasn't long in coming.

"Don't give me any of your crap, Quigley, I don't want to hear it. Get those kids inside where it's cool, and don't ever pull a dumb stunt like that again."

"Yes, sir, Captain Nolte."

I went back outside and called them to attention. "Class, I hope we don't ever have to do this again; however, we will be out here again tomorrow if you turn into a bunch of zombies again."

Divorce

I have never felt more alone than I did after my divorce. Even though it was probably the right thing, it hurt deep inside. I felt like I had lost my best friend, and that I would never find another. And even though she was the one that asked for it, she cried every time she saw me for years. I never understood her.

You had to justify a divorce at the time, so she had a friend say she had an affair with me. I didn't understand her rush. I vaguely realized that I could not truly love another while I was all wrapped up in myself. I lived in a small world. As I became aware of others, the world expanded, and became a safer and more interesting place. I had grown some since entering the service, but I was still trapped in my inner self at the time of my divorce.

It had been coming for a long time, but it was still painful. She did not accompany me on my tour of duty in Cocoa Beach, Florida, so I had already been alone for three years. We were married 13 years, but if you subtracted all of the separations, we spent less than 6 years together. I think the divorce rate in the Navy is probably one of the best-kept secrets in the history of the world.

In spite of the fact that she threatened to divorce me while I was on the Enterprise, I do not believe the separations were the problem. I was simply too immature to understand and accept my responsibilities. The fact that I found other women irresistible didn't help.

Between child support and my pledge to help Carla get her bachelor's degree, I literally did not have enough left to live on even though I lived in the barracks for free. I got a job tending bar at the Chief's Club across the street from the barracks. It wasn't a smart move. I drank all my mistakes, and the more I drank, the more mistakes I made. I became known as the dancing bartender. I never left the club alone, and I was frequently late for work. My reputation as a master craftsman was being replaced by that of an irresponsible drunk.

"I am having so much fun, I would pay to work here," I was fond of saying. At the end of my first month when I received my credit card bill for booze and motel rooms, I discovered that I was paying to work there. I bought a two-bedroom house, and stopped drinking at the club while I was working. It took time, but I rebuilt my reputation for craftsmanship and reliability. I was still considered to be a troublemaker. It took a long time to shake that off, and some people would say I never did.

When the chiefs threw a party, I would make about $50.00 in tips. That was good money in 1970. Occasionally I would have to work a party at the Mustin Beach Officer's Club. The most I ever made at the O' Club was $15.00. I have long suspected that they teach a course in "cheapness" at the Naval Academy.

Captain Nolte's secretary was a big blonde with big boobs and a pretty face. "Russell," she said, "I need a second job, but I am afraid to work at the Chief's Club even though I hear they tip well."

"What are you afraid of, Debbie? You certainly don't have any trouble handling yourself around here."

"You know, I hear a lot of stories about chief petty officers."

"And I suspect most of them are true, but I never heard of them doing bodily harm to a barmaid or a waitress."

"I need to do something. Will you introduce me?"

"Of course."

All the girls wore hot pants and halters—this was before male chauvinism was invented. Debbie was a knockout in hot pants and the instant favorite of all the chiefs. They flirted with her and teased her unmercifully.

She had a rough couple of weeks until she mastered the art of remembering seven or eight different drinks and the two or three tables for which they were destined. Things were smoothing out, and she seemed to be enjoying herself by the time we had our biggest party of the year.

She was doing great. She had made over $100.00 in tips, and she still had an hour to go. And then she slipped with a full tray of drinks. She hit the floor hard and all of the drinks spilled on top of her. She was soaked from head to toe.

I rushed to her aid, but I couldn't get to her. There must have been fifteen chiefs on the floor with her, but they weren't trying to help; they were licking the drinks off her body. One chief, who couldn't get to the trough, picked his drink off the table, stood over her, and poured it on her crotch. There was a mad scramble to see who could lick it off. Debbie looked over at me, started crying, and said, "You lied to me."

She lit into me when she saw me at the Photo School the following Monday.

"I assume you are going to quit?"

"No," she said, "I made too much money to quit; they must have thought I was going to put them on report or something; they kept pushing money into my pockets until the bell rang."

"Well then, what's the problem? If you survived last Friday, you can surely take anything else they could possibly do to you."

In spite of the distractions at the chief's club, it was a long time before I really felt good again.

Checkups

The Dental Department really had it together. They were actually notifying us when it was time to come in for a six-month checkup. I had never seen this at any other command. I was impressed.

My name was on the list, but since I had full dentures, I didn't think they really wanted to see me, so I gave them a call. "No, Chief Quigley, you don't have to come in."

The following month I received a phone call from Master Chief Langford, the "A" school officer. "Chief Quigley, your name is in the dental checkup list again. There's an asterisk after your name. Apparently, you were supposed to go last month. How about taking care of this. I don't have time to baby-sit you guys."

"Master Chief, they said I didn't have to go because I have full dentures. I'll call them again."

"You do that, Quigley."

I called. "I'm sorry, Chief Quigley. It won't happen again." But, of course, it did.

Master Chief Langford called again the next month. "Quigley, what is wrong with you? I made a simple request that you take care of your personal business on time and you screw around for three months and it still isn't taken care of. What do I have to do, take you by the hand and go down there with you?"

"I'll take care of it immediately, Master Chief."

"See that you do."

I took care of it.

"Captain Nolte? This is Captain Strussel. I'm in charge of the Dental Clinic. I'm calling to tell you that you have one smart-ass chief in your command. I'm referring to Russell Quigley. He put his dentures in a plastic baggie and stuck them in guardmail envelope with my name on it. I am a busy man, Captain, and I don't need that kind of crap from any of your chiefs."

"Captain Strussel, I will attend to it immediately." He did.

Pretty Dog

Pretty Dog was called Pretty Dog because he liked to be called Pretty Dog. Ten-year-old Lorna Thompson changed his name from Rex to Pretty Dog when she noticed that his ears stood up and his front legs danced excitedly whenever she said, "pretty dog."

Lorna and Pretty Dog were inseparable. Pretty Dog would even go to her school to greet Lorna when she came out of the building, and then walk her home. It could be a nuisance sometimes. Whenever Lorna stayed after school, either Fred or Dianne Thompson would have to drive over and pick up Pretty Dog. Pretty Dog would get in the car, but if they tried to walk him home, they literally had to drag him all the way.

When Lorna was hit by a truck while riding her bike, Pretty Dog was there, running along behind. He seemed to know she was dead because he didn't go for help as he had before; he just lay down beside her and cried the way dogs cry.

When they said Pretty Dog could not come into the funeral parlor, Fred and Dianne simply said they couldn't go in without him; he's family. They stood outside and greeted friends and relatives as they came in. It was only a few minutes before management caved in and invited Pretty Dog in.

Pretty Dog comforted the Thompsons in their grief. Whenever they cried, he put his head in their laps and cried with them. "Are you crying for Lorna, or are you crying because I'm crying?" asked Dianne.

But as the months rolled on, Fred and Dianne realized that Pretty Dog never went outside except for necessities, and that he didn't dance when they called his name. They came to believe that he needed someone to replace Lorna. They decided to give him away. When they heard the Navy needed dogs and preferred German Shepherds, they thought the program would be perfect for Pretty Dog. Not only would he have a constant companion, he would receive training and have a job to do. He would be active again.

Pretty Dog blossomed all over again. He loved his work, and he danced whenever his handler, ABE1 Mike Hollis, called his name. He became famous for his ability to sniff out drugs in cars, planes, packages, and most of all in barracks. Pretty Dog greatly reduced the amount of drugs on base, and sent many young sailors home to their mothers. Pretty Dog enjoyed his work, and he enjoyed being around people. Unlike most Navy dogs who only respond to their handlers, he soon began dancing for anyone who spoke his name. Everyone liked Pretty Dog.

Pretty Dog lived with Mike, his wife Jane, and his two boys, three and a half year old Jacob and one and a half year old Randy. Randy couldn't quite say Pretty Dog. What he said sounded more like Pree Dee, which the family, except for Mike, shortened to Pee Dee. Pretty Dog, or Pee Dee, quickly became one of the family, and went everywhere with them.

If sailors were going to do drugs, they knew better than to do them on base; that is, except for our students at the Naval Schools of Photography, who came and went within a few months and weren't always aware of Pretty Dog's reputation. Pretty Dog would always find a bunch of pot in our student barracks. Most of it was hidden in common areas like the ceiling, so we didn't actually catch many students; however, we did manage to confiscate most of their pot on a regular basis.

Captain Nolte despised drug users, and was really frustrated when we found so much pot, but couldn't take anyone to mast. After every visit by Pretty Dog, Captain Nolte would assemble the chiefs and scream at us, "You guys aren't doing your jobs. Real chiefs would know who is using pot and who isn't, and get them out of the Navy before they get killed on a flight deck or cause someone else to get killed."

The Navy's policy was to discharge anyone caught using drugs, no second chances. If you turned yourself in, you could get counseling and stay in the service, but no one wanted to be marked as a drug user, so the program wasn't working very well.

A couple of us got together after one of Captain Nolte's tirades and bounced it around until we hatched a plan. We would set up an interrogation table in one of the empty rooms, and talk to each student after his or her room was inspected. After a few students were interrogated, we would spread the rumor that some of the students were talking and naming names.

Pretty Dog found pot everywhere: stuffed into radiators, taped to fire extinguishers, inside socks hanging in the cleaning gear locker, and, as always, above the ceiling tiles. After a room was inspected, we called each student's name over the loudspeaker, and told him to report to the interrogation room.

"Are you using drugs of any kind?"

"No, sir, Chief Quigley."

"Do you know of anyone in your room using drugs?"

"No, sir."

"Would you tell us if you did?"

"I, um, um well, I guess I would."

"Dismissed."

That's pretty much how all the interviews went; however, while I was talking to students, my colleagues were circulating around the barracks, "You guys better 'fess up, because your shipmates are squealing on you. We have a list of names a mile long. You either turn yourself in, or you're out of here."

It worked much better than we thought it would. We only had 211 students, and 57 of them turned themselves in. We also got an unexpected bonus. Several of the students started actually giving us names. That gave us probable cause and we alerted the proper officials. Eventually, most of them were caught.

The captain was not allowed to punish those who turned themselves in, but he couldn't resist lecturing them.

"Men, your duties as Navy photographers will ensure that most of you spend some time on the flight decks of Navy aircraft carriers. I just can't tell you how dangerous a place to work a flight deck is. We lost 37 men on my last Med cruise. Good men. Men who were paying attention. I can't imagine working on a flight deck with even one man bombed on pot. The thought scares me to death."

They seemed to be impressed; although our next inspection did not go so well. Pretty Dog found just as much pot as before, but our ruse didn't work the second time. The students must have figured out what happened before because nobody turned themselves in.

One hapless student, Mark Thurgood, returned from a dental appointment, and was caught by surprise. Pretty Dog alerted on the startled student, and promptly attacked his ankle. Mark had a bag of pot stuffed into his sock, and Pretty Dog would not let go of his ankle even when called by his handler.

The student's ankle was in bad shape by the time we got Pretty Dog off him. His parents tried to sue the Navy, but it never got anywhere. The judge said their medical expenses were unnecessary because Mark was still in the Navy, and his pain and suffering were not more than he deserved.

We were on the second deck and just about finished when Pretty Dog alerted on a window that looked out on a cement terrace about 30 feet below. A student had put his pot in a sock, leaned out the window, and used a thumbtack to secure it to the outside of the building.

Pretty Dog stepped through the window as if he were stepping over a small hedge.

He was gone before we knew it. He received several medals, and we buried him with honors at the Barrancas National Cemetery, a few blocks away. I hadn't cried for a dog since I was a kid, but I cried for Pretty Dog.

Rally Around the Flag

Rochester Institute of Technology (RIT) looked more like a prison than a college campus. I noticed the flags at half-mast, and I wondered who passed away. I was excited. I'd wanted to come to RIT's Photographic Process Control Technician course ever since I was on the *Enterprise*. It had the reputation of being one of the most difficult courses in the Navy, a year of chemistry, a year of statistics, and a semester of sensitometry all squeezed into ten weeks of summer. We went to class eight hours a day, five days a week.

The "A" School officer wanted to introduce quality control (QC) into "A" School, so he asked me if I wanted to go and then write the curriculum when I got back. I jumped at the chance. I needed both chemistry and statistics for a BS degree, and I wanted to learn QC.

The dorms were coed, which was an education in itself. I was heading for the shower wrapped only in a towel, when a young lady came up behind me and snapped off the towel.

Embarrassed, and thinking it was one of the guys, I spun around cursing a blue streak.

"Welcome to RIT," she said, holding out my towel and not batting an eyelash.

"Thank you," I mumbled, reaching for the towel. She giggled and walked off.

My classmates were great, two ladies and eighteen men. We got along famously, and when the course proved to be as difficult as its reputation, we formed study groups, and studied until 11 p.m. every night except Fridays. Friday nights were party time.

The professors were the most impressive men I have ever come across. They made us feel like we were the most important people in the world. They were gifted teachers and truly loved their profession. I think they admired us because it took a great effort for average sailors to get through such a difficult course.

I loved our Friday night parties. We bought beer and refreshments and invited the professors and their families. They flattered us by never missing a night and they really seemed to enjoy themselves. I always joined the poker game with professor Tom Berry. He had a reputation of being a world-class player, but we never got burned. One night while I was getting a beer, I caught Mrs. Berry giving her husband a signal.

"What's that all about?" I asked.

"I give him a signal when I'm ready to go home. He likes about 20 minutes to return all his winnings plus a little extra. It's his way of saying thanks and contributing to the party fund."

Dr. Tim Henderson was the most fun. After several beers, he would open these huge glass doors to the balcony and begin place-kicking beer cans through the opening. He would close the doors a little after each beer and by the end of the evening the opening was barely wider than the can. It was amazing. He was as graceful as a ballet dancer, and he never missed, no matter how many beers he had.

We soon realized that the flags were not at half-mast because someone died; they were being flown upside down and at half-mast to protest the Vietnam War. We were warned about the anti-war sentiment. In fact, we weren't allowed to wear our uniforms on campus. However, Staff Sergeant Ben Chiarella and I put on our dress uniforms after class and went out and turned all the flags right side up and raised them up to the tops of the poles. We would have to do it again every few days, but we kept it up all summer.

Summer passed all too quickly, and soon I was back at the photo school.

The Supply Chief

The supply chief, Diane Kalavoda, was a sharp lady with a sharp tongue. She asked me to come to her office soon after I returned from RIT.

"So, Russell, now that you're a QC man, can you tell me why I have to pay $35.00 for calibrated light bulbs for the sensitometers when I can purchase uncalibrated light bulbs for $2.00 each. After all, we are only a training command for Christ's sake."

"Gees, Di, I never thought about it. The light bulbs are calibrated to ten decimal places. That does seem like a little much. If you can get me a dozen light bulbs, I can run tests on them for consistency from bulb to bulb."

"I just happen to have a whole case of $2.00 light bulbs. How will you test them?"

"Well, I'll expose several sensistrips with each light bulb, average the readings, and then plot them on process control charts. We will know precisely what the variances are from bulb to bulb."

"Russell, we are spending one hell of a lot of money on these calibrated light bulbs. I can buy a lot of film and paper with the money we would save."

"I'll get right on it, Di."

I ran all the tests and plotted all the variables. They looked like straight lines on the process control charts. The differences between light bulbs were about one fifteenth of an f/stop. I could not imagine it making a difference at a training command. I wondered if it would make any difference in the fleet. I couldn't wait to tell Di.

"Hey, Di, glad I caught you in. I tested those light bulbs. There is no practical difference between them. The difference is about a fifteenth of an f/stop. That would only be of interest to a film maker."

"That's great news, Russell. I won't order any more calibrated light bulbs."

"Not so fast, Di. I can only speak for "A" School. You need to run it by Commander Wiley, over at "B" School."

"I'm not speaking to that pompous ass, Russell. We do not get along at all."

"I'll talk to him. I'll show him my test results. I'm sure he'll go along."

I made an appointment to talk to Commander Wiley.

"Chief Quigley, I'll tell you the same thing I told Chief Kalavoda, not only no, but hell no."

"But, sir, my tests results show—"

"I don't give a damn about your test results, Quigley. If you don't understand how important those calibrated light bulbs are, then we really wasted our money sending you to RIT. Without calibrated light bulbs, our readings would be all over the place. The staff and the students would instantly know something was wrong. You tell Kalavoda that if I catch her changing light bulbs, it will be her ass. You understand?"

"Yes, sir. I understand."

I told Di what Commander Wiley said.

"Russell, I'm going to tell you something, and if you tell the commander, it really will be my ass. I changed his light bulbs two years ago. I just wanted to know if it made any difference."

Scene Brightness Range

My photographic process control course for "A" School students was not going well. The main stumbling block was a four-hour lesson on logarithms, but the whole course seemed too difficult for them. I called Dr. Tim Henderson at RIT.

"Russell, if I were teaching at that level, I would forget about powers of ten and tables of mantissas. Use a simple table of logarithms based on the number 2 to coincide with the doubling relationship of f/stops and shutter speeds. You know, .3, .6, .9, 1.2, 1.5, 1.8, 2.1, 2.4, 2.7, and 3.0. That way, you can relate everything to f/stops and shutter speeds. I would also use eleven step wedges in your sensitometers, so that your sensistrips have the same relationships as your table of logarithms."

"Fantastic, Tim, I think you have solved my problems. Thank you very much. How is everything at RIT?"

"Everything is great, Russell. We've just been talking about visiting your school. Think you could set it up for us?"

"I'd be happy to. I'll get right on it."

"Okay, Russell, I hope we see you soon."

The Captain said no to their visit. I think I was the wrong person to ask for it.

I rewrote all my lessons around Tim's ideas and you could just see the light bulbs going on. I added the logs .15, .10, and .05, so that students could interpolate a half f/stop, a third f/stop, and one-sixth f/stop. This gave them all the accuracy they needed.

I was so proud of my students' accomplishments that I got caught by Commander Wiley bragging that my students could compute scene brightness ranges in their heads while "B" School students fiddled with their slide rules. Commander Wiley stopped the first student that came along.

"Have you been through Chief Quigley's QC classes?"

"Yes, sir, I have," said Airman Apprentice Charles Cook.

"Good. You two come with me."

We followed the commander to his car and rode to "B" School with him. "B" School was in an old hanger on

Ellison Field about five miles away. We walked into the lounge and found two petty officers on a smoke break.

"Have you guys finished the QC block?"

"Yes, sir, we have."

"Good. I want you to break out your slide rules and solve a scene brightness range problem."

"Yes, sir."

Commander Wiley proceeded to give us all the parameters of a typical scene brightness range problem. All Airman Apprentice Cook needed to hear was the light meter readings for the brightest and darkest objects, which were f/4 and f/22. He counted five f/stops between them, multiplied 5 by .3, and quietly told Commander Wiley that the scene brightness range was 1.5. The "B" School students were good; it only took them three minutes to get the same answer using their slide rules.

I was bubbling with pride and turned to gloat, but Commander Wiley was nowhere in sight.

"Well, Charles, I guess we have to find our own way back to building 1500. You did good, Charles. You did real good."

I don't Do Windows

Some students broke into the school through a basement window and stole half a dozen enlarger lenses. They were worth about $20.00 each, and were literally worthless to anyone without a number of enlargers. Certainly not enough to risk going to the brig for, but the students were never caught. Considering all the cameras and other high value items they could have stolen, these were not our brightest students.

Master Chief Langford's solution was to weld the lenses to the enlargers, in case we ever had another group of students as dumb as this group. The real damage came as a result of the broken window, which we couldn't get fixed. The floor would flood every time it rained, and the wall under the window was crumbling. We couldn't begin training until all the water was mopped up, and if it rained all day, we had to mop all day.

Public works claimed that it wasn't worth their time to fix one window, and that we would have to wait until at least 10 percent of our windows needed repair. Cracked windows didn't count. We had plenty of cracked windows. I realized the solution was to bust out all the cracked windows. Then we could get our leaky basement window fixed.

"Quigley! What the Sam hell are you doing?" It was Captain Nolte.

"Well, sir, I was—"

"Don't bullshit me Quigley. I saw what you were doing. I saw it with my own eyes, or I wouldn't believe it. It's bad enough I have to put up with students breaking everything, but I will not tolerate a chief petty officer deliberately breaking windows. What the hell were you thinking of?"

"Well sir, Public Works wouldn't—"

"Quigley I told you not to bullshit me. I know what I saw. I'm calling Public Works. They're going to fix each and every window in this building, and you are going to pay for it. You understand?"

"But, sir, I was just try—"

"Damn it, Quigley! Not another word. I don't believe in taking chiefs to mast, but if you say one more word, I will make you an exception."

"Yes, sir."

All good tours come to an end. I received orders to the USS *Midway* (CV 41). I really enjoyed teaching, but I also enjoyed the thrill of being on the flight deck during flight quarters. Leaving my children behind was always painful, so I left the Photo School with mixed emotions.

THE USS *MIDWAY*

The USS Midway (CV 41) was commissioned on September 10, 1945. Named for the Battle of Midway, she stood the watch for 47 years. More than 200,000 sailors served aboard her. She served off the coast of Vietnam, in the Persian Gulf, and during a number of other conflicts.

Midway was home ported in Yokosuka, Japan, when I came aboard. She was bigger than the Wasp and smaller the Enterprise; she was just the right size, and we got along fine. The Midway was my biggest challenge; she had a 27-man photo lab with only 12 men to run it.

Work

When work would allow us, my friend Chief Electrician Bobby McAllister and I would meet for lunch in the chief's mess. Bobby was more than a little overweight, and the Navy was starting to get serious about physical fitness. Bobby was meticulous about his appearance, and when he manned the quarterdeck, you could not leave the ship unless your uniform was perfect.

Part of Bobby's job was to check on the generators periodically, which meant that he had to climb 11 flights of stairs periodically. One hot day, Bobby came into the mess after one of these episodes, soaking wet from top to bottom. Knowing how he felt about his appearance, I immediately began busting his chops about his disarray. I guess I went too far because he exploded.

"You damn photographers don't even know what work is."

"Of course we do, Bobby, we photograph it all the time."

BM3 Joe Maderatz

Most of us liked Zumwalt's suggestion boxes. Finally someone was going to listen to us. The idea that we could submit a suggestion and receive an answer from the captain was mind-boggling, especially since there were so many things that needed improving. I was probably one of the first to offer the captain the benefit of my experience and expertise. To my surprise, he not only did not appreciate it, he seemed angry with me.

What could I do? Such a great program, but the captain's intense dislike for it made it a risky proposition. There was only one thing to do. Develop a fictitious character. Enter BM3 Joe Maderatz. We conspired with the personnelmen to give him a personnel record, and we conspired with the corpsmen to give him a medical record—we gave him 19 cases of the clap.

We gave Joe a unique personality: extremely sincere, hard working, totally dedicated, patriotic beyond belief, and dumber than dirt. We made him so dumb and so dedicated that it would be impossible to get mad at him, but the captain would still be required to answer him. It took Joe six years to make third class, and he hasn't progressed since.

Deer Captin Polk ser.

I nose yoo ar bizy bt I can get anytheng to eet bord yore ship! I now yoo have 2 messes yoo aren't usen. Why? I men look arond captin. Yoo gots peple to fed. Why don yoo bee lak Macdonolds an hav a lt of hot dowgs an harmbergers an fresh frys an thinggs thet ar fas. I laks werken fer yoo captin an I don mine werken 16 ars a day bt I cud werk beter if I cud eet.

Respekfuly
Joe Maderatz
BM3   USN.

"NOW HEAR THIS. NOW HEAR THIS. PETTY OFFICER MADERATZ REPORT TO THE BRIDGE. PETTY OFFICER MADERATZ REPORT TO THE BRIDGE."

I wondered what they would do when he didn't show up. A call to the Personnel Office: the captain asked for Joe's record. A note in the Plan-of-the-Day: 5. Attention BM3 Joe Maderatz. The captain wishes to thank you for your excellent idea. We will open up the portside aft galley and serve hot dogs, hamburgers, and French fries beginning Monday. If it catches on we will open up the other side.

Liberty in Yokosuka
Petty Officer Lance Davidson could speak Japanese, write using Kanji, and go on and on about Japanese customs and philosophy. He said the Japanese were terrified of being different or of being left out. Lance also said that a favorite saying in Japan was, "The nail that sticks up gets hammered down." Lance came by his knowledge honestly; he had been married to a Japanese woman for eight years. There was, however, trouble in paradise. Lance was still madly in love with Hideko even though she had moved out of their house six months earlier.

He said Hedeko still loved him, but family, friends, and acquaintances ostracized her for marrying an American. I knew some Japanese were prejudiced. I had already entered a bar without noticing a small sign that said, "Japanese only." Since the sign was in English, it was obvious whom it was aimed at. Lance tried for many months to win her back, but there came a day when he said, "Well, I've got to have a woman. I can't stand living alone. I'm going to have to go downtown and pick one out."

"Just like that?" I said. "How long is it going to take, ten, fifteen minutes?"

"Yeah, if I find someone I like at the first place I go. Actually, it will take ten or fifteen minutes to know one way or the other. If she says no, it will take me another ten or fifteen minutes to find out about the next woman I zero in on."

"No way," I said. "I haven't made out since I got here, and I'm no slacker when it comes to picking up women."

"Would you care to make a wager, Chief? Say twenty bucks."

"You're on, Lance. There's one little condition. If you succeed, you have to tell me your secret."

"Agreed. When do you want to start?"

"Tonight would be fine."

Lance started volunteering helpful information as soon as we got into the car. I rather think he would have been glad to share his secrets if I had just asked. However, it's more than a bit awkward for a chief petty officer to ask a second class petty officer how to make out with the ladies. The bet was working just fine.

"Chief, the first thing you have to realize is that women in Japan are second class citizens. They are not participating in the 'great economic boom' that is going on in Japan. They are paid less than men just like in the States. They are not encouraged to own businesses, and a Japanese man will not work for a woman. They are also not encouraged to go to college, which is one of the reasons why there are so many 'buy me drink' girls in Japan."

"Another problem for Japanese women is that Japanese men don't want to get married until they are well established. What all this means is that Japanese women are left on their own for a long time without a terrific income at a time in their lives when they are most desirable."

I was beginning to see Japanese women in a whole new light, but we arrived at our first club, so I would have to wait for the rest of my questions."

If you want to drink alone, it is more convenient to sit at the bar. We were looking for company, so we sat down at a booth. The "buy me a drink" game is an expensive one, so we came prepared. I thought the game was just for Americans, but Lance said Japanese men play this game too.

"Chief, it's possible to get a buy me drink girl into bed for a one-night stand but it is expensive. The only way is to get these girls to really drink with you. To do that, you have to buy a fifth of good American scotch and wait for one of them to join you. Once you're both snockered, you can usually coax her into bed for a hundred bucks. These girls are not hookers, but most of them are in a bind financially, and they don't have any hang-ups about sex. You'll see how it all fits in with my method before the night is over. You've probably been trying to romance them and that isn't going to work. They're not interested in a real romance with an American for the same reason my wife left me."

Two young ladies soon joined us. I bought the first round of drinks. The girls spoke good English and the conversation was quite lively. I kept my eye on Lance while he was looking at every girl in the place except the one next to him. I asked the girl I was with to dance, but Lance excused himself and intercepted another lady on her way to the bar. He talked with her for a few minutes and then came back to our booth and asked the other girl to dance.

Lance winked at me while buying the next round of drinks. There was no way I believed he made a connection, and I couldn't wait to get out of there, and hear what he had to say. Lance was anxious to leave too, so we excused ourselves and headed back to the ship.

"I'm not going to believe anything you tell me Lance. It could not possibly have happened that fast."

"It's not a sure thing, Chief. Her name is Mitchiko. She said she thinks it will be okay, but she has to see me in the daylight and talk to me for a while. She said she doesn't want to live with a grumpy American."

"Well, I'm not going to pay up until I visit you at her place."

"Chief, you're going to owe me a lot of interest by the time I invite you over."

"Okay. Okay. Here's your twenty. Now tell me what happened back there."

"Well Chief, it's like I've been telling you all along. These women aren't looking for romance with American sailors, but they like sex and have no taboos about sex before marriage. However, what they really want is someone to share expenses and that is what I offered Mitchiko. Oh, I told her I found her attractive, but I don't think that had anything to do with her decision. It's just like selling cars, Chief. You just keep trying until you make a sale."

"Well, I'll be damned. You were right about one thing. I was trying to romance them. No wonder I couldn't get to first base."

"I have an advantage, Chief, and it's something you should think about. I speak Japanese. Most Americans think it's too difficult, and don't even try. It's not. It just takes a little persistence. Japanese are really impressed with Americans that take the time to learn to speak Japanese. It also pays to learn a little Kanji, and if you really want to impress them, show them some origami that they haven't seen before."

I had just the ticket. I knew how to fold a dollar bill into a bow tie. I studied Japanese. I learned to write a little Kanji. I was never again lonely in Japan.

In a Fix

I heard that we took enough pictures in Vietnam to map both North and South Vietnam 28 times a day. I don't know if that's true, but I do know we took a lot of pictures, most of them aerial reconnaissance. All that film and all those prints had to be processed and that took a lot of chemistry. One of the more troublesome chemicals was ammonia thiosulfate, what we called fixer, because it was used to fix prints. Ammonia thiosulfate removes unexposed and undeveloped silver from negatives and prints.

We used ammonia thiosulfate in our machine processors. We used sodium thiosulfate, a milder chemical, referred to as hypo, when we processed by hand. I accidentally got a whiff of concentrated ammonia thiosulfate one time on the *Enterprise*. I have been very careful ever since. It burned my nose, my mouth, my sinuses, and my lungs. Every germ in my body saw it as an opportunity to attack, and I was down hard for a month.

Congress declared the cessation of all U.S. military operations in Southeast Asia on August 14, 1973. I checked aboard *Midway* in June 1974, so I wasn't surprised to see the surplus fixer in the photo lab; however, I was concerned. One hundred and twenty bottles, safely packed in rugged cardboard boxes, were neatly stacked three high throughout the photo lab. It was difficult to get around. I called supply to see if we could turn them in, but they said that they had been unable to find anyone who would take the chemistry. Then I called every photo lab in the Pacific. Subic Bay took 20 bottles off my hands. I asked about throwing it over the side. The XO said, "No way." It had little to do with the environment back then. It had to do with dollars and cents.

"Chief Quigley, this is your last warning. You've got to find a more appropriate place to store that chemistry." It was Lieutenant Junior Grade Bill Nelson, the zone inspection officer. "The XO says the chemistry has to be gone before the next zone inspection."

"Mr. Nelson, that chemistry isn't going anywhere. Supply won't take it, and I've contacted every photo lab in the Pacific. Nobody wants it and the XO, himself, said I couldn't dump it overboard."

"Chief Quigley, if you can't handle it, I'll just have to handle it for you."

That hurt, but I couldn't think of anything to say, so I decided to wait and see what he did. I didn't have to wait long. A working party showed up at the photo lab that very afternoon.

"Chief, is that the chemistry we have to move? I understand your guys are supposed to help us."

"Yes, that's the chemistry. Where are you going to put it?"

"We found a space on the other side of the ship, Chief."

"Is it heated? That stuff freezes at 60 degrees."

"Hell no, it ain't heated. It ain't a void, but it's close."

"Hold up, guys, I've got to call Mr. Nelson. He can't put this chemistry in an unheated space."

"Chief, we've got to get started. If that space ain't satisfactory, we'll just have to move it again. Mr. Nelson said to get this stuff out of the lab this afternoon. It was a direct order, Chief."

Half of the chemistry was already gone by the time I got in touch with Mr. Nelson. "Sir, I don't think you realize how bad this stuff is. If one of those bottles breaks, it is going to be a real nasty situation. We'll be in a fix."

"Chief, I'm telling you for the last time, it isn't your problem. I told the XO I would take care of it, and I have."

He hung up on me. The photo officer was off, so I wrote a memo to Commander Burton explaining the danger, but he never answered it. Oh well. It wouldn't be cold for a few months. Maybe I could talk some sense into them by then. But of course I couldn't. I mentioned it to Commander

Burton whenever I saw him. The temperature dropped to 40 degrees. There were no bottles cracking. I began to feel like I was hollering, "wolf." Commander Burton told me to forget about it.

"You didn't put it there, so don't worry about it. If anything happens, it will be Mr. Nelson's fault. He was the one brown-nosing the XO."

I agreed to let it go. I mean, Commander Burton was right. It wasn't my problem. I did all I could. The warning was right there on the boxes, and I did point it out to everyone. And besides, it was my birthday. I was sad enough without worrying about someone else's problem. My children were in Pensacola with their mother, the former Mrs. Quigley. I missed them, especially when it was time to celebrate. I wondered what we would be doing if we were still together. I decided to get drunk. I knew just the place, a little saki bar downtown. If there is anything the Japanese do well, it is drinking saki, and they are good company.

The *Midway* photo lab was authorized 27 people, and I only had 12. When I contacted BUPERS, they said it wasn't their problem. My XO had requested the billets be transferred to X Division. The XO had also cut the photo lab budget. I shut down a large color processor because it costs a fortune to run and because I didn't have enough people to do the maintenance. Then I went on a scavenger hunt for automatic printers. I had the lab automated and able to be run by 12 men by Christmas.

Christmas eve was a killer. It was the family thing again, except this time I didn't even feel like getting drunk. I like the Japanese, but they don't do Christmas, and I didn't have anyone else to do Christmas with, so I stayed aboard. There were only three of us in the lab, two young photo mates, who didn't have enough money to go home, and me. I was expecting a nice, quiet evening. I was in for a surprise.

BOOOM! BOOM! BOOM! BOOOOM!

BONG! BONG! BONG! BONG! THIS IS NOT A DRILL. THIS IS NOT A DRILL. THERE HAS BEEN A CHEMICAL EXPLOSION ON THE MAIN DECK, AMIDSHIPS, STARBOARD SIDE. ALL NONESSENTIAL PERSONNEL STAND CLEAR. AWAY THE FIRE PARTY. AWAY THE DAMAGE CONTROL TEAM. ALL EMERGENCY PERSONNEL DON OXYGEN BREATHING APPARATUS BEFORE APPROACHING THE AREA.

I was wondering which photographer to send when the phone rang.

"Chief Quigley?"

"Yes."

"The Doc says don't send any photographers, essential personnel only. This is real bad stuff, Chief. There are all ready five casualties. They're down in sickbay right now. They're hurt bad. Nobody knows what this stuff is, but I got a nose full, and I can tell you it's bad."

"Tell them it's ammonia thiosulfate, photographic fixer. The best thing they can do is dilute it. They need to dump a whole lot of water on it, and then pump it over the side if possible."

"Thanks, Chief, I'll get right on it."

I don't know what, if anything, was ever said to Mr. Nelson, but nobody ever said a word to me.

More than I Ever Wanted to Know

I had spent the morning shopping at the Navy Exchange and decided to stop at the base cafeteria for lunch before going back to the ship. It was crowded, but I managed to get a seat just as a young man was leaving. I was about halfway through my sandwich when I noticed a gorgeous woman standing with her tray looking for a place to sit.

I waived for her to join me. She said she was Sara Addison and that her husband was Jim Addison. She seemed genuinely grateful for a place to sit. We had an animated conversation about Japan and the homeport program.

"This is so much better than being back in the States with two small children and no husband. We get to see Jim all the time even though he is terribly busy. He is an NIS agent for the *Midway*."

My ears perked up at this revelation because the XO was on my case about drugs in the photo lab. It was rumored that some of my sailors were smoking pot. The XO was frustrated with my inability to catch them. He also thought that Leroy Johnson, one-half my quota of blacks, was dealing hard stuff. I thought the young man was using something because he always looked sleepy, but I was positive he wasn't dealing. He was the most homesick sailor I had ever met, and he religiously put $25.00 or $30.00 in the safe every payday for a round trip ticket to New York City.

She was as pleasant to talk to as she was to look at, so I sipped my coffee and stretched my sandwich until she was finished with hers. We said our goodbyes and I went on back to the ship.

I should have known who he was when he walked into the lab, but I didn't make the connection. A man in civvies stands out on a Navy ship even in port.

"Hi. I'm Jim Addison. I stopped by to thank you for being so kind to Sara. She said you two really hit it off."

"It's always a pleasure to talk to a pretty woman, and if she is as bright and interesting as Sara, it is a double pleasure."

"Thank you, Russ. I can see why she wanted me to ask you over for dinner. Do you think you could come over Friday? She wants to show off a new recipe for pork roast."

"I'd be delighted."

"Great. This is a pretty big space you have here. Mind showing me around?"

"Not at all." He was interested in photography and surprised at all the equipment we had. He also seemed interested in my photographers, and talked to them at length about their work. I was looking forward to dinner with Sara and Jim.

She had reason to be proud of her pork roast. It was succulent. Both Sara and Jim were interested in photography. They were on a mission to see and photograph all of Japan. They showed me their point and shoot cameras and said they wanted to upgrade.

"What is the best 35mm camera?" Sara asked.

"Well, I like both Cannon and Nikon, but really, nowadays you can't buy a bad Japanese camera. They are all good. Be sure to get a good zoom lens, though. You will never go back to a normal lens again."

"What is a zoom lens?" asked Sara.

"Well, I guess I should have brought my camera, so I could show you. It is a variable focal length lens that lets you vary the image size from wherever you are."

"What other lenses should we get?" asked Jim.

We talked about cameras and photography for a couple of hours. It was the most fun I'd had in a long time, and I was looking forward to taking them out to dinner in the near future.

Sara finally excused herself to do the dishes, and Jim and I started talking about the drug problems on the *Midway*. I told Jim I was sure I had problems in the lab, but that I didn't know what to do about it.

"We brought dogs in one night and searched for hours, but we didn't find a thing."

"Don't worry, Russell, if they're dealing or using, we will catch them. The XO and I are making lots of changes. There aren't going to be any drugs or drug users on the *Midway* if we have our way."

I wondered how they thought they could pull that off.

"You know, one of the most frustrating things for us has been waiting for months for drug paraphernalia to come back from the lab in Tokyo. Half of the time it comes back labeled 'Insufficient Residue.' That's nonsense. Everyone knows what a pot pipe is used for. Well, we're just not going to put up with that anymore. From now on when we pick up drug paraphernalia, it is automatically going to be marked positive for drug residue."

I couldn't believe my ears. I was stunned. I couldn't say a word; I just kept listening. Jim went on and on about what he and the XO were doing to rid the *Midway* of drugs. Eventually, Jim realized that I was no longer a part of the conversation, and that maybe he had said more than he should have.

"Well, Russell, we'll have to do this again soon."

That was my signal to leave. Sara came in from the kitchen and we said our goodbyes. I never saw them again.

Standard Stock

One day when we were in port, the photo officer, Chief Warrant Officer, Bud Bruggeman, called in sick. It seems he had what was called Kato Plains hay fever. I didn't see him again for five months, during which I heard he almost died. That made me the acting photo officer as well as the leading chief. I didn't think much about it until the Operations Department head, Commander Burton, warned me to be wary of the IS Officer, Lieutenant Snitzel. Lieutenant Snitzel asked the XO if he could take over OP Division since we shared a common area. We didn't really share a common area; the photo lab had a back door that led to the IS Division spaces.

The XO thought it was a good idea, but Commander Burton said, "No, Chief Quigley will do just fine." We kept the back door locked, but of course Lieutenant Snitzel had a key. He took to roaming about the photo lab at will. He wasn't exactly an authorized visitor, but I could hardly challenge the ship's intelligence officer.

I gave the crew the same warning Commander Burton gave me. "Be polite, but don't get friendly." Lieutenant Snitzel sensed he was getting the cold shoulder and was miffed. Rather than just staying away, he came over more and more often.

"Chief Quigley, I want you to move that paper shredder into my office. I need it more than you do."

"No sir, Mr. Snitzel, I can't do that. We use it every day to shred classified material. All of our scraps are washed and dried and shredded before we take them to be burned. I'll be glad to order you one; it's a standard stock item."

"Chief, I need one right now. Order one for yourself if you need to, because that one is going in my office."

"No sir, I don't have the authority to give up custody."

"No problem, I'll assume the responsibility. My people will be over in a few minutes to pick it up. They'll sign for it."

The ISs were known as Snitzel's snots. The ISs, like the CTs, did not have to stand any of the ship's watches; there was some resentment. We never saw the CTs, but we had to work with the ISs. Rumor had it that they were all OCS dropouts. Anyway, they came for the shredder.

"Mr. Snitzel said we didn't have to sign for it. He said he will explain to Bud when he gets back."

I did a slow burn, but I wasn't anxious to get into a pissing contest with the Mr. Snitzel. I didn't order a new one, because I didn't think Mr. Bruggeman would have any difficulty getting his back when he returned.

One of my troops asked, "Chief, do you think those Intelligence Specialists have enough intelligence to operate our shredder?" We all laughed, but it turned out that they didn't. One of them was curious to see what it would do to a nickel.

"Chief Quigley," said Lieutenant Snitzel, "I want your repairmen to fix this machine and return it to me ASAP, and don't make any remarks."

"Yes, sir," I said. I only had one camera repairman, but he took it apart.

"Chief, it's going to need a new blade. That nickel did a number on it. There is no way I can fix it."

"Okay, order a new blade. Hopefully, it will take a few months."

Three days later, there was a brand new paper shredder in my office. I called supply. "Brown, why do I have a new paper shredder when I only ordered a blade?"

"Chief, that paper shredder is a standard stock item. We have plenty of them in the warehouse on base. I would have to order the blade from stateside and it would take several months."

"Brown, is there any way you can make sure it takes several months?"

"Chief, I don't understand. The blade costs $89.00. The shredder only costs $150.00. Why would you want to order a new blade when it would take months to get here?"

I explained.

"Wow! Why didn't he just order one? If he'd said it was an emergency, I could have walked it through and had it for him in a matter of hours. Leave it to me, Chief; it'll be next Christmas before he gets a new blade for his shredder.

"Thanks, Brown."

I hid my new shredder in the film development room. I didn't have to worry about Lieutenant Snitzel finding it because he stopped coming around.

Two for Me, Two for You

The seventies were difficult years for people in the military. The Vietnam War was unpopular, and the military was unpopular long after the war was over. And there was the ever-increasing friction between whites and Afro-Americans. The situation was so tense that the Chief of Naval Operations ordered that all racial incidents, no matter how small, be reported to him within 24 hours.

There was a riot aboard an aircraft carrier on the West Coast. Several hundred men were involved, and the ship was incapacitated and could not get underway. A congressional investigation ensued. I was surprised at the insight congressmen had into military operations. They blamed the entire chain of command; however, they placed the primary responsibility on the commanding officer. Since the commanding officer reported the incident to the Chief of Naval Operations, he waited to hear from the Chief of Naval Operations before he took action. Congress reasoned that if the commanding officer had sounded "general quarters," the riot would have been nipped in the bud.

Congress also found that Afro-American strikers were routinely given the most difficult assignments aboard ship. This prompted a new policy aboard the *Midway*. We called it the two for me, two for you policy. Every division was given two Afro-American strikers. My two guys did not want anything to do with photography.

Elmo said to me, "What the hell is going on, Chief? I was perfectly happy pushing airplanes around the flight deck. I was striking to be an Aviation Boatswain's Mate, and that is exactly what I want to be. No offense, Chief, but I joined the Navy to do a man's job, not to be no photo pussy, no offense."

Rodney felt the same way, except he didn't care what his job was as long as it had something to do with airplanes. I was furious, not just because these two men were pushed into jobs they disliked, but also because it would not take me more than 15 minutes to find two Afro-Americans that wanted to be photographers had I been given the opportunity to look for them. And I really needed help; I had 12 people to run a 27 man photo lab. Well, that's not true anymore; now I have 14 people.

To make matters worse, the XO believed that the "two for me" were dealing drugs. It wasn't long before the photo officer, Warrant Officer Bruggeman, and I were summoned to a screening mast for Roger and Elmo. The XO went on and on without presenting any evidence. All he talked about was who my guys were associating with, and that, "We know that those men are dealing drugs."

"I can't believe what I'm hearing, XO. You're railroading these guys because they know some guys you believe are dealing drugs?"

I didn't see his face turn red. I didn't even see him turn the podium aside. I did see his fist coming at me, but not in time to duck. The XO was in his late forties, but he still packed a punch. My head snapped back and smacked into a steel bulkhead. I slid straight down the bulkhead and sat on the deck.

"Chief, I'm not railroading anybody. These men are dealing drugs, and I'm going to prove it." The XO motioned to the chief master-at-arms, and they both disappeared.

Chief Warrant Officer Bruggeman was stunned. He said he had never seen an officer hit an enlisted man before. "I guess you know you have his career in your hands. I saw it happen, so if you tell the CO, his career is over."

I could not bring myself to turn the XO in. I shouldn't have accused the XO of railroading my guys even though that's what I thought he was doing. I was sure my men were not dealing drugs. Elmo was so homesick that I knew he would have gone home if he'd had drug money to buy a ticket.

About a year after I left the *Midway*, I heard Elmo was doing hard time in a federal penitentiary for dealing drugs. Perhaps I should have turned the XO in.

Operation Frequent Wind

The *Midway* moved through the night and into the war zone off the coast of Vietnam. It seemed more like a summer storm than a war, lightning flashing and thunder crashing. But we knew it was real. We had left the air wing behind. In its place were six USAF CH-53s and four USAF HH-53s. USMC CH-53s from the *Hancock*, loaded with marines, formed the first wave, departing about 30 minutes before launch time, in order to be on the ground and provide security for the main evacuation force. We were about to evacuate American citizens, South Vietnamese at risk, and various third country nationals. The operation was code named "Talon Vice" until the name was compromised by its publication in a news magazine. It was renamed "Frequent Wind."

The *Coral Sea*, *Enterprise*, and *Hancock* were with us along with about 50 other ships. It was an impressive sight. *Blue Ridge* was the command ship. We had been on and off alert constantly for the last two weeks, so when it finally came over the loud speaker, it took a minute to sink in.

"DEEP PURPLE. DEEP PURPLE. THIS IS NOT A DRILL. THIS IS NOT A DRILL. COMMENCE OPERATION FREQUENT WIND. COMMENCE OPERATION FREQUENT WIND."

I went topside to see what I could see. The sky was full of South Vietnamese helicopters descending upon us like locusts, looking for a place to land. Our helicopters cleared the deck just in time. There was much confusion: some of the South Vietnamese did not speak English, and they came in whenever they saw an opening. All of their helos were overloaded, most with refugees, some with heavily armed, panic stricken military troops. One of the pilots terrorized everyone by landing next to the island with only a few inches clearance on either side.

"GENERAL QUARTERS. GENERAL QUARTERS. ALL HANDS MAN YOUR BATTLE STATIONS. ALL HANDS MAN YOUR BATTLE STATIONS. THIS IS NOT A DRILL. THIS IS NOT A DRILL. GENERAL QUARTERS. GENERAL QUARTERS.

Refugees were pouring from the helos onto the flight deck. Aviation Boatswain's Mates were signaling refugees to move as if they were moving aircraft and it worked. The refugees were searched, disarmed, and moved below decks in rapid order.

The chief master-at-arms was in charge of inspecting all packages and confiscating all weapons. One short and stocky Vietnamese in civies was reluctant to open a large, old and tattered, leather suitcase. When it was clear he could not proceed without divulging the contents, he got down on his knees, opened the case slowly, placing his arms over the contents, so nothing would be lost to the wind. The Chief Master-at-Arms called two sailors over to count it. They said it contained over $500,000.

The CIA helicopters were easy to spot as were the pilots, but this one was different. He handcuffed a briefcase to his wrist before leaving his helo. He marched straight for the open hatch on the island. The Chief-Master-at Arms interceded, "I need to look in your briefcase, and I need your gun before you go any further."

"No," said the pilot.

"Sir, the captain has ordered us to disarm everyone coming aboard and to inspect every package."

"No."

The chief master-at-arms went for his 45. Even one handed, the pilot was quicker. They stood face to face with their weapons pointed at each other's gut. I was about ten feet away. I raised my camera slowly. I was ready to shoot, but I was afraid to because the flash might set one of them off. A lance corporal rushed over and snapped a rifle to the pilot's temple.

"Sir, you can't go inside with a weapon," the chief master-at arms repeated. "And I need to see what's in your briefcase."

"No."

Everyone around them stopped moving. The flight deck was slowly paralyzed. The only one showing any emotion was the lance corporal who was visibly trembling.

One of our pilots stepped out of the island and on to the flight deck and hollered, "The captain said to let him come up." No one moved. He walked closer. "The captain said to let him come up as is."

The chief-master-at arms slowly holstered his 45 and stepped aside.

Rumors were rampant. The North Vietnamese were going to attack with small torpedo boats. Tan Son Nhut Air Base was burning. A South Vietnamese flotilla with 30,000 refugees was on its way to meet us. I left two photographers in the photo lab, put two in the hangar bay, two on the signal bridge, and the rest on the flight deck.

Refugees began pouring into the hangar bay where they were deloused and sprinkled with white powder. Yeomen, personnelmen, and others were busy recording names and other pertinent data. The refugees were then taken to designated spots in the hangar bay where hundreds of canvas cots and blankets were waiting for them. Getting them all fed, to and from restrooms, and bedded down was a real challenge.

Our own helicopters began returning. The ship was awash in refugees. We took hundreds of pictures. Many of them would move you to tears. Some of us were on the verge of crying anyway; we had never lost a war before. On 30 April 1975, the Republic of Vietnam ceased to exist.

The Midway moved over 7,000 evacuees, plus 989 Marines. Many helicopters were pushed over the side during the evacuation. The first ones were pushed over the side to make way for more incoming helicopters. Then they were pushed over the side to make way for a South Vietnamese Colonel and his family to land in a Cessna O1 Bird Dog, a small observation plane. And finally, they were pushed over the side to make room for 105 F-5 fighters that were flown out of South Vietnam and landed in Thailand.

All told, nearly 50,000 people were rescued from Vietnam. It was, I believe, the largest rescue mission in history. The Secretary of the Navy presented the Navy Unit Commendation to the Commander, Task Force 76. Operation Frequent Wind gave birth to a new medal: the Humanitarian Medal.

Powdered Milk

When the helos stopped flying, and the last refugees were safely nestled in the hangar bay, the door to the photo lab flew open, and two sailors with a stretcher full of multi-colored bricks wrapped in plastic came barging in. A civilian rushed right in behind them and began speaking to no one in particular.

"We need a picture of this stuff in a hurry." The two corpsmen set the stretcher down in front of the studio, and before I could speak, the civilian said, "Start putting those bricks on that table."

"Wait a minute," I said.

"We're in a hurry; I told you."

"Back off," I said, grabbing the corpsmen and pulling them back from the table. I threw the bricks back onto the stretcher, and said, "If you want a damn snapshot then take your stuff out of here and shoot it yourself.

"All right. All right, but make it quick."

I reached up and pulled a background paper down and over the table. A clean foreground and background is one of the primary differences between a snapshot and a professional photograph.

The door flew open again, and a first class petty officer with a master-at-arms band stepped in carrying a sawed-off shotgun.

"Where in the hell have you been?" asked the civilian. "You're supposed to be protecting this junk."

"I got lost. You guys moved too fast."

It was an easy picture to set up and shoot, but I took my time just to irritate the abrasive civilian. He was probably from NIS, but he was not one of the regulars. I assumed the stuff was heroin. Why else all the fuss and the shotgun.

"How soon can I get the pictures?"

"How soon do you need them?"

"I need them right now, just as fast as you can make them."

"It will be at least two hours. You will have to sign a job order."

"I'm not signing any job order."

"Sir, I'm not about to release these pictures without a signature on a job order authorizing the shoot and another signature on the job order when you get your prints."

My office man, hearing the fuss, stepped around the corner with a completed job order on a clipboard and offered the man a pen. He refused to budge.

"John," I said, "Write up the job order and take it to the executive officer and tell him I can't shoot these pictures without a signature, his orders." The civilian took the pen and signed, "Aberto Faggini," on the job order.

About an hour after the man left, the captain made an announcement over the loud speaker:

"NOW HEAR THIS. NOW HEAR THIS. THIS IS THE CAPTAIN SPEAKING. THERE IS A RUMOR GOING AROUND THE SHIP THAT WE HAVE HEROIN ONBOARD. NOTHING COULD BE FURTHER FROM THE TRUTH. SOME OF OUR PILOTS WHO WERE OPERATING OUT OF THE JUNGLE WERE CARRYING POWDERED MILK, AND THAT'S WHAT STARTED THE RUMORS. I REPEAT, THERE IS NO HEROIN ONBOARD. THAT IS ALL."

I had the crew make duplicate negatives and put them in the safe, and then I called Mr. Faggini and told him his pictures were ready.

Mr. Faggini looked at his pictures, nodded his approval and said, "I will need the negatives."

"Okay." I added the negatives to the job order and said, "I need your initials here." He hesitated, so I added, "No initials, no negatives." He initialed the job order and I gave him the original negatives. The duplicates were still in the safe when I transferred.

BM3 Kenneth Sterling

Boatswain's Mate Third Class Kenneth Sterling was as dedicated and loyal a sailor as any I had ever known, so when he was accused of deliberately sinking a 30-foot sloop that had come alongside for help, I just had to talk to him and find out what really happened.

"Kenny, I ain't believing you sank that boat on purpose. What really happened?"

"Damn straight, I sank it. I sank it on purpose. And, I told the admiral I sank it on purpose too. Did you see those people? They were starving, dehydrated, and sick. Doc said that a mother and her baby weren't going to make it through the night."

"I thought they brought the mother and baby on board and took them to sick bay."

"They did, Russell, but they were going to put them back on board as soon as they were treated."

"Why didn't they just bring them all on board, Kenny?"

"They said they couldn't because we were not in international waters. We were in Thailand's waters, so we could steal back our planes that South Vietnamese pilots were flying into Thailand. There were too many people on that little boat; that's why I knew it was going to sink."

"Geese, what did you tell the admiral?"

"I said, 'Admiral, if you can steal 105 aircraft from Thailand, you can damn sure pick up a few refugees that they don't want anyway. Besides, ain't nobody gonna argue with a United States aircraft carrier.' He wasn't happy, but he didn't put me on report."

"Wow! You have got some nerve, Kenny. You have got some nerve."

It Ain't Over until it's Over

I put in my papers to retire with 20 years of service under a "save pay clause" in a bill passed by congress to decrease the COLA for retired pay. Congress said that anyone who was eligible and wanted to retire could do so. I took 30 days leave, and visited all of the colleges in Manila. I chose the Philippines because I didn't want to make the mistake again of not having enough money to finish. I enrolled in the University of the Philippines. I paid my tuition and some special fees they only charged Americans.

To my astonishment, BUPERS disapproved my request. I quickly wrote a letter asking how they could ignore a congressional mandate. I received a rather terse answer, "Reference Transfer Manual." Well the Transfer Manual is several inches thick, so I didn't stand a prayer of finding out why I was the only man in the Navy that wasn't allowed to retire in the summer of 1975.

Well, like the man said, "It ain't over until it's over." I received orders for the combined services photo lab at the Kadena Air Force Base in Okinawa.

KADENA AIR FORCE BASE

The Naval Air Facility (NAF) was across the field from the main base. Although the buildings were new and impressive, they were all that was left of the Naha Naval Air Station, which was in the process of being returned to the Japanese. The combined services photo lab at Kadena had its own building and 41 photographers and draftsmen. I was just getting acquainted when I was called to NAF to meet the captain.

"Senior Chief," said Captain Farnsworth, "I want my own photo lab and I want it located on our side of the base. It takes too long to get a photographer from main side. Besides, I'm not getting the response from those folks that I'm used to.

"I want you to draw up some plans for a small photo lab. You can leave a couple of people over there, but I want the bulk of my photographers on my side of the base."

"I'm sorry, Captain, but we can't build a photo lab without NAVAIR's permission. They just closed several illegal photo labs on the West Coast last month."

Perhaps I should have given it more thought. Captain Farnsworth's face was bulging and so red I thought it might explode. In a way it did.

"What the hell kind of chief are you, Quigley? You're supposed to help me solve my photo problems, not be a part of them."

"Sir, NAVAIR just issued a bulletin with a warning that they are looking for unauthorized photo labs."

"Senior Chief, that's my problem. Your problem is designing a photo lab."

"No, sir, I am not going to have anything to do with an unauthorized photo lab."

Captain Farnsworth was a big man—he reminded me of Commander Bunch—so when he stood up and came around the desk, I thought he might hurt me. I stood up. He stood toe to toe and looked down into my face.

"Quigley, I have a serious problem. Half my chiefs are still at Naha wrapping things up for me. That only leaves my maintenance chiefs to stand Officer-of-the-Day (OOD) watches here in the terminal. Since our mission is flying, I can't really spare my maintenance chiefs, and, since you don't want to be my photo chief, you're going to solve that little problem for me. Quigley, your new desk is out there in the lobby. You can see it from here; it's the one with the OOD sign behind it."

I was totally demoralized. The OOD watch for NAF was a glorified receptionist. It was the most boring job I ever had. It made me realize why I still loved photography after all these years: every job is unique and has a different set of problems to solve.

The only pleasant part of the job was the captain's secretary, Linda. She was a pleasant woman, and she was unusually nice to me. In time I realized that being the captain's secretary was only a sideline. Her real job was finding eligible bachelors for single Filipinas. First, she reviewed their records to obtain their marital status. Then, she made friends with them, gathering as much information as she could. The final step was to consult with her friends to determine who should be paired with whom.

She pared me with Melanie Alonzo, a piano teacher at the Ryukyo Music School. She had studied for six years at the University of Sto. Tomas Conservatory of Music, and was a gifted pianist. I wondered why I was pared with her; she was way out of my league. Our first date was a disaster. Our second date was also a disaster; however, I did agree to take her to a Filipino dinner dance. I was just going to forget about it, but Linda kept reminding me of our date and telling me that I couldn't stand her up.

"You don't do that in polite circles, Russell. If you really don't want to go with her, you have to call her and tell her."

Well, I couldn't do that, so I assured Linda that I would take Melanie to the dinner dance. I discovered that she was a different person when she was surrounded by friends. She was animate, articulate, funny, and just plain fun to be with. We were inseparable from then on. She taught me how to love myself as much as I loved her. It was a new beginning for me, but it was the beginning of the end of my stories, for I was getting into less and less trouble.

Back in the Saddle, Again

"Chief Quigley, this is Master Sergeant Bob Lowry. I need to know if you can come back to the photo lab. We are in hot water because we can't produce quality portraits. For about a year, we have had a war going on between the portrait man and the film processing man. They both blame each other for the problem. Anyway, we heard you were a photo quality control person; can you help us out?"

"Master Sergeant Lowry, I would like to help you, but I am really in the doghouse with Captain Farnsworth because I won't help him set up a photo lab over here. It would take a miracle for him to release me."

"Chief, General Marshal, himself, relieved Chief Master Sergeant Burkette over this problem. I don't think it's Burkette's fault because he is a draftsman and doesn't understand the photographic process. Anyway, when I told the general you were a quality control technician, he said I should do whatever it takes to get you back. I know he will be happy to call Captain Farnsworth."

"That would be great, Master Sergeant. I can't wait to get back."

"Quigley," said Captain Farnsworth, "I have most of my chiefs back from Naha, so I have decided to send you back to the photo lab. I'll build my own photo lab without your help, thank you. You're not a team player, Quigley. I really don't want you around."

"Yes, sir, Captain."

It was good to be back in a photo lab. I was the senior man, but it was not clear whether or not I was going to be in charge. It was evident that the Air Force did not really want to turn over their photo lab to a sailor. I decided to give their portrait problem top priority.

Staff Sergeant Udager was in charge of the portrait studio. He really seemed to know what he was doing, and was positive all of his problems were Airman Cauley's fault.

"Who is Airman Cauley?" I asked.

"He's the young kid that runs that film processing machine in the lobby. He doesn't know what he is doing. Look at my negatives."

I looked. Something was wrong all right. The density and contrast varied from thin and flat to dense and contrasty.

"Staff Sergeant Udager, all I have to do is read a few of your negatives with a densitometer and we will know whether the problem is your exposure or Airman Cauley's film processing, but I would like to talk to Airman Cauley first."

"It's that simple? All you have to do is read a few of my negatives? Chief, I've had this problem for over a year—my evaluations have suffered because of it."

"Yes, it really is that simple, Staff Sergeant. I will be glad to show you how it is done, if you like. That way, you would never have to go through this again."

"I would like that, Chief."

Airman Cauley, a young black man, was just as sure that it was not his fault. I asked to see his sensistrips.

"My what?"

"Your sensistrips—the test strips that you process with your film."

"I don't do that, Chief. Staff Sergeant Mueller does that. He's our QC man."

I was flabbergasted. I knew the Air Force had a tendency to over specialize, but I couldn't believe that this man's whole job was just running this processor. How can you run a film processor without knowing how it works? I found Staff Sergeant Mueller in the QC lab, which was located in the farthest corner of the lab.

"Staff Sergeant Mueller, I'm Chief Quigley. I would like to see your process control chart for the film processor in the lobby."

"Don't have one, Chief. Don't need it. All my machines are running fine."

I couldn't tell if this was arrogance or ignorance talking, but I knew I found the problem.

"Staff sergeant, let me have your sensistrips for the last few days, so that I can build a process control chart."

"There in the corner, chief. Help yourself, but you're wasting your time. You won't find anything wrong."

I looked in the corner and saw a pile of sensistrips. It was obvious that they weren't in order so I asked him to plot his next ten sensistrips.

"Chief, I told you it ain't necessary to do that, besides, I don't work for the Navy."

I unplugged his densitometer, picked it up, and carried it out of the room.

"Hey, Chief, you can't take that. I need it to do my job."

"You don't need it anymore, Staff Sergeant. I am the new QC guy."

I set the densitometer on a table in the lobby and proceeded to show Staff Sergeant Udager and Airman Cauley how to read negatives. We quickly determined that the processor was the problem.

"Staff Sergeant Udager, as you can see, all of your negatives are well exposed and very consistent."

Airman Cauley was upset. I tried to assure him that it wasn't his fault, but he could not be calmed. He sulked for several days.

I marked one of the rollers on the processor and counted the number of revolutions per minute. I repeated the count several times without getting the same number twice. I called the camera repair shop and asked for the senior repairman to come to the lobby.

"Good morning, Chief. I'm Petty Officer Ross. What can I do for you?"

"Ross, how long has it been since you serviced this machine?"

"Chief, I have a dozen cameras to fix, and they keep calling me over to the flight line to repair the squadron's aerial photo systems. I know the systems belong to the Aviation Electronics Technicians now, but they are having a hard time catching on to them."

"In other words, you haven't checked this processor in a long time. I don't want you or your crew to go home until it is fixed. You understand?"

"Yes, perfectly, Chief. We'll get it fixed."

After several hours, Petty Officer Ross came to my office. "Chief, you've got to see this. You ain't gonna believe it."

He showed me a small compartment within the machine that was full of gunk.

"What is it, Ross?"

"It's what left of two batteries. This is a forty thousand dollar processor, and the speed is regulated by two D cells."

"You're right. I don't believe it. Can you fix it?"

"I'm not sure, chief. It's awfully corroded."

"Well, give it your best shot. If you can't fix it, we'll be processing a lot of film by hand."

Petty Officer Ross was able to repair the processor. I was put in charge of the photo lab. Imagine, Chief Master Sergeant Burkette had his career ruined by a couple of D cells.

The Ghost and Mister Kwan

Master Sergeant Lowry was the first to tell me about the ghost. "Chief, you might as well hear about it from me because you're going to have to deal with it sooner or later. The troops think there is a ghost in the photo lab, and I don't mind telling you, I'm one of them."

I looked at him in disbelief. "Ghosts?"

"Yes, ghosts. You know, this lab was built on a makeshift memorial for a number of Japanese soldiers that were killed here. Mr. Kwan objected strongly when they started building on this spot, and he was furious when the Americans continued to build here. He said he was with the soldiers when they were killed. He said we would be sorry."

"How long ago was that?"

"About 15 years ago. I was an airman first class. This was my first overseas duty station."

"And you believe in this ghost?"

"Yes, there are too many things happening in this lab that just can't be explained any other way."

"For instance?"

"Well, one day I was setting up fresh chemistry in the film processing room for an important job. The lady who usually developed was out sick. I didn't mind that she was ill, but the room was a mess and I couldn't tell how old the chemistry was. I was angry and I was slamming things around. When I was ready to process the film, I locked the door and turned out the light. Well, there was a terrible noise. I jumped, and I turned the lights back on. All my film-processing tanks were tipped over, and the chemistry was running down the drain. It's a small room. There is no place for anyone to hide, and the door was still locked."

"I'll be damned. I never heard of such a thing." I asked around, and sure enough, several people had similar stories to tell.

I forgot all about the ghost. Then, one day I heard Staff Sergeant Alice Fortner, who worked in the print room, screaming at the guys in the print finishing room.

"That's the tenth job in a row you guys messed up. There is no way that many prints are getting lost between the print room and here."

There was a water-filled light trap that allowed prints to be pushed out from the print room directly into the finishing room.

"We haven't lost a single print," responded an equally angry young man.

"What seems to be the trouble here?" I asked.

"We are losing prints between the print room and the finishing room," said Alice. "It's probably that damned ghost."

"Mr. Ghost," I said, feeling a little silly, "how about moving over to the film developing room so that we can get some work done."

"Chief," said Alice, "this isn't funny. I am working on a rush job, and this is the second time I have printed it."

"I'm sorry, Alice. I'm not used to working with ghosts. I'll stay in the finishing room and keep an eye on your prints, so that you can get this job out." Half an hour later, I personally took her prints from the light trap and put them on the dryer. I followed the job until it was delivered to the front desk. I was just about to tell Alice that her rush job was on its way to the customer when Staff Sergeant Ernest Shelby came screaming out of the film developing room. His face was white and his eyes were bulging.

"I ain't never going back in there. Chief, I ain't never going back in there."

"What happened?"

"I was in the room, by myself, the door was locked, and someone grabbed my ankle. I ain't never going in there again, Chief."

"I guess I'd better have a talk with our ghost. I don't know what I'm going to say, but surely, it won't hurt to talk to him. Has anyone else tried to talk to him?" No one answered. I went into the film developing room. A crowd followed me to the doorway.

"Kwansan, I don't know if you are still with us, or if you are with the souls resting here, but either way, I need your help. I need for you to tell them that we are sorry. We are sorry they were killed, and we are sorry the lab was built on their resting place. Tell them that we are soldiers like they were, and that we are just doing our jobs. Tell them that we cannot leave, and that we don't want them to leave either. We just want them to rest in peace. Tell them that the war is over, that our countries are getting along well, and that we would like to get along with them too. Tell them that we lost a lot of good people too, and that we hope they are also resting in peace."

We didn't have any more trouble with ghosts, but I always felt a chill when I went into the film developing room.

Don't Let Them Get Your Goat

The naval base at Naha was built by the Japanese for the Americans after World War II. When the base was completed, the mayor of Naha gave the base commander a pair of goats. It was a traditional Japanese gift full of tradition and meaning. Goats were only given to people whom you wanted to prosper. It was a thoughtful gift, and the base commander expressed his gratitude.

The goats were a nuisance at first; they like to eat the grass down to the nub, and they will chew on anything at least once, but when someone suggested that they be transported to an island on Kadena Air Force Base where munitions were kept, they were soon forgotten. The goats multiplied over the years and eventually became a herd, and then they became several herds.

Even the Japanese forgot about the goats and how they came to be on the Air Force base. Japanese workers on the base began wondering why the Americans needed so many goats, and why didn't they ever milk them, and why didn't they ever eat them? Soon the whole town wanted to know why the Americans needed so many goats.

And then one day, it occurred to them. Of course, they are there to protect the Americans from nuclear radiation. If the goats start dying from nuclear radiation from the hidden stockpiles of nuclear bombs, then the Americans would evacuate, leaving them with another Hiroshima. The central government of Japan denied the existence of any American nuclear bombs on Okinawa, but they also denied the existence of the blackbirds (SR-71s) that many Okinawans had seen and photographed.

There were many protest rallies outside the gate and in the city of Kadena. Protests became an everyday affair, and protesters were flown in from all over Japan. The Kadena Air Force commander knew how the goats had come to be on his base. He refused to meet with the protesters, but he did release the whole story to the press, which refused to publish it, so they were at a stand off.

The armed services agreement with Japan allowed Japanese to come and go as they pleased. They harvested every square foot of unused land, sugar cane mostly. Anyway, when hundreds of Japanese protesters poured through the gate, there was nothing the gate guards could do to stop them. They were loud and angry, but civil. They marched through the base and over the bridges and onto the island. They came prepared. They had plenty of food and a loudspeaker system that could be heard all over the base.

The commander was thoroughly annoyed, but ordered that no one interfere with the protesters. However, when he heard they stayed overnight, they really got his goat. He ordered the Seabees to dismantle the bridges. The protesters stayed another night before anyone tested the waters to see if they could get across. The river was man-made and very shallow, about waist high on the shortest protester. They were still angry, but they left more quietly than they came. There were no more protests.

I Ain't Your Nigger

There were eleven sailors in the photo lab. My favorite was a young black man named Bruce Gilmore. He was a second class petty officer that was always smiling and always pleasant. One day when I was terribly busy, I asked Bruce to get me a cup of coffee.

"No way, Chief, I ain't your nigger."

I was shocked. I looked up. He wasn't smiling. My mind went to general quarters. I shouldn't have asked him for a personal favor, but I wasn't prepared for this. I froze in my chair. Then suddenly, the smile was back on his face and he was pointing to Master Chief Bob Lowry.

"I'm his nigger, Chief. You'll have to ask him if I can get you a cup of coffee."

I looked over at Bob and saw that he was trying to keep from laughing. Apparently, he had been through this before. I knew I was going to have to play along, but I almost choked on the "n" word.

"Bob, would it be okay if your nigger got me a cup of coffee?"

"Sure, Russell. As a matter of fact, you can keep him. I won't be needing him anymore."

"Okay, Chief, how do you like it? Black? Cream? Sugar?"

"Black would be just fine, Bruce."

An hour later, I was summoned to the Personnel Office where I met an angry Air Force captain. The sign on his desk read, Captain McAdams.

"Chief, I understand you called a black man in your lab a nigger. I don't know what it's like in the Navy, but I can assure you that we don't tolerate such language in the Air Force."

"Sir, I can assure you that it was said in jest. It was in response—"

"I don't care what it was in response to, you can't call anyone a nigger and get away with it. I'm placing you on report."

"Captain, I wish you would talk to Petty Officer Gilmore before—"

"I don't have to talk to anyone, Chief. What you did was wrong and you're going to pay for it."

"Sir, you can't put me on report for such a serious charge without talking to everyone involved. I can assure you that Captain Farnsworth will not entertain a report chit without statements from everyone involved." I was bluffing, but it worked.

"Okay, call Petty Officer Gilmore and ask him to come over."

I was glad to see Master Sergeant Lowry with Petty Officer Gilmore, but I was surprised to see Airman Cauley.

"Airman Cauley, what are you doing here?" asked Captain McAdams.

"I came over to tell you that I made a mistake. They were just—"

"You didn't make a mistake. That kind of language isn't allowed under any circumstances."

"Captain McAdams, if that's true, then you will have to put me on report also because I said it first."

"That's different; you're black."

"Why is it different? They wouldn't have said it if I hadn't said it first."

Master Sergeant Lowry chimed in, "You will have to put me on report too, Captain. I told Chief Quigley he could have my nigger; I said I didn't need him anymore."

"Don't use that word in my office."

"I guess you will have to put me on report also," said Airman Cauley. "I said it when I told you what they said."

"All right, already. Nobody's on report, but knock it off, okay?"

"Well, Chief," said Petty Officer Bruce Gilmore, sporting his biggest smile ever, "I guess that means I can't be your nigger anymore. You will just have to get your own coffee."

A Compromise

Captain Farnsworth was flabbergasted when he learned that most of his operating funds were in the form of allowances to be spent at Air Force facilities. It meant, among other things, that he could not afford to build his own photo lab. However, he came up with a compromise that gave him what he wanted most: photographers at his beck and call. Captain Farnsworth knew the value of publicity and its effect on promotion.

His plan was simple. He bought two Nikon cameras complete with extra lenses and flash units, and then ordered me to teach his yeomen how to use them. I turned that chore over to Petty Officer Bruce Gilmore because I knew he liked to teach, and because he was the epitome of diplomacy.

I also told Bruce to add the equipment to our NAVAIR inventory. All photographic equipment belongs to NAVAIR no matter who buys it. I sent along a copy of the instruction because I knew Captain Farnsworth would not be pleased.

I received a call from the captain: "Quigley, why did you put my cameras on your inventory? I paid for those cameras out of my OPTAR; you don't have any connection to these cameras. They are mine and you are not going to use them, ever."

I explained the NAVAIR instruction and the function of our inventory to Captain Farnsworth. He was not happy.

"Quigley, in addition to your miserable attitude, I just plain don't like you."

The captain's plan worked fine for nearly a year. His yeomen became pretty good photographers. They covered all events on their side of the field and sent their film to us to be processed and printed. We did the lab work, filed their negatives, and then returned their prints. The yeoman kept their cameras in their desks, which, unfortunately, were not locked. One night, they simply disappeared. The captain was beside himself. He accused me of stealing his cameras. He was even more upset when NAVAIR asked Commander Johnson of the local Naval Investigative Service to investigate.

Married Again

I proposed to Melanie. I had never met anyone who made me feel so good about myself and so happy to be alive. I could not imagine living without her. To my pleasant surprise, she said yes.

The Navy does not seem keen on sailors marrying foreign nationals. There are lots of roadblocks and the paperwork is endless. It requires about six months to meet the Navy's requirements under the best of circumstances. I was afraid that the paperwork would not be finished before I received orders, so I tried to bird dog the paperwork. I believed my package had been in the Naval Investigator Service (NIS) office for about two months, but when I went over there, no one seemed to know anything about it.

One day, after getting the run-around from NIS, I returned to the lab and was greeted by a group of Japanese men standing around the lobby and jabbering excitedly. We were exchanging greetings when Master Sergeant Lowry came over and said they were waiting on Commander Johnson from NIS.

"There has been an ugly murder on base. We are on our third photographer. The first two got sick. They even had to take Sandra to sickbay. A first class petty officer was bound and gagged and shot in the back of the head with a shotgun. It was probably a robbery because he disappeared last Sunday after picking up the receipts from all the clubs."

"Who's over there now?" I asked.

"Petty Officer Ross. He said he had shot dozens of bodies and that nothing bothered him."

Commander Johnson came in and bowed to the Japanese men. They bowed in return, and the conversation continued, but in English.

"How soon can we get a look at the negatives?" asked Commander Johnson.

"About an hour after the photographer returns with the film," I replied.

"What! He isn't back yet? It's been over three hours since I called."

"Well, sir, I understand we are on our third photographer."

"Well, you should have known better than to send over a woman. Pretty damn stupid if you ask me." The commander was obviously annoyed. The Japanese had jurisdiction and had wanted to bring their own photographers. Commander Johnson suggested that they all go to lunch at the "O" Club. The Japanese men smiled for the first time and followed the commander out the door.

Petty Officer Ross returned with four rolls of color film to be processed. He asked to be excused for the rest of the day. The film was processed and proofed by the time the investigators returned from lunch. They spent over an hour looking at the pictures and then gave us a huge order and left.

The following day, just before Commander Johnson returned to pick up his pictures, I received a phone call from Linda, the captain's secretary.

"Russell, I just got a phone call from my friend at NIS. She said they were told by the captain to lose your paperwork. You'd better get over there and do something about that before its too late."

"Thank you, Linda." I was still fuming when Commander Johnson came through the door.

"Commander Johnson, I'm afraid we've lost your pictures. They were in the safe last night, but now, we can't find them anywhere."

"What the hell are you talking about? You want to cause an international incident? You'd better be joking or you're in a world of shit. The Japanese are already cussing us out because we sent the man's wife back to the States. They think she was involved, and we can't legally make her come back."

"Sir, I understand that Captain Farnsworth told you to lose my paperwork, you know, the clearance package on Melanie Alonzo. It will be a whole lot easier to find your pictures after you find my paperwork."

"Chief, that sounds an awful lot like blackmail. You must know you could lose your career over these pictures. This murder is a very sensitive issue with the Japanese. Give me the damn pictures before I have to write you up."

"No, sir. You aren't getting the pictures until after you've located my paperwork."

"You're making a very serious mistake, Chief. If I leave here without those pictures, you will be on report."

I didn't budge. He glared at me.

"You know, Chief, you are wrong. Captain Farnsworth did not tell me to lose your paperwork. It left my office weeks ago."

He left without another word. I figured I would be a civilian soon. What I didn't know was whether or not I could salvage my retirement.

Commander Johnson returned in about 20 minutes. Here is your paperwork. It's finished. You are free to get married. I apologize. The captain did tell one of my staff to lose your paper work. The captain and I will have serious words about his going behind my back. Now, may I have my pictures?"

I reached under the counter, picked up his order, and set it on top.

"It has never been out of my sight, sir."

"Chief Quigley, don't assume for a minute that I approve of what you did to me. You could have come to my office and told me of your suspicions."

"Yes, sir."

We were married soon after that incident. The base chaplain had Melanie and I take personality profiles, and then warned us that we were both take-charge people, and that we would have to work it out between us. It wasn't a problem. She is much more take-charge than I am, and much more organized too. It's wonderful. You can't believe how spoiled I am.

My anger has been replaced with contentment, and I am slowly learning what is and what is not important in life. I have learned to concentrate on my responsibilities and let other people worry about theirs. I am having fewer and fewer run-ins with other people. Consequently, I have run out of stories.

Well, there was that one time at sub school. The submarine base at Groton, Connecticut, is located on a narrow strip of land between the Thames River and a mountain. It literally has no room to expand. As submarines got bigger and more complicated, they needed more and more support. Every time a new facility was added, there was less room for parking. By the time I arrived, E4s and below could not park on the base, and I had to come to work an hour and twenty minutes early just to get a parking place.

I had been TAD to Washington, D.C., for two weeks when COMSUBLANT scheduled a visit to sub base. Every day I was gone, the captain posted the following message in the Plan of the Day: The subject of parking is not open for discussion during COMSUBLANT's visit. The "All Hands" meeting with COMSUBLANT was scheduled for the morning I returned. Between sub school and sub base personnel, the auditorium was packed.

As soon as the admiral finished speaking, he asked if there were any questions. I stood up and was immediately recognized.

"Senior Chief Russell Quigley here, Admiral. I would like to know why we entrust nuclear ballistic missiles to people who can not even manage parking."

About the Author

David W. Griffiths' naval career spanned 32 years and 5 months, during which, he photographed presidents, astronauts, pilots, ships, planes, events, and lots of people doing lots of things. He became addicted to being where the action is. He attended Basic Photography School in 1954, Advanced Photography School in 1966, Photographic Statistical and Chemical Quality Control School in 1970, Motion Picture School in 1977, Photographic Equipment Repair School in 1978, and the Robin Perry Creative Color Workshop in 1985. His favorite medal is the Humanitarian Medal, which he earned during the evacuation of Saigon.

He received his Bachelor of Science Degree in Occupational Education with an emphasis in photography from Southern Illinois University just before he retired from the Navy. He used the "G.I. Bill" to obtain a Master's in Vocational Education, and went to work for the Chief of Naval Education and Training as an Instructional Systems Specialist. For the next fifteen years, he developed Training Task Inventories, monitored contracts for computer-based training, and assisted chief and senior chief petty officers in developing nonresident training courses. Mr. Griffiths says it was a privilege to work with men and women of their caliber.

Mr. Griffiths says his stories were easy to write because they were inspired by true events. He believes his stories ended in 1977 when he met and married Perla Lumawig Mogol, who promptly put out the fires and calmly went about the business of teaching him how to forgive, how to love, and how to put first things first.

Made in the USA
Lexington, KY
21 April 2015